Don't
Bring Home
a White Boy

Don't Bring Home a White Boy

And Other Notions That Keep Black Women from Dating Out

KARYN LANGHORNE FOLAN

GALLERY
BOOKS

NEW YORK   LONDON   TORONTO   SYDNEY

GALLERY
BOOKS

A Division of Simon & Schuster, Inc.
1230 Avenue of the Americas
New York, NY 10020

Karen Hunter Publishing,
A Division of Suitt-Hunter Enterprises, LLC
598 Broadway, 3rd Floor
New York, NY 10012

First Karen Hunter Publishing hardcover edition February 2010

For information about special discounts for bulk purchases, please contact Simon & Schuster Special Sales at 1-866-506-1949 or business@simonandschuster.com.

The Simon & Schuster Speakers Bureau can bring authors to your live event. For more information or to book an event contact the Simon & Schuster Speakers Bureau at 1-866-248-3049 or visit our website at www.simonspeakers.com.

Designed by Aline C. Pace

Manufactured in the United States of America

10 9 8 7 6 5 4 3 2 1

Library of Congress Cataloging-in-Publication Data

Folan, Karyn Langhorne.
   Don't bring home a white boy : and other notions that keep black women from dating out / by Karyn Langhorne Folan.
      p. cm.
   1. Interracial dating.   2. Man-woman relationships.   3. African American women—Psychology.   4. Blacks—Race identity.   I. Title.
   HQ801.8.F65   2010
   306.73089'96073—dc22   2009016068

ISBN 978-1-4391-5475-5

CONTENTS

Don't
Bring Home
a White Boy

INTRODUCTION

It was New Year's Day 2004, and I'd made a resolution.

In the summer, I would turn forty years old. I was alone with my then eight-year-old daughter, and as much as I loved her company, she could hardly be my only companion for the rest of my life. She was growing up.

I'd been divorced for four years. My ex was Daniel Wynn, an internationally known painter and artist, a black man nearly twenty years my senior. Even though I had been his third wife (yes, I know, but like so many women I thought, "It will go differently for me"), I'd married Daniel because I admired so many things about him: his outgoing personality, his amazing talent, the history he'd lived through. He was a child of a significant era in American history, growing up in deeply segregated Jacksonville, Florida, and coming of age in the angry 1960s. He'd lived in Oakland, California, for a time and briefly joined the Black Panther Party. He'd sold art to Muhammad Ali when Ali was at the top of the boxing world, and hung out in the Washington, D.C., clubs where Roberta Flack got her start. Devastatingly handsome even in his later years, he'd been a professional model for a while. He'd met the queen of England and traveled through Europe. When we married in

November 1995, he was interesting, creative, temperamental, and still fighting, still angry, and I loved him and everything he stood for, even though I grew up in a very different era.

I was born on August 24, 1964—almost a year to the day after Dr. Martin Luther King's famous "I Have a Dream" speech on the Capitol Mall and only a few weeks after President Lyndon B. Johnson signed the Civil Rights Act of 1964, the most sweeping and dramatic racial legislation since Reconstruction. During the early years of my childhood, America changed dramatically, erupting in volcanic demonstrations that changed us as a nation both physically and psychologically. But I was a kid: I didn't know a world before "Black Power." I didn't know a world that hadn't included integration. I didn't know a world that didn't believe me fully capable of achieving King's dream. I didn't know the world that my parents and teachers did: a world that had limited people who, like me, were born black.

So in 1969, when I went to kindergarten in Fairfax County, Virginia, my school was already integrated; I learned with white and black kids from the beginning. I lived in a mixed-race neighborhood from the beginning. I learned from kindergarten about diversity and difference—not segregation and separatism. Sure, occasionally there were incidents on the playground, and I had my share of race-related run-ins with students and teachers alike. But I also had white friends and went to their houses to play, and they came to my house too. I lived in a mixed world where people all got along—if not altogether comfortably, certainly quietly enough.

These were the 1970s—the era in which women's roles changed dramatically too. No more were we limited to "helper" roles in our careers (as nurses, secretaries, and teachers) or at home. I absorbed from grade school that I could expect an equal role in my career and my household. I learned that I had choices . . . from the beginning. So, when Daniel and I met, I was an attorney—a graduate of Harvard Law School, no less. I was comfortable with my role as an educated, up-and-coming black woman.

Daniel and I were married for five years before things completely unraveled. In 2000, when our daughter was four, we divorced. Far from wanting to jump back into the dating scene immediately, I then spent four years trying to understand what had gone so wrong between us—and raising our daughter on my own.

Finally, as 2004 began, I felt I understood my role in the failure of my first marriage and that I was ready to stick a toe in the waters of a new relationship. But what was I looking for? What did I really want in a man? Past the superficial qualities of good looks and a nice body, what should my next partner in life be like?

Like most women do when confronted with a major life decision, I consulted my girlfriends. My friend Paula Langguth Ryan,[1] who is also a spiritual adviser and life coach, suggested I make a list.

"Write down everything you want him to be," she suggested. "All of the qualities that are important to you in a man."

"And then what?" I asked, always anticipating the next step.

She shrugged. "And then nothing," she said. "Live your life. Let God do his work, and don't get in the way of it."

I confess to being more than a little skeptical of this plan. Everyone knows that nothing happens to people who sit on the sidelines of life; I didn't want to be that woman, forever waiting for Mr. Perfect to show up on my doorstep. But the idea of a list appealed to me and I went to work. I spent some time on it, carefully considering each item and asking myself why each thing was important to me. Some of the first things I wrote down didn't stand up to scrutiny and were replaced by other concepts that I decided were more true to what I hoped for in a husband. I wish I still had it; I don't. But it was something like this:

1. Someone to cherish me, to love and appreciate me, not just for the things I do for him, but for everything I am, warts and all.

2. Someone to love my daughter, to respect that another man is her father, but to provide her with a father figure in her life.

3. Someone financially secure, who does work he loves and who is ambitious in achieving his life goals.

4. Someone who cares about his body, is physically fit and healthy, but not obsessed with his appearance.

5.   Someone who is well educated, having at least a master's degree, and who is still engaged in learning through reading, travel, and talking to others.

6.   Someone who likes to be at home with his family; a quiet, homebody soul.

7.   Someone who is open-minded about others' beliefs on religion, politics, and worldview.

Then I followed Paula's advice: I folded the list up carefully and stuck it in the bottom of my lingerie drawer, where it stayed for quite a while.

The part of Paula's advice that I didn't follow was the "do nothing" part. As a goal-oriented American woman who had made a decision, I went to work. I asked my black girlfriends if they knew anyone to "fix me up with." I made efforts to become more involved at the church I attended then—a predominantly African American institution—hoping I might strike up a conversation with an eligible bachelor. And, in this age of computerized matchmaking and social networking, I paid for membership in an online search company, found a cute picture that I thought showed my nearing-forty advantages in the best light, and put up a profile, listing my accomplishments.

The "ask friends if they know someone" alley was a dead end: most of my black girlfriends (and white ones) were single and looking too. If they found a good black man, chances were pretty good they wouldn't be passing him my digits. They'd be keeping the brother for themselves.

And the church didn't work either. I met some very nice men, but they were married or I wondered if they might be gay. At any rate, I didn't meet anyone who seemed interested in my interest.

But the internet worked. In fact, it worked too well. I got lots of interest from brothers who apparently didn't read my profile. Crude, rude come-ons that spoke to nothing I was hoping for in a man. I wondered, did these guys just respond to every black woman who put up a profile? Did they just look at the pictures but not read the words attached? Could they read? I couldn't tell from some of the replies, which were poorly written, ungrammatical disasters. Call me picky if you must, but I'm a

Harvard-educated lawyer. Was it too much to ask a man to approach me with some finesse? I'm not talking about poetry, but polite, complete sentences would have been nice.

These dudes didn't even get answered, let alone a chance to prove themselves.

I did go on a couple of dates, though. The first was with a brother around my age, also an attorney, with the shortest stature and the biggest ego since Napoleon. I'm short, so his height wasn't an issue, but his attitude was a complete turnoff. He seemed to think I should feel honored to have been invited to spend a moment basking in his presence. Since I wasn't, the date was a hopeless waste of time.

The second man I met was a dude who dreamed of being the next Sean Combs . . . but considering that the guy was already forty, living in D.C.—not New York, Los Angeles, or even Atlanta—and didn't have any connections in the music industry, I wasn't impressed with his chances. Outside of hoping to churn out bestselling artists, he didn't seem to have many interests. At the end of the date I discovered why he contacted me: he wanted to know if I knew any entertainment lawyers who could "hook it up" for him.

Then there was the guy I talked to on the phone but never actually met—thank God—who kept asking questions about my eight-year-old daughter. The one who, I discovered after a few clicks on the internet, had been convicted of an unspecified child sex offense and would have his name on the sex-offender registry for another decade.

A few white guys also responded to my profile, and I met a couple of them too. After all, I've had a multicultural life. I grew up on military bases (my father was an Army officer) and the military is well known for being a bit more racially progressive than the civilian world. I had even had a crush or two on a white boy here or there, and a couple have had crushes on me. But nothing had ever come of any of that. Even in my relatively integrated, relatively progressive upbringing, I'd absorbed that an occasional date outside of the race was okay . . . but anything more serious was highly unlikely.

Still, I figured since I was doing so badly with the chocolate, I'd give the vanilla a try. I had a couple of nice dates, but no real love match. But the experience encouraged me to broaden my horizons. I'd never considered dating a Hispanic man, for example. Or an Asian one. Maybe my search for romance was too narrowly defined. Maybe I should open myself up to the world—and every kind of man that might be in it. I decided to join one more dating site: one that focused on interracial relationships.

Interestingly enough, I still got lots of winks and replies from black men on the interracial site. I'm not sure if they thought I was something I'm not, but once again, I worried. Was it possible that these men didn't know how to read? Or did they simply disregard what they read and replace it with what they wanted to believe to be true? Perhaps they were simply supremely confident. Maybe they even wanted to discourage black women from meeting men of other races on the site. I don't know.

I also got some creepy replies from white men that suggested some kind of fetish for big butts and brown skin. All of these I ignored: I wasn't interested in any "the darker the berry, the sweeter the juice" come-ons from white guys interested in "booty calls"—any more than I was entertaining any "booty call" requests from black men. Months went by and I began to wonder if I'd join many of my African American girlfriends as yet another manless woman over forty.

And then I got an email, polite and in complete sentences, from a gentleman named Kevin. He introduced himself, commented on all the items in my profile, and confessed that he was impressed and a little intimidated to correspond with a woman of my many achievements. I was flattered and charmed and . . .

I answered him.

We exchanged pictures, and I remember thinking that looks-wise, he was just okay. With his white hair, he looked older than the fifty he claimed to be, and he didn't seem like the kind of white guy I could ever be physically attracted to. But he wrote such interesting emails! Emails full of stories about his job (which he loved and had become quite financially successful at), about his travels (he'd been in the military like my own father, studied Russian, then visited that country, then taken time to travel in South America and learn Spanish), about the books he was reading (he loves history, while I read more fiction), about his life growing up as the oldest of six kids of Irish immigrants in Boston (a city I had lived in myself for three years). After weeks of respectful, funny, intelligent emails, he asked if he could call me. I said yes.

He was charming on the phone. I found I liked talking to him as much as I had liked reading his emails. His stories were even better when he told them aloud, and I found myself looking forward to hearing from him. He made me laugh—then complimented me on the sound of my laughter, saying it was "infectious" and "beautiful." He also had an interesting point of view on the world. I liked him. So, after a few weeks of phone calls, when he asked if he could take me to dinner one night, I knew I would ask my sister to babysit and go.

Even though we lived about thirty miles apart, he didn't ask me to meet him somewhere; he drove across town and picked me up. When I opened the door, I was once again a little disappointed: Kevin was well built but had that fair, reddening skin that just never appealed to me. I have been attracted to white men before, but they always had a little color to them: swarthy Italians and Greeks, or guys who worked outdoors and had tanned faces. By comparison, Kevin was so . . . white. Compared to my ex-husband, Daniel—who still had his unlined café au lait skin and model good looks—he was something of a step down on the handsome ladder. But I shouldered my purse and headed out, reminding myself of our good conversations. Besides, it was just dinner. It wasn't like I had to marry him, right?

But I'm getting ahead of myself.

We had a great date. We already knew each other because of weeks of calls and emails. We knew we had enough things in common to connect and enough differences to keep each other intrigued. He took me to a fancy steakhouse and paid the bill without hesitation. We walked around a bit, talking as easily as old friends, then he drove me home and said good night at the doorstep without so much as a handshake.

I didn't know what to make of that. You know how guys are these days: if they pay for dinner *for* you, they act like they've paid for something *from* you. Kevin's courtliness was both refreshing and confusing. I wondered if he was all that into me. I wondered if chatting with a black woman on the phone and via internet were fine, but sitting across the table from her—with others staring with interest—was a different thing for a Southie boy who grew up in the late 1950s in Boston.

But then, I also wondered about my own feelings. I wondered if I could really see myself being physically intimate with him. If he had tried to kiss me, would I have pulled away?

He called—not the next day, but later the same evening—to tell me what a great time he'd had . . . and to ask for another date. I actually had plans to meet another of my internet responders the following week, but I wasn't that excited about it. Instead, I told Kevin yes and emailed the other guy no. Once again, we had a lovely time. Once again he was an absolute gentleman.

Weeks went by and every weekend Kevin and I went out together. We went to museums and clubs, restaurants and movies. We talked every day, we laughed, and we got acquainted. There wasn't that bang of immediate chemistry, and he never once crossed that line. I never felt nervous. I never felt like I had to pretend to be something I wasn't. I never felt uncomfortable. Our conversations were easy and natural. I didn't feel like I had to apologize for my education or intelligence or compensate for my achievements; he had a master's degree in international relations and worked in the financial industry. He read voraciously: history, politics, and social science. He spoke two languages in addition to English. And he picked me up for every date, paid for everything, and at the end of every date, disappeared into the night with a warm hug and nothing more.

He was my friend.

It started to make me nervous. I wasn't sure how I felt about him, but in spite of how much fun we had, his gentlemanly manners made me wonder if, romantically, he wasn't sure about me either.

We started including my daughter in our dates, spending Saturday afternoons at the aquarium or the zoo. Kevin and Sierra got along like a house afire—helped by the fact that Kevin quickly figured out her favorite things and brought frequent gifts. I remember watching him on his knees on my living room floor, playing with Polly Pockets or some other girly toy, listening to her prattle on about how to play with dolls. And I remember the day they raced through the zoo, then raced back to me, hugging me simultaneously. I remember how clearly it hit me: "I like this man. I like him a lot."

My mother had always told me that real love was "a quiet thing." I'd felt swept away with Daniel: an immediate romantic fantasy led my heart faster than my brain . . . and ended with the same flash and explosiveness. What I was coming to feel for Kevin was its exact opposite.

I liked him. I respected him. I felt good in his presence. I missed him when he left and was glad when we were together again.

But then there was the physical side. Not just the question of sex, but the whole question of being intimate with someone so . . . white. I worried about how we looked together. I was unsure of what my parents would think, what my ex-husband would say when he learned a white man was spending so much time with his daughter. But mostly I wondered about Kevin himself. Why hadn't he made some kind of move toward intimacy? He seemed to like me too, but maybe I was wrong.

I'm not exactly a wallflower, but I dislike "Where is this relationship going?" conversations. Instead, I decided to take matters into my own hands. After the zoo date, while Sierra was upstairs taking her bath, I wrapped my arms around him and kissed him.

And he kissed me back, passionately, with real desire. If my child hadn't been just upstairs, I'm pretty sure I know where that kiss would have led.

"I was waiting for you to do that," I said when our lips finally separated.

"I wanted to," he replied, "but I wasn't sure you did. Besides, I wanted you to be sure that I'm here for more than that. I know I've found a good thing here. And I'm not going to do anything that would cause me to lose you."

I loved that answer. I loved the respect it showed for me . . . and the intention it revealed.

But now that we were officially "in a relationship," I started to notice things I hadn't before: the way some black people—especially men—stared at us when we went out together and how I sometimes felt uncomfortable under the directness of their gaze. Like I was doing something I shouldn't be. Once, as we strolled together after a lovely dinner in Baltimore, a car full of black men honked at us.

"Come back, sister!" one of them yelled out of the window. "Come back!"

"If you have children, they'll be confused," one of my black girlfriends told me.

"I just think it's the ultimate in self-hate," said another.

And then there were my parents. Kevin wanted to meet them, and after hearing me talk about him for so many months, my parents were curious about him too. I'd told them about him, including that critical racial detail, and they'd seemed unfazed. Given how I'd described how caring he'd been to me and my daughter, I thought they'd like him instantly.

They didn't. In fact, our dinner together was strangely silent. My mother is the sort of woman who is usually the life of the party, but she barely said a word and hardly made eye contact. I knew there was trouble ahead.

"I just don't like him," she said later.

"Is it because he's white?"

"I don't know." She hesitated, and I remembered the many conversations we'd had in which she'd doubted the possibility of true happiness with a white man. She'd grown up in segregation and had had plenty of negative encounters with whites to justify her feelings. "I just . . . don't like him," she repeated, then clammed up and wouldn't say another word.

My father simply shrugged. "You're grown," he said, but he couldn't seem to bring himself around to any real warmth toward Kevin either.

It was strange: here I was, happy in a relationship for the first time, and instead of being happy for me, my parents seemed cautious and withholding. It bothered me, but my father was right: I was a grown woman. It was my happiness at stake, not theirs. They'd lived in a different time—a different world than the one I had known. I had to do what was right for me.

Of course, you know the end of the story. Kevin and I married in 2005, almost a year to the day after our first email contact. We now have a daughter together, as well as Sierra, who refers to him as "Dad."

And my list? When we bought our house and moved in together as a family, I found it in the bottom of my lingerie drawer. I was surprised by both what I had written and what I hadn't. Of the criteria I had written, my husband met every single one. What I hadn't written was the word "black," even though I had assumed it at the time.

My friend Paula was right: I needed to get out of my own way and let God bring my happiness. And he did.

My purpose in telling you my story is this: I have heard every notion in this book against "bringing home a white boy," and I'm glad I had the

good sense to look at Kevin beyond race and do it anyway. My purpose in writing this book is to challenge black women to look for love
beyond racial boundaries—and to stop letting some of the notions that
have bound our thinking about interracial relationships keep us from
happiness.

So many of us are single and don't want to be. And yet many black
women I know have been approached by white men—white men who,
they admit, are kind, thoughtful, intelligent, and secure—and have rejected, solely on the basis of his race, even the *possibility* of finding out
what that man might have to offer them. After writing an essay on the
anniversary of Loving Day that was published in the *Washington Post* in
June 2008, I knew I had to explore this phenomenon in more depth. To
refresh your memory, Loving Day commemorates the 1967 *Loving v. Virginia* ruling, in which the Supreme Court struck down a Virginia law
preventing blacks and whites from marrying each other. My essay focused on the interesting fact that although the Lovings were a white
male/black female couple, most black/white marriages today—more
than forty years later—are black male/white female. Even more interesting is the fact that, although the most recent census available reported
that 70 percent of black women are single, black women have the greatest resistance to marrying "out" of the race.

I received hundreds of comments in response to the essay, from read-
ers as close as my own neighborhood and as far away as Europe and
Africa. I received letters from black women who felt they had (once
again) been portrayed as angry and racist for refusing white men. I received letters from black men who admitted their discomfort with seeing a "sister" with a white man. I received letters from white men who
told stories of being rebuffed for reasons both straightforward and spe-
cious by black women in whom they had expressed a romantic interest.
And I received emails from black women and their white husbands
who had experienced varying levels of acceptance and disapproval—
sometimes from surprising sources.

The number and the intensity of the responses made me realize that
interracial marriage between black women and white men is a topic that
still generates a great deal of controversy, even in the twenty-first century. Although black men married to white women certainly face their
problems with acceptance in our race-conscious society, black women

and their white spouses seem to face even greater disapproval—if their relationship is allowed to flourish to the point of commitment at all.

What keeps black women from exploring relationships outside of their race, forty-three years after the Lovings' marriage was recognized as a legal union? Why is it that, at a time when the pool of eligible black men is at an all-time low and the pool of single black women is at an all-time high, black women hesitate to look beyond their race for marriage partners? Does marrying interracially really mark a black woman as a "traitor" to our black men? Is a white husband really an emblem of self-hatred? Does the history of sexual oppression that white men imposed on black slave women over the centuries negate the possibility of happiness with a white spouse today? And what about the children?

This book is an exploration of all these questions. It is an attempt to delve deeply into the roots of black women's cultural resistance to white men. It's an effort to harness the theories and emotions behind the controversy, analyze them, and offer them up for deeper discussion. The title reflects the long-standing cultural message stamped deep into every black daughter: "Don't bring home a white boy." At least on some level, these cultural messages play a role in why so many African American women are single. I called this book *Don't Bring Home a White Boy* because it intends to examine even-handedly the cultural messages that discourage black women from interracial dating. But I have to admit, this book is also an advocacy book for my black female sisters. Black women have given much to the struggle against racism and paid a high price for it—in our silence about the treatment we often receive at the hands of black men, in the negative ways we are portrayed in our own communities, in church teachings that advise us to forgo our needs for love and romance and choose community service instead.

Black women have more choices than we realize, and it's time to pursue *all* of them, just as black men do. This book is written in the sincere belief that it's time for African American women to broaden their horizons beyond black men and become open to experiencing romantic happiness with any man whose character and interests are compatible with their own . . . even if that man's skin happens to be white.

A WORD ABOUT WORDS

Throughout this work, you will see the terms *black* and *African American* used interchangeably to denote American persons who are descendants of African slaves. Although I use both terms, my preference has been for the term *black* for a reason pointed out to me by my teenaged daughter. Asked about her ethnicity, she declines to say "African American" because, in her words, that phrase better applies to her friends whose parents emigrated from African countries. Many of these young people were born in this country, but they have strong family ties to Africa. "Those are the *real* African Americans, Mom," she tells me. And I think she has a point. Most American blacks have a far more attenuated connection to their African ancestors, and this country being both a cultural melting pot and a nation fascinated with racial and ethnic categorizations, the term fails to define our experience accurately.

Of course *black* fails on that level too. "Black people" are folks of every shade and hue, from cream to ebony, ecru to ink. One word cannot possibly address the richness of skin tone and experience that is a part of our culture.

My father used to say, "You don't really know a thing until you can call it by its right name." Racial identification is a thing that we as a nation are still struggling to fully "know," understand, and appreciate. I make no claim to "know"; I'm still asking questions. But until I can do better, *black* and *African American* are the words used in this book to describe American people who are descendants of African slaves.

NOTION 1

*After Slavery, I Would **Never, Ever** Date a White Man*

> *Personally, I would never ever "date out." If you know anything about the history of black women in this country—about the way we've been treated by white men—it just seems wrong to even consider a white man as a possible partner. I'd feel like I was dishonoring all my ancestors who suffered rape and sexual abuse at their hands. For me, it comes down to this: my foremothers had no rights, no say over who used their bodies. They couldn't stop them [white men]. But I have the power now and I can say, "You won't get this [body]. You'll never get this."*
> *—From a conversation with a sister-friend, December 2008*

Although slavery ended almost one hundred and fifty years ago, it's very much alive in the consciousness, in the sense of history and place of African American people. And while scholars sometimes debate the prevalence of the rape of slave women by white masters, overseers, and other white men, the anecdotal evidence suggests that if rape wasn't common, it certainly wasn't rare. Almost every African American family with an oral history has some story of a white owner or overseer who fathered children with a black woman.

Because of the legal status of slaves, it is generally assumed that these children were the product of rape: black female slaves, as property, had no rights protected by law—not even rights to their own bodies. It wasn't a crime, therefore, for a white man to have sex with a slave woman, even by force. For that reason, as explained by Harvard Law professor Randall Kennedy in his book *Interracial Intimacies: Sex, Marriage, Identity, and Adoption*, many scholars and historians believe that any sexual encounter between an enslaved woman and a white man could fairly be characterized as rape.[1]

Even after slavery, black women had little or no legal protection against white men. Through Reconstruction and Jim Crow segregation, black housekeepers and hotel workers were at particular risk, since they worked in isolation around white men and would have no witnesses or support if they alleged crimes in court. In an essay published in the compilation *Other Souths: Diversity & Difference in the U.S. South, Reconstruction to Present*, Danielle L. McGuire examines the nexus of sexual violence against black women at the beginning of the civil rights movement. "The sexual abuse of black women . . . was an everyday occurrence," McGuire writes, based on her interviews with black women who grew up in segregation.[2] She quotes Ferdie Walker, a black woman who grew up in the 1930s and 1940s in Fort Worth, Texas, as saying that it " 'was really bad and it was bad for all black girls.' "[3]

White-on-black rape, sexual assault, and intimidation continued for nearly one hundred years after slavery ended. But by the mid-1950s, even in the Deep South, black women were gaining a legal voice.

In 1959, in Tallahassee, Florida, against the backdrop of the 1955 Montgomery, Alabama, bus boycott and the growing momentum of the civil rights movement, four white men abducted and gang-raped Betty Jean Owens, a young black woman. The men were arrested and pleaded innocent to the charge, even after they had signed a confession—joking to themselves that they would never spend a day in jail. After all, they were white men. Their victim was just another "nigger girl" and they were just "having some fun." But they were wrong. They were ultimately convicted for the assault: it was the first time in Florida history that white men were ever convicted of rape against a black woman. McGuire summarizes the impact of the case:

The arrest, trial, and conviction of Owens's white rapists by an all-white jury marked a dramatic change . . . the verdict not only broke with southern tradition but fractured the philosophical and political foundations of white supremacy by challenging the relationship between sexual domination and racial inequality.[4]

The case of Betty Jean Owens is within memory for many living African Americans and is a testament to just how much things have changed in our nation's race relations in fifty years. Today the opportunity to pursue justice for rape seems a given for most American women, regardless of the victim's race or the race of her attacker. But only fifty years ago, a black woman bringing a charge of rape against a white man faced an uphill battle.

In her book *Black Feminist Thought*, Patricia Hill Collins writes, "Freedom for Black women has meant freedom *from* White men, not the freedom to choose White men as lovers and friends . . . given the history of sexual abuse of Black women by White men, individual Black women who choose White partners become reminders of difficult history. . . . Such individual liaisons aggravate a collective sore spot because they recall historical master/slave relationships."[5]

Hill Collins sums up the black community's resistance to BW/WM relationships succinctly. This is the history most black folks grew up with and some experienced. This is also the history that has best served an important goal: rallying men and women from all walks of life—and all races—to the cause of ending segregation and racism. Stories of slavery and its horrors, stories of brutality and cruelty have been important instruments in unifying black people around their common goal.

But focusing on the horrors of slavery, of Reconstruction and Jim Crow—and on a black/white paradigm that paints all whites as oppressors and all blacks as victims—omits a broader discussion of the sexism black women face from men in our own communities. It distances black women from the sexism that women of all races endure at the hands of men of all backgrounds. It casts all whites (white men in particular) as evil, powerful abusers and all blacks (black women in particular) as weak and powerless. It ignores the roles of African nations in the slave trade, and it glosses over the greed that can drive all human beings, regardless of race. Avoiding these facts creates serious collisions with the realities of the present.

The present reality is that black women have come a long way, baby.

Black women have continued to march, fight, and struggle, gaining greater and greater ground both legally and socially. Black women have thrived in spite of efforts to limit us or to force us into the backseat. Name any walk of life—law and politics, literature and medicine, engineering and military service, film and music, art and philanthropy, even outer space—and there's a black woman who is a leader in the field. In spite of the efforts of some to place us at the bottom of the social hierarchy, we, as Maya Angelou wrote, "still rise."[6]

Present realities put black women and white men on a new footing with each other in this multicultural world. In just fifty years, we've gone from powerless to substantially more powerful—and not just in terms of our legal status. "Nigger gals" are running corporations, are members of Congress and media billionaires. A white defendant in a criminal proceeding might expect to square off against a black female prosecutor and plead his case before a black female judge! We've chipped huge holes in the system of white male authority that existed when Betty Jean Owens's case went to trial, and while the fight against inequality and injustice continues, the progress we have made is nothing short of outstanding.

Don't believe it? Still only see the problems? Then consider these email comments from Angela Shaw, one of the first black women to graduate from Harvard Law School. She has traveled the world and seen both its wonders and its horrors:

> I don't know a single black American woman who would trade places with the women around the globe . . . I've looked into the eyes of the little girls [like the ones in] *Slumdog Millionaire*. I thank God every day for blessing me with having been born a black American woman. I don't deny that there are unique challenges that we face regarding our appreciation of our own value, but there is no other ethnic woman (including and especially white women) on this planet that I would trade places with.[7]

So much has changed for black women in a mere half century that our identities are struggling to catch up. In one way, it's easy to understand why so many of us black women cling to the notions of generations past. History, after all, is what grounds us. It gives us a connection to place and people. It is a part of who we are. But history is, by its very definition, the past.

The present realities are that the old-fashioned notions of white = oppressor, black = victim aren't as clear-cut as they used to be. The present realities are that black American women are more powerful, more relevant, and on more equal footing with men of all races than ever before in history. The present realities are that sexism presents as great a stumbling block for black women as racism—and that men of all races can be guilty of it. The present reality is that black women are more likely to face sexual violence from black men than from white men, and that black-versus-white thinking keeps us from fully addressing that problem in our community. Finally, the present reality is that black women are not limited to men from only one race; we have the option of choosing our romantic partners out of the entire global village of men if we so choose, based not on their race but on their individual qualities and characters.

BLACK MAN, WHITE MAN, GOOD MAN, BAD MAN

The men did what they wanted to the women when I was a girl [growing up in the 1940s and '50s]. I remember my uncle used to beat my aunt so badly she could barely walk. He had a bunch of children by her . . . and several others with other women who lived nearby. Even at the end of her life, when she was very ill, he forced himself on her sexually. He said that was all she was good for. Until the end of her life, she defended him. "Black men got it hard," she'd say. But it seemed to me then—and now— that she had it even worse.

—Name withheld

Basing our rejection of white men as potential partners on the legacy of slavery puts all kinds of limits on black women's identities, forces every white man we meet into a narrow box (robbing him of an individual identity as well), and suppresses important and necessary dialogue between black men and women about our treatment within the black community. Although the slavery notion is intended as a means of sustaining black unity, at the end of the day it may cause as many problems as it solves. Here's why:

Lawyers know well that to craft a good and persuasive argument, you have to find a way to neutralize difficult or contradictory facts. You craft a strategy and put your best ideas forward, sweeping the secondary ones to the side. Then you "sell" your key arguments to the relevant audiences—judge, jury, the general public. It's how cases are won.

As a part of the "case" for the success of the civil rights movement, the black leadership made a conscious choice to present a unified front against white oppression (and to choose certain people to represent it), and that meant minimizing the popular impression among white people that black men were violent, hypersexual "animals." For black women, that meant keeping silent about some of the dirtier of our personal racial laundry: the domestic abuse, incest, and sexual violence that occurred against women and children in the black community—just as it still does throughout American culture today.

Did you know, for example, that nine months before light-skinned Rosa Parks refused to give up her seat in the back of the bus for a white passenger, Claudette Colvin did the same thing? Colvin was fifteen years old when she was dragged off a Montgomery, Alabama, city bus by police officers for refusing to give up her seat to a white passenger, but she was considered "too dark" to represent the civil rights movement, too "feisty," too poor. During the legal challenge that followed her impulsive refusal to comply with Jim Crow laws, she also discovered she was pregnant. The father? A married black man who, some sources say, raped Colvin, then lied about it. Instead of becoming the voice of the bus boycott, Colvin was shunned, was expelled from school, and ultimately had to leave Montgomery just to find work.[8]

It's not a story most people know, but it is an important one, for two reasons. First, it was Colvin's lawsuit, *Browder v. Gayle*,[9] that ultimately desegregated public transportation in the same way that *Brown v. Board of Education* desegregated schools, and second, because it illustrates the concerns involved in the shaping of a movement. Colvin didn't represent the image the leaders of the civil rights movement hoped to project; in fact she had several liabilities. The saddest of them was the ostracism she faced as a pregnant teenager, an ostracism that becomes even sadder if the rumors were true and the child was conceived as a result of rape, not by a white man but by a black one. Justice for this crime against Colvin never came: indeed, she was sacrificed entirely for the goals of the civil rights movement.

Other crimes were suppressed for similar reasons. Perhaps you re-member the late James L. Bevel, the minister and civil rights leader who was a close confidant of Dr. Martin Luther King Jr. Bevel was a front-and-center figure in the civil rights movement of the 1960s. He organized the 1963 Children's Crusade in Birmingham, Alabama, and was a leader of the Freedom Rides to desegregate public accommodations through-out the South in the early 1960s. He helped organize the March on Washington in 1963 and the Selma-to-Montgomery march in Alabama in 1965. Along with civil rights icons Jesse Jackson and Andrew Young, Bevel witnessed the April 4, 1968, assassination of Dr. King in Memphis, Tennessee.[10]

In 2008 he was convicted of raping his teenaged daughter repeatedly over a two-year period in the 1990s. His daughter brought the charges out of fear that her father might also sexually abuse her younger sister. When she testified against him, he accused her of "disloyalty" and as-serted, "Someone has plotted to destroy my reputation, my being."

He showed little remorse for what he'd done to his own daughter, referring to having sex with her as "education" conducted for "scientific purposes."

Eldridge Cleaver, writing in *Soul on Ice*, his 1968 internationally best-selling manifesto of black power and aggression against white people, delineated how he developed his strategies for revenge rapes of white women. He acknowledged that for "practice," however, he raped a few black women first—making clear his disdain for the sisters who had struggled beside him to end segregation.[11]

These men are icons in the fight for racial parity between blacks and whites. But their callousness toward black women casts them in a very different light. The lives of Reverend Bevel and Eldridge Cleaver make an important point: we cannot generalize about which men have black women's best interests at heart, and which don't, on purely racial lines.

Black women don't focus on this violence that is perpetrated daily against us because, for a great deal of the past one hundred and fifty years, we have believed being silent was "for the good of the race." For the good of the race, we pretended that gender inequalities were a lesser problem. For the good of the race, black women kept silent about the crimes committed against them by black men, because revealing those crimes might hinder the fight to obtain racial justice for all black people. Black women knew that if they leveled charges against them, black men would face especially harsh treatment from a racially unjust system. To protect black men from that system, black women swallowed their hurts and suffered in silence.

Certainly, in the period between the end of the Civil War and the close of the civil rights movement, most black women perceived racism—not misogyny and sexism—as the greater evil and so willingly signed on to the effort to end that great wrong. They hoped that once the uphill struggle against segregation and racism had been addressed, the black community would be free to address and heal gender-related issues.

This sacrifice speaks to the depths of loyalty and commitment that black women have demonstrated to black men and to the black community as a whole. But despite the fact that black women who gathered in congregations in churches provided much of the money and muscle of the civil rights movement, credit for their service to the movement and the expected shift to healing the community issues of violence against them have proved hard to come by. Even as the last vestiges of the Jim Crow system began to fade away and the Black Power movement began to challenge white privilege and preach that "black is beautiful," black women were forced aside. Black men, newly empowered by the end of segregation and the advent of affirmative action, made it their first priority to enforce the same kind of patriarchal limitations on black women as white men had. Two of the Black Power movement's most brilliant and loyal women, Elaine Brown and Angela Davis, have written about being kicked out of the cause for not being deferential enough to the men. Black women who identified themselves as feminist—writers, scholars, and thinkers like Michele Wallace, bell hooks, Alice Walker, and many others—were harshly criticized by black men for demanding better treatment for black women.

The civil rights campaign would hardly be the first time women's concerns were ignored, minimized, or swept under the rug. Whether the perpetrator is white, black, Asian, Native American, or Hispanic, violence against women is as American as baseball and apple pie. As acclaimed novelist Pearl Cleage wrote in the essay "The Other Facts of Life,"

> In America, they admit that five women a day are killed by their husbands, boyfriends, ex-husbands or lovers. That doesn't count the women killed during random rapes, murders, robberies and kidnappings. In America, the main reason women are ever hospitalized is because they've been beaten and tortured by men. More than for childbirth. More than for cancer care. More than from heart attacks. In America, thousands of women a day are raped and/or tortured and abused by men in as many ways as you can think of, and don't want to, including beating, shooting, scalding, stabbing, shaking and starving. The facts indicate that we are under siege, incredibly vulnerable, totally unprepared and too busy denying the truth to collectively figure out what to do about it.[12]

Right now, a black woman is being abused by a father, brother, boyfriend, or husband—a black man who professes to "love" her. Chances are good she won't speak out against him. Most of the time, although friends and family know, they won't intercede to help her. Most of the time these men won't be prosecuted. Black women are still protecting black men, even men in the media.

Black folks are adept at blaming the victim—especially when the victim is a black female and the perpetrator is a black male. Remember the 1992 rape conviction of boxer Mike Tyson? How many folks said eighteen-year-old beauty pageant contestant Desiree Washington shouldn't have gone to his room at two a.m.? What did she think would happen? How often did you see "Free Mike Tyson" T-shirts after a court of law found him guilty and sentenced him to six years in prison? The black female victim's conduct was heavily scrutinized, as was her decision to prosecute for the violation. In some corners, the consensus seemed to be that Desiree Washington "deserved" to be raped simply for putting herself in Mike Tyson's line of sight and that the real crime was that she, a black woman, had turned a black man over to the criminal justice system.[13]

And what about singer R. Kelly, accused of having sex with two underage girls? Although he was acquitted of child pornography charges in 2008, rumors still abound on the content of the sex tape that allegedly shows the singer having sexual relations with a minor. The allegations did nothing to harm his career: *Double Up*, the album released during the controversy, was his most successful ever.

Or the even more recent controversy between singers Rihanna and Chris Brown? A frightening number of *black women* have theorized about what Rihanna might have done to *deserve* a beatdown—as though there were ever a situation when a young man beating up a young woman were justifiable!

Perhaps you don't need to look to the headlines at all. Maybe in your own family, in your own life, there was a pastor, a neighbor, a family member—a black man close to you—who was a predator and abuser. Perhaps you told your mother, your aunt, or another older female. Were you believed and supported? Or were you told to keep quiet? If you'd been raped or sexually assaulted by a white man or boy, would the reaction to your plight have been different?

One woman I corresponded with told this horrific story:

I don't know the full story, but my maternal grandmother was killed by her husband, my grandfather. This was done not in one act of violence, but in a lifetime of beatings that hastened her death. He deprived me and most of my cousins of getting to know Madea, as she died in a hospital at the age of 44. I will be 44 on my next birthday and I can only imagine that her entire life was a miserable existence. While she was in the hospital dying, my sister as a child remembered another woman in their home, in their bed. Even now, I don't know how many aunts and uncles I truly have.

Another tragedy of my grandfather was the fact that he gave my twelve-year-old aunt to a man several years his senior. The man had had sex with her (child rape) so [my grandfather figured the rapist] might as well take her as his wife (one less mouth to feed). My poor aunt had fifteen children and grew up with them. Could/Should/Would she have protected her 8 daughters from several years of sexual molestation under different circumstances? I don't know. I do know that [the man she married] molested all his daughters, even fathering some of their children. He even had access to his granddaughters as well. This is the life they had grown to accept. Some of them are messed up to this day.

In both examples, we are talking rural Alabama in the 1950s and '60s, where they (the women) felt helpless and felt that [this abuse] was their lot to suffer. They didn't even consider the law because of Jim Crow and for fear of even more abuse from whites. I don't begrudge my aunt as she is so simple-minded and sweet, but I still know women even from that time who would never have allowed it. At the same time, I have legions of relatives who knew this abuse was going on and not one lifted a hand to help my grandmother or my aunt. Maybe they accepted it too, but I know today, I would sound the trumpet. I would blow the whistle loud and risk alienation. My heart hurts for some of my female relatives who endured these wretched lives. They stood by these black men who used, abused, tortured and mistreated them. Again, who were they going to tell? It was life as usual. [It was] a secret that everyone knew.[14]

While it is certainly true that black female victims of violence may not receive fair treatment from the legal system, it's also true that they don't receive fair treatment from their own communities. Consider, for example, the shocking 2008 case of an eleven-year-old Milwaukee girl raped over the course of hours by twenty different men and boys between the ages of thirteen and forty while another teenaged girl and an adult woman watched. Everyone involved was black. Most of the males were convicted with sentences of between three and fifteen years. The forty-year-old man was sentenced to twenty-five years in prison, the teenaged girl to three years in juvenile hall. Six others were not brought to trial for lack of evidence.

The case is extraordinary not only for its sheer brutality but also for community reaction to the young victim. Quoted in an MSNBC.com report, one neighbor said of the sentencing of the perpetrators, "Five years? Ten years? That's ridiculous. They (are) getting time for nothing. That girl, she knew what she was doing."[15]

The fact that the girl in question was only eleven—still a child—

seems not to enter into the equation. "She asked for it" and she got it, and so do all black women from other blacks when we step outside the box we've been labeled to fit into. What's particularly ironic is that this is the exact same box that whites built for black females during the slave trade, the logic that excused rape and other mistreatment: we're hypersexual, little better than animals. We asked for it and we got it, and we have no right to complain about it. While the community clearly feels the outrage of that treatment by whites in the past, complaining about our treatment by our brothers in the race can still buy us harsh criticism now.

These cases—both the high-profile and the desperately, quietly unknown—illustrate our obsessions with race and sex in vivid ways. When black men rape black women or girls—even when all the evidence is there—it's a matter for silent shame; the victim is expected to suffer quietly and to bear her scars inwardly. When the perpetrator is white, however, the black community is ready to mobilize behind her—even if the evidence isn't there.

RALLYING AGAINST THE EVIL WHITE MAN, GUILTY OR NOT

In their book *Gender Talk: The Struggle for Women's Equality in African American Communities*, scholars Johnnetta Betsch Cole and Beverly Guy-Sheftall tackle the double standard of the black community when it comes to race and sex:

> They are up in arms when white men abuse Black women because they want it known that Black women's bodies will no longer be the terrain for white male physical or sexual aggression . . . any white man who violates a Black woman's body violates Black men and the "property interest" in that Black woman's body. However, when the abuser is a Black male, the response is less politically strident, and often politically defensive, because the assault on the Black woman . . . is sometimes understood to represent an assertion of Black male masculinity which, it is argued, is a response to white male racism.[16]

In other words, when black men abuse black women in the same ways white men did under slavery, their conduct is a response to white racism, which effectively offers an excuse for the black man. The question is, just what difference does the race of her attacker make for the black woman who has been brutalized? Does it in any way change the physical and psychological pain of the attack?

Like Cole and Guy-Sheftall, I would argue that it does not—and encourage black women to take a fresh look at how they perceive violence against women. Many of us have absorbed a cultural idea that accepts behavior from black men that would never be tolerated from a white perpetrator. These cultural ideas aren't true. They are more accurately described as mythologies that continue to shape our world in terms of black/white and victim/oppressor—even when these labels don't apply.

The article "Blacks' and Whites' Perceptions of Interracial and Intraracial Rape," published in the *Journal of Social Psychology*, explains how race and sex have been twisted into "mythologies" in our slavery-damaged perceptions. During slavery

> the rape of a Black female slave by her White owner was ignored or condoned. In contrast, a Black man having sexual relations, even if consensual, with a White woman was severely punished and often executed. Vestiges of those reactions to rape have remained . . . however, most rapes do not conform to the myth of interracial rape; 93% of rape cases involve people of the same race.[17]

The evidence of our mythology (though perhaps *pathology* would be a better word) is evident in two other relatively recent headlines: the twin rape allegations of Tawana Brawley and the Duke lacrosse team.

In 1987, in Wappingers Falls, New York, Tawana Brawley, a fifteen-year-old black girl, was found huddled in a garbage bag, her hair and body smeared with feces and racist graffiti. She alleged that six white men, including a police officer, had abducted and raped her. The case became a national rallying cry for African Americans from all backgrounds. In *Interracial Intimacies*, Kennedy writes:

Although the putative victim exhibited a suspicious evasiveness from early on in the evolution of this bizarre saga, a broad cross-section of African Americans fervently embraced her and insisted upon her honesty. They did so in part because her alleged ordeal evoked terrible collective memories of white men's sexual brutalizing of black women under the tolerant gaze of white officials.[18]

A grand jury ultimately refuted Brawley's allegations, finding little evidence consistent with any sexual intercourse of any kind (no genital trauma, no sperm); Brawley was seen at a party during the period in which she claimed to have been "abducted"; an eyewitness spotted Tawana as she climbed into a Dumpster, wearing a garbage bag. Brawley was sued for defamation by one of the men accused and was ordered to pay almost $200,000 in damages for what was soon widely determined to be a hoax.[19]

Similarly, in 2006, Crystal Mangum accused three white Duke University lacrosse team members of raping her at a party. The claims unraveled and were dismissed a year later, when photographs, eyewitnesses, and rape kit evidence conclusively refuted Mangum's story. Furthermore, the district attorney charged with investigating and prosecuting the case was disbarred for "dishonesty, fraud, deceit and misrepresentation"—a first in the state of North Carolina.[20]

Black folks are sensitive to both the Desiree Washington/Mike Tyson and the Tawana Brawley/Duke scenarios in different ways. In the case of Desiree Washington, a popular reaction was "How could you do that to a brother?" and for the Brawley/Duke situations, the reaction was "We believe her no matter what." The difference isn't the crime—the violence of rape remains tragically the same—but the race of the perpetrators. Race makes one allegation of rape something to be silenced; race makes another allegation something to be rallied around. We hold to the notion of white/black rape and arrange our lives in protest to it. We're making up for the abuses of slavery, we say. We're telling white men, "You took this once, but now you can't have it." Fine, if only it really made a difference to our grandmothers and great-grandmothers.

But it doesn't. Those days are gone and nothing we do now changes them. However, our grandmothers and great-grandmothers also suffered daily at the hands of nonwhite men, and so do we. Our everyday realities prove that those of us who are attacked will most likely be a victim of a black man in our lives. Many of us already have been.

I don't mean to demonize all black men, nor do I mean to grant white men a pass. The point is a larger one that reaches beyond racism and history—and a smaller one that reaches to the most intimate and personal of decisions a woman makes. That point is this: white men have abused black women, and black men have too. The point is that black women have internalized the idea that, for the good of the race, we loudly condemn one rape and completely deny another. The point is that accepting these party lines about race, sex, and violence limits our choices, suppresses the dialogue about gender issues between black men and black women, and continues to foster the idea that black women's bodies are not our own.

THOSE WHO LOVE US

The hard legacy of what her foremothers endured during slavery isn't something any African American woman is likely to forget. But it may be easier to focus on the crimes of the past than to take a hard look at the truths of the present. Fighting racism has been the focus of our attentions as a people for so long, we've chosen not to look at the misogyny that pervades our culture, both black and white. In short, some black women still choose to demonize all white men rather than look objectively at the facts of our modern times, which are these: some men, whatever their race, are bad for us. And the converse is true as well: some men, whatever their race, are good for us.

It's just that simple, and it's always been that simple.

It's a little-known fact that, even in segregation—even in slavery days—white men and black women lived as family units. Tempting as it may be for the purposes of intraracial unity to characterize all interracial unions prior to the civil rights era as rape, the evidence gathered by Harvard Law School professor Randall Kennedy demonstrates that it just wasn't so. In probate records and other court documents, he recounts stories of white men who purchased slave females, freed them, and then lived openly with them as husband and wife, although laws at the time prohibited marriage.[21]

White men continued to enjoy privileged access to black women as Jim Crow custom generally permitted such pairings not only for sexual purposes, but also as the nucleus of stable, family-like relationships. According to journalist Ray Stannard Baker, "White men in many communities, often prominent judges, governors, wealthy planters, made little or no secret of the fact that they had a Negro family as well as a white family."[22]

I know this to be true from a story my mother told me about a childhood visit with her father and mother (my grandparents) to her father's family's farm in North Carolina in the 1940s:

This old white man came to visit us, and he greeted my father with genuine affection. He seemed really happy to meet me and wanted to take me with him into town, to buy a present or something, I can't remember now. We waited for the bus together and I remember feeling a little uncomfortable: I had lived my whole life in segregation and I didn't have any idea what to say to this old white man. When the bus arrived, we got on. The bus driver, who was, of course, a white man, eyed me with an ugly look and said, "You sit in the back," but the white man corrected him sharply. "She'll sit with me. She's my grandbaby and you'll leave her alone." The white bus driver backed right down. I understood later that my grandfather had two families, a white one in one county and a black one in another, and he supported both of them, though he definitely made a concerted effort to keep them geographically separated.

How many white male/black female "families" were there before 1950? How many white men lived "double lives" like my greatgrandfather? No one really knows. Cases like these pose challenges for historians because formal documents (like marriage licenses and birth certificates that named white fathers) were illegal. But one study, "Black-White Interracial Marriage Trends, 1850–2000," which culled data from census reports taken over a span of one hundred and fifty years, concluded that

interracial marriages (including common law marriages) were uncommon, but not necessarily rare, prior to the end of Reconstruction. While the increase in the size of the free black population due to Emancipation reduced the visibility of interracial marriage among blacks, declines in the underlying propensity to intermarry only occurred after the end of Reconstruction. White policing of the color line in the South and "latent" racism in the non-South contributed to a drastic overall decline in . . . the out-marriage ratio between 1880 and 1930. . . . With the atrophy of the Jim Crow state after 1930, the frequency of interracial marriage increased briefly before stabilizing with the Civil Rights period. With the twilight of the Civil Rights era, the frequency of the interracial marriage began to increase at a steady exponential rate.[23]

Kennedy uncovers several other cases, including the white Yazoo County, Mississippi, sheriff who married a black schoolteacher, and the former slave owner who married his slave mistress after the end of the Civil War, explaining to the army chaplain who performed the ceremony, "I am already married to her in the sight of God."[24] In another case, during the Jim Crow era, a black woman living with a white man in Mississippi told an interviewer,

A few words of the marriage ceremony, what do they mean? I feel I'm living a great deal more decently with a union based on love than some who are married before the law and I don't feel that I've heaped any disgrace on Jim [her son]. He's got a dad and a good one who is doing everything possible to be a good dad to him. And we live in our little shack, happily, and according to my standards, decently.[25]

Recent books explore the nuances of relationships between black women and white men in slavery times and beyond. Historian Annette Gordon-Reed's critically acclaimed book *The Hemingses of Monticello: An American Family* chronicles several generations of the relationship between the family of Thomas Jefferson and his slave Sally Hemings. In *Passing Strange: A Gilded Age Tale of Love and Deception Across the Color Line,* Martha Sandweiss uncovers the unusual love story of acclaimed nineteenth-century geologist Clarence King, a white man who pretended to be a black man to marry and father children with Ada Copeland, a black woman. In *The House at the End of the Road,* W. Ralph Eubanks tells of his grandparents: a white man and a black woman who built a life for themselves and their children in south Alabama in 1914, in defiance of the cultural norms of the times.

While no one argues that these cases were common, they do add an important element to the discussion of interracial relationships. Even during the darkest nadir of this country's race relations, black women have on occasion chosen white men as spouses—when those white men have revealed themselves to be the most desirable partner in that woman's eyes.

On a similar point, just as we tend to emphasize a "group evil" in the acts done by some white men in our racial past and choose to ignore a fuller picture that places blame and credit on individuals, we also tend to emphasize the "group" powerlessness of black men in the face of racism and excuse from individual responsibility some black men. This is both false and dangerous for us women as human beings. As Kennedy points out, no one is ever completely without power:

> The obscure black man who is relatively powerless in many situations can in a blink reveal himself to be rather powerful in relation to others whom he is in a position to hurt. For at least a moment, every rapist is powerful in relations to his victim. It is simply untenable to claim then, that blacks and other discriminated against people of color have no power. And because blacks, like all responsible individuals, have some power, their moral hygiene, like everyone else's warrants close, careful attention.[26]

By using slavery as an excuse to deny ourselves even the possibility of attracting white men, black women are still suffering, still silent, and still protecting others—and still seeing our struggles in terms of blacks against whites long after white men have ceased to be our biggest threat.

ROLES OF OTHER BLACKS IN THE SLAVE TRADE

One additional thought: a black woman who believes that slavery should limit who is acceptable mating material should rule out not only white men but men who are from certain parts of Africa—and their descendants.

Africans had a significant role in the slave trade—a truth that goes largely unmentioned when slavery is discussed by African American blacks. Writes Tunde Obadina, director of Africa Business Information Services, in his essay "Slave Trade: A Root of Contemporary African Crisis,"

> At the initial stage of the trade, parties of Europeans captured Africans in raids on communities in the coastal areas. But this soon gave way to buying slaves from African rulers and traders. The vast majority of slaves taken out of Africa were sold by African rulers, traders and a military aristocracy who all grew wealthy from the business. Most slaves were acquired through wars or by kidnapping . . . Africa's rulers, traders and military aristocracy protected their interest in the slave trade. They discouraged Europeans from leaving the coastal areas to venture into the interior of the continent. European trading companies realized the benefit of dealing with African suppliers and not unnecessarily antagonizing them. The companies could not have mustered the resources it would have taken to directly capture the tens of millions of people shipped out of Africa. It was far more sensible and safer to give Africans guns to fight the many wars that yielded captives for the trade. The slave trading network stretched deep into Africa's interior. Slave trading firms were aware of their dependency on African suppliers. The Royal African Company, for instance, instructed its agents on the west coast of the continent that "if any differences happen, to endeavor an amicable accommodation rather than use force." They were "to endeavor to live in all friendship with them" and "to hold frequent palavers with the Kings and the Great Men of the Country, and keep up a good correspondence with them, ingratiating yourself by such prudent methods" as may be deemed appropriate.[27]

And of course, a fully enlightened historical discussion of Africa must also include the ironies of Liberia, a nation formed by African Americans who emigrated to the United States at the end of the Civil War and set up a class system of haves and have-nots that mirrored the injustices they had left.

The fully informed black woman knows the blame for the horrors of slavery goes far beyond skin color and deep into the greed of the human soul.

Taken together, all these facts complete the picture and deflate the slavery notion against pursuing partners outside the race. The struggle now isn't between black and white—or even between male and female—but between those who treat us well and those who don't. Reverend Lisa Vazquez, author of the black female empowerment blog "Black Women, Blow the Trumpet," offers these words toward a fresh analysis of how to move past both slavery and the unaddressed gender issues between black men and black women:

> The actions of black men as a whole have caused many black women a lot of pain, and have produced a lot of anger. At some point, we have to move *forward*. You can let it go any day you want to. May I point out one fact that may help some of my sistas get over their bitterness? White people will not apologize for slavery and racism. Black men will not apologize for all that has happened. Waiting for remorse to be shown only allows resentment to fester.
>
> My advice to all black women: *Stop waiting* for an apology from black men and *stop waiting* for an apology from white people. We won't be getting one.
>
> We can choose to move onward and to seek self-actualization. It all begins with a mirror. . . . Slavery isn't a defense for anything. Slave conditioning isn't an excuse for anything. We have a choice every day we wake up to dismantle class conditioning, slave condition-ing, black self-hatred, and any other dysfunctional conditioning that we have internalized. *We have a choice to make.*
>
> When I hear black people tell me, "in slavery, we were taught to hate ourselves," and "in slavery, our families were always being split up," I often reply, "and now that we can interpret the histori-cal conditioning, what is the choice we decide on *today*?" [28]

FORGET THE MEN: IT'S ALL ABOUT THE WOMAN

Vazquez believes that black women have some "reinterpreting" to do in order to make peace with the past and to open themselves up to accepting a brighter future. Reinterpreting means taking a fresh look at the notions that govern our lives, including notions about whom we date, whom we marry, and whom we love. In her essays, she encourages black women to "dismantle" ideas that limit them to all-black choices.

Evia Moore, founder of the ezine Black Female Interracial Marriage, dedicated to "empowering black women to make long-range choices that promote and protect their interests 'first and foremost,' " has written extensively on the issues surrounding black women and mate selection, arguing that black women must learn to choose men based on "quality," not race. In email correspondence, Moore, who has a background in mental health, addressed the slavery argument as a question of black women's "woundedness":

> The woman who really wants to be in a relationship with a quality man, but who is making this sort of "because of slavery" response is making an argument that is entirely emotional. She is in pain and is expressing her woundedness. This attitude mostly springs from the lack of opportunities to heal. Most [African Americans] have not had a chance to heal [from the effects of racism] because the topic of race is so volatile—and the topic of black-white interracial relationships/sex is about as volatile as it gets.
>
> The "slavery" response is also about fear—fear MAINLY of social ostracism (on some level) by other blacks, fear of white men, fear of rejection by white and other non-black males, fear that a white male can't love a black woman, fear of being hurt by a white or non-black male and then having to face the ridicule of the black community. It's also about a . . . lack of self-esteem (Am I pretty enough? Am I good enough? Am I lovable?) and a fear of leaving the familiar black comfort zone. (Do I dare to take a chance on finding a mate who might be of a quality beyond my imagination? . . . What if I fail?) [The fears and insecurities go] on and on . . .

In her book *Rock My Soul: Black People and Self-Esteem*, black feminist scholar bell hooks makes similar points about the "woundedness" of African American people—women in particular—and the difficulties associated with healing the ongoing legacies of racism. Citing psychologist Nathaniel Branden's *The Six Pillars of Self-Esteem*, hooks writes, "Many young black people who feel victimized by racism are more willing to articulate the cause of their pain than to consider taking any actions that would eliminate that cause. This is the behavior that is self-defeating and self-sabotaging." Branden describes the sort of thinking that might lead a black woman to refuse to "date out" even more explicitly:

> Sometimes people who are essentially dependent and fearful choose a form of self-assertiveness that is self-destructive. It consists of reflexively saying "No!" when their interests would be better served by saying "Yes." Their own form of self-assertiveness is protest—whether it makes sense or not. . . . While healthy self-assertiveness requires the ability to say no, it is ultimately tested not by what we are against, but what we are for . . . self-assertiveness asks that we not only oppose what we deplore but that we live and express our values.[29]

Or as Vazquez writes,

Fear is the slave chain for the black woman now.

Resentment is the slave chain for the black woman now.

Denial is the slave chain for the black woman now.[30]

Ultimately, the slavery notion is rooted in fear. What if a white man could make us happy and treat us well? What would happen to the safety of our belief in the "black family" or the "black community"? Will we still be loved and accepted if we marry outside the race, or will we have betrayed something important that can never be recaptured? Will we still be "black women" if we align with men of other cultures? And even more important, if this notion is wrong, what other concepts in our belief system may also be in jeopardy?

These are the real questions at the root of the idea that we, as black women, should never partner with white men "because of slavery," and these are the real fears that black women must address within themselves as they reexamine both history and present realities and make new choices.

My belief on this issue is simple:

When black women who want to be in relationships, who want to raise families, who want to share all the love inside them with a man reject possible partners who might be good for them and to them *solely on the basis of race*, they may be throwing away their best chances for happiness with both hands. If they never marry, if they never have those children they dream of, if they never give that love inside them, they are failing to express some of their fundamental values. In the end, they deprive not only themselves but the whole community of the beauty of a fully actualized life.

Black women can no longer afford to use a difficult-to-document history as the basis for ruling out a substantial section of the marriage/relationship market. It's time to see history through a wider lens, and the present with our eyes wide.

I'll leave you with the words of my friend, playwright Mona R. Washington, a smart black woman who has dated men from all over the world. On using slavery and the assumption of racism to exclude certain partners, she said, "You can't blame a child for who his parents were. It's something none of us have any control over. If you want to be judged on the content of your character, start by approaching others on the same grounds."

NOTION 2

I'm Looking for My Good Black Man

> *Nothing but a black man will do.*
> > *—From an anonymous email to the author*

> *I ain't down with the [chocolate-vanilla] swirl.*
> > *—Daamon Speller,* A Box of White Chocolate

I want to tell you the stories of two of my friends. I've changed their names but not their circumstances. Perhaps their stories will sound familiar to you.

First, there's Mimi, a woman I've known most of my life and whom I have the utmost love and respect for—except, perhaps, for her choices in men. Mimi seemed to move from one bad relationship to the next. For years she was with a good-looking physician—we'll call him David—who couldn't seem to get a grip on the meaning of the word *faithful*. David was married when they met, but that didn't stop him from pursuing her. And why not? She was in her late twenties, attractive, college-educated, with a good job, making a professional salary. Mimi was the sort of woman many men would find appealing, with an easy smile, an athletic figure, a quick wit, and an outgoing, free-spirited nature.

But she hadn't dated much since college, so the attentions of this older, attractive, married man were intriguing.

"We worked together and he made my days so much fun. I never meant it to go that far. You have to know I'm not the sort of woman who goes around stealing other women's men," she told me. "But at the same time, I was lonely, and at the beginning, he was so charming. We always had such a great time together. We'd go to lunch or drinks after work. He told me his wife didn't understand him, and even though that's one of the oldest lines in the book, I believed him."

Mimi's "friendship" with her married man deepened into a romance that ultimately got them both fired, broke up his marriage, and began a rocky ten-year relationship between them. "I hoped he would marry me, since now he was free," she confessed. "But he said I was a 'home wrecker' and he wasn't sure he could trust me. I guess I felt he was right—even though he was as guilty of destroying his marriage as I was. My own guilt kept me in turmoil, so I didn't press the issue when he prowled around, pursuing other women while living with me."

Years went by, years of fighting, breaking up, getting back together over and over and over again. With her fertility declining and commitment nowhere in sight, Mimi started to talk about leaving, to talk about seeing other men and letting this guy know he wasn't the only game in town.

"At my new job, there was another guy. He was very different. Not as charming or as handsome. Just nice. Funny. Smart. He liked me. He kept asking me out for a drink. But I never went. I told him that I'd been burned badly in an office relationship before, and that was certainly true. But that wasn't the real reason I turned him down and I think he knew it. The real reason was he was white, and even though I thought he was nice, I just couldn't leave a black man—even one who was treating me badly—for a white one."

And she didn't. Instead, she dated the black guy for several more years—through the entire decade of her thirties—and suffered through many more turbulent confrontations over his other women until, finally, he dumped her for a younger version and moved away.

Mimi's story—and her reason for refusing the attentions of a white office mate—aren't unique. Consider Tabitha's story:

Tabitha was a successful manager in her midthirties. She had a winning smile and one of those open personalities that made her the natural confidante of just about everyone she met. With a trim, petite figure and a wardrobe of beautiful clothes that maximized her assets, she should have been sought after by men of every description.

And she was, but Tabitha had a certain kind of man in mind. "He has to be tall, brown-skinned, great teeth, financially secure, and well educated," she admitted, waving a set of elegantly manicured nails. "Anyone else need not apply."

But when one of the lawyers—we'll call him Tim—at the association she worked for approached her with an invitation to dinner, she hesitated. He fit her criteria exactly: six feet three inches tall, nice looking (though a little older than she), financially secure, well educated. They knew each other from the office and he had the reputation of being compassionate, respectful, thoughtful, and smart.

He just wasn't "brown-skinned." In fact, his skin color couldn't be described as anything darker than "pale pink."

Tabitha went on the date with Tim, reluctantly, mostly because she felt that completely refusing him would have made the office environment uncomfortable. She was hoping that their evening together would make it obvious to him that a relationship wouldn't work out.

"He's a good guy," she reported the next day. "He was a good listener, a perfect gentleman, and made me feel really at ease. We laughed and had a really good time. But we're not going out again. He's not my type. I mean, he's fine as a friend, but he's white. I can't imagine having a serious relationship with a white man. I can't imagine sleeping with a white man. It's just not something I can see myself doing."

Tim pursued her . . . until he realized he was getting absolutely no encouragement and even less traction. That was a decade ago. Unfortunately, Tabitha is now in her late forties and still single, still looking for a serious relationship with a tall, handsome, financially secure, and well-educated black man.

A GOOD BLACK MAN

"There are so few good black men out there."

"All the good ones are taken."

"The white women take all the good ones."

These comments and others like them are repeated so often they have become the chestnuts of black female conversation. When black women gather and the discussion turns to men, invariably these words are uttered (in one version or another) and amen-ed to universal nods of approval. The topic has attracted so much attention in recent years that it has gone from sister-girl conversation to the mainstream, with articles in major national newspapers like the *Washington Post*,[1] a book called *How to Find a Good Black Man*[2] (which encourages black women to dress nicely, to avoid toting the baggage of past relationships, and to offer to pay for their share of dates), and an hour of conversation with "good brothers" on the *Tyra Show*.[3] Even the reigning queen of talk has skin in the game. "It's the numbers," Oprah told her audience in a show in April 2007. "The numbers are not there. It's like everyone is waiting for a certain cut of meat and it's just not available!" She encouraged black women to "explore what's out there" if they hope to find the man of their dreams— and to widen their romantic horizons to include men of other races.

Census figures indicate that nearly 70 percent of all black women are single and waiting for their good black man.

Where is he?

Imprisoned by a racist society? In the arms of a nonblack woman or another man? Have we sent Mr. Good Black Man into hiding by being "difficult" or placing unrealistic and unfair demands on him?

What happened?

Theories abound. There are, indeed, numbers that point to the disparities between the professional, educational, and social achievements of black women and those of their black male counterparts. Some theories reflect the differences in choice and mate selection criteria that widen the gap between black men and black women. And still others blame us black women ourselves (unfairly, to my way of thinking) for attitudes and behaviors that limit our ability to attract that elusive good black man. Each of these reasons is discussed here, but ultimately, they all point to one possible solution. Oprah is right: we need to cast a wider net.

SHORTAGE: WHERE HAVE ALL THE GOOD BLACK MEN GONE?

The shortage of good black men—or at least their absence from many black women's lives—is hardly news. For a variety of reasons, throughout the history of African Americans, black men have been unavailable to their women, often for reasons far beyond their control. Certainly, slavery separated black men from their families and had a detrimental influence on the black family. Similarly, the harsh Jim Crow laws of segregation and the racial caste system that limited the opportunities available to black men before the civil rights movement sometimes made it difficult for black men to support their families. Sometimes frustration and shame drove these men to leave their women completely. In other cases, long work hours, war, or incarceration were the causes. Still, government figures reveal that in 1950, 62 percent of black women were married, compared to only 28 percent in 2008.[4]

Here's my take on what happened.

After the civil rights reforms of the 1960s and 1970s, black men and women both gained greater access to opportunities in employment and education. Girls born in the first generation after segregation were instilled with a limitless sense of their own opportunities—and acted on it. The result? According to the *Journal of Blacks in Higher Education*, in 2000 black women earned college degrees at twice the rate of black men, and 437,000 black women held master's degrees or higher, compared to 275,000 black men.[5] These women—now in their forties—hold jobs of responsibility and make money, and a good number of them are single and waiting for black men with similar education and income.

The fate of black men of this same generation has been less educationally focused and less economically prosperous for several reasons. Popular theories to explain the education and income gap between black women and black men include wars—particularly Vietnam, which eroded the numbers of a generation of black men[6]—and the rise of the drug culture, beginning with heroin in the 1970s and culminating with crack cocaine in the late 1980s and early 1990s. Stricter prison terms for drug dealing incarcerated black men for relatively petty offenses for decades[7] and lowered their chances for employment after their release. Thanks in part to mandatory minimum sentencing laws enacted in the late 1980s, black men make up 6 percent of the general population but over 50 percent of the prison population. According to the Sentencing Project, on any given day in America, one out of eight black men in his twenties is in prison, more than are enrolled in colleges and universities. Not surprisingly, a 2003 Northwestern University study found that black men with criminal records faced significant disadvantages in wages and employment.[8]

The results of these statistics are what we commonly refer to as "the numbers":

- According to the 2006 census report, 70 percent of African American women are single, compared with 54 percent of white women and 60 percent of African American men. Nationally 43 percent of adults are single.

- A half million more black women than men are college graduates.

- Black women hold a large lead over black men in enrollments in professional programs (medicine, law, business, etc.).[9]

- Between 1970 and 2001, the overall marriage rate in the United States declined by 17 percent; for black people, that drop was 34 percent.

- According to 2004 Bureau of Justice Statistics numbers, 12.6 percent of black males in their late twenties were in prison or jail, compared to 3.6 percent of Hispanic and 1.7 percent of white males.

Taken together, these statistics suggest a decline in the marriage pool of eligible black men for certain groups of black women—specifically educated women, interested in dating black men with college or advanced degrees. Add to these declining numbers recent studies that suggest that women have stronger same-race preferences than men,[10] and you have the makings of a problem that will mean more and more single black women—not just now, but for decades to come.

DEFINE *GOOD*, PLEASE

Black men get angry with black women when they complain about the shortage of "good black men." There are lots of us out there, they complain. We're good guys. What on earth do you ladies want?

They have a point. This discussion goes beyond numbers: it strikes at the heart of the differing definitions men and women have of the word *good*. It speaks to what women really want from their men—and don't always feel safe admitting.

A "good black man" translates to a long and detailed list of attributes that go far beyond his personality and whether he has a criminal record or a job. The "real deal" list for educated black women is a man who

- is at least as well educated as she is (more education than hers is a plus);
- makes at least the same income that she does (making more money would not be sneered at);
- is as intelligent, well spoken, and informed as she is;
- is attractive and reasonably fit;
- is drug-free and physically and emotionally healthy;
- has a good personality;
- has compatible interests and religious beliefs;
- is manly and firm (not thuggish or abusive, but not "soft" either);
- holds similar views on sexual intimacy and children;
- is monogamous;
- is free of emotional baggage; and of course
- is black.

Black women aren't searching for just *any* "good black man": they are searching for an amalgam of qualities that compose an ideal. A misfire on any cue, whether major or minor, ends the game, since, as many sisters are fond of saying, "I can do bad on my own." This seems to be particularly true in the dating game. As Evia Moore, founder of the interracial website blackfemaleinterracialmarriage.com, writes, "If he's not on your level, drop him. He won't be comfortable in your professional circle or your expanding social circle. He can't provide for you and any children that may come of your union. He can't protect you and your children, because in today's world, physical muscles don't amount to diddly . . . in today's world, you need a man who mainly has *intellectual* muscles . . . and a good amount of financial muscles, too."

Financial and educational muscle is a requirement about which many black women and men disagree.

Black men attack the "real deal" list on several levels, but especially the "intellectual and financial muscle" requirements. Black women's list, they argue, reveals them to be "gold diggers" or "bougie." But those labels don't make the critics right or the black women who have such criteria wrong. Recent studies suggest that while black women would prefer to date and marry black than nonblack men, we are unwilling to date any man when there are economic and educational disparities.

In short, there will be no romance without finance, but this is a charged topic for many black women.

As Vazquez asserts on her blog,

Many black women have been taught that "only scheming gold diggers care about social mobility and financial security." This perception is deeply flawed. There are many women who are not gold diggers who value the construction of marriage that allows for women to prioritize socioeconomic mobility.[11]

While the concept of gold digging is discussed more fully in Notion 7, the idea of economic parity within relationships further complicates the search for a "good black man" under the criteria on the "real deal" list. "I had a list—or at least, I knew what qualities I wanted in a husband," writes Monique Fields, a twenty-seven-year-old black woman who lives in Birmingham, Alabama, and works as a journalist. "I knew I wanted a man who was respectful, trustworthy, responsible, taller than me, thin or physically fit, had a college degree, professional, ambitious, attractive to me and attracted to me. I like to joke that I received everything I wanted. I didn't specify a color and that left the door open." Before meeting her husband—a white man—Monique had mostly dated black men.

"It wasn't that I couldn't find black men who met my criteria. I found them—a lot of them," she continued. "But they didn't want much to do with a nerdy journalist who didn't—and still doesn't—drink alcohol. Those men were in high demand and had their pick of black women. Commitment also was an issue. I wanted to date one person at a time, and didn't have any tolerance for clubbing and other parts of the dating scene. I'm sure that cut down on my prospects considerably, but I had to be myself. I didn't want to change who I am just to have a man in my life."

Monique met her husband at work at the *Montgomery Advertiser* newspaper.

> He was an editor; I was a reporter. I used to kid him about the ties he wore. We were friends for a long time, and I didn't think much about it until he got one too many beers in him one day and confessed [to stronger feelings]. Our first date was hamburgers at a fast-food place. We dated, but I didn't think he wanted to get married. We are both children of divorced parents. Finally after several years and me moving all over the country for grad school and for different jobs, I found a job in Florida that I really wanted to take. I told him it was best we split, especially if we weren't going to get married. He dropped his fork. I went home; he parked outside my dad's house all night and waited for me to come out of the house at 5 a.m. He said, "Don't date anyone in Florida until I get a chance to come down there and talk to you about marriage." That was July 3, 2000. He proposed on October 6, 2000, and we were married March 3, 2001.

Monique's "real deal" list had the criteria that black women often don't want to admit to: money, education, commitment, stability. Though some men like to give us the guilt trip about them, black women should stop apologizing for expecting a man to bring to the table fidelity, education, and, if not financial security, some ambition or plans for his future. As any woman who has found herself financially supporting a man knows, wanting a man to have his own isn't always about getting a share of what's his. It's about protecting what's *yours*!

And men have their lists and are often quite frank about it. Any woman who's heard a man utter the phrase "no fat chicks" knows that men's lists can sound every bit as limiting and harsh as women's. When I was in law school, I briefly dated a fellow student, a black male who informed me on our second date that he considered me "marriage material" because I "met all his criteria." Those criteria included that I was "short, light-skinned, and from the South," since, according to him, southern women were more "traditional" and usually "deferred" to men.

That was our last date.

I think he's still single, but the point is that he had his criteria and was unapologetic about them. Unfortunately, when black women name their criteria, black men respond with attacks. Women who ask for— even demand—more from black men are deemed "difficult," "too masculine," and "too independent."

Consider this young black woman's thoughts, posted on dearblackman.com, about the double standards that plague relationships between black women and black men:

> *Lately, I've been rather reflective on my singlehood. In the past, I've been that desperate woman clinging to the emotionally abusive man. I admit nothing compares to the warmth of another. But given the various prospective BM I meet, I'm cool with being ice cold [to them] right now. The last guy I met was over 300 lbs. and 5'8". He had a 14-year-old daughter and lived with his "ex-girlfriend." He did her laundry, but was also allegedly a member of the Marine Corps. Oh yes, and he supposedly owned a trucking business. We happened to be alone in an elevator, and he asked what was necessary to get my number. Then, there was another prospective, he was 5'4" and just had a newborn, and he wasted no time telling me his baby was the top priority in his life. He asked me what I thought about that. I briskly told him, "Sorry, but right now, I play second to no one. Not even a baby!"*
>
> *Maybe my rejections of these two BM were selfish and shallow. Maybe I'm just too picky. I mean I could have settled on either of these two gentlemen, and it would break my 6 years' involuntary celibacy. But if I weighed 300 lbs., I highly doubt that many brothas would be checking for me. If I lived with my ex-boyfriend and did his laundry while trying to rap to another guy, I'm sure I would be quickly dismissed. If I were a single mother, never married as many BW are, I'm sure many BM would*

avoid me like [a disease]. So, why should I have to settle for either of them? Why is it still so commonplace for BW to extend the benefit of the doubt to BM? Why do older BW still train younger BW to accept this because "men will be men"? See, I told my grandmom about the guys with the babies, and she nonchalantly said men . . . do tend to make babies. My problem is perhaps these men would be more apt to want to commit to the "baby-mama" if they didn't have the option of seeing other females so quickly after getting another female pregnant.

What if the script was flipped, and [after children] men didn't have options for years? Some BW can break up with a man, and not have an alternative option for years. Then some women get desperate and end up settling for the first man that pays them a compliment, after enduring so many years of thirsting for someone's touch and admiration. What if all females, especially BW, stopped dating "baby-daddies" who weren't divorced?

Or just maybe, if more BM were told to "close their legs" as much as BW [are], then perhaps there would be significantly fewer "baby-daddies." What if we stopped dating the very same "overweight" guys, who have the audacity to criticize women for developing cellulite? Maybe if we as women didn't create so many freedoms for men (i.e., cat fighting, know-ingly playing mistresses, stealing another's man, etc.), just maybe this would fix at least 50% of the lack of stability and longevity in relation-ships.

Perhaps men wouldn't feel so comfortable with infidelity if they weren't sure their woman would always take them back. That a woman would always be there to forgive, as "that's what a female does," and if not, they can holla at that other woman over there.

Maybe I'm too feminist, but I hate the "natural order" that as a female I'm expected to measure a man on a scale different from the one he applies to me. If he's "fat," that should be okay, but if I'm "fat," then it's a no-go? What???!!![12]

This young woman's post speaks to the frustration more and more women feel about the double standards applied to them by black men. Black women shouldn't apologize or capitulate on any item on their "real deal" list. Men have such lists as well: they have preferences and turn-ons that guide their decision making in selecting sex partners and mates, and for the most part, they pursue their preferences and requirements without penalty or criticism. We're entitled to our preferences and requirements, just like everyone else, or we would be if the black community didn't have so many double standards for what is expected from black women as opposed to black men. And nowhere is a double standard more apparent than in interracial dating.

A DOUBLE STANDARD: BLACK MEN HAVE CHOICES, BLACK WOMEN DO NOT

It was August 24, 1955, and a fourteen-year-old black boy named Emmett Till and his cousins were visiting relatives in Webb, Mississippi, when he allegedly whistled at a white woman working at the counter of a candy store. Insulted, the woman told her husband, who organized his brother and another man to take retribution. They abducted Till, beat him, gouged out one of his eyes, shot him in the head, tied a seventy-five-pound cotton gin fan around his neck, and dumped his body in the Tallahatchie River.[13]

The discovery of Till's body three days later sparked a national outcry that stoked the fires of the nascent civil rights movement. Emmett Till's case wasn't the first: since Reconstruction, black men had been subject to vigilante violence and lynchings for even the slightest perceived disrespect of white women. Tuskegee University experts estimate that between 1882 and 1959, over 4,733 lynchings of African Americans occurred in the United States. Although not all of those lynchings involved allegations of rape made by white women, lynching is tied to that crime in the African American consciousness.

Like the case of Betty Jean Owens, the case of Emmett Till resonated with the African American community and provided a catalyst for action. But unlike the Owens case, Till's murder and the centuries of racially charged sexual stereotypes underlying it seem to have had less of an impact on black men than they have had on black women. In spite of the numbers of black men falsely accused of sex crimes by white women—and despite the numbers of black men killed as a result—black men no longer hold on to the legacy of slavery and Jim Crow by refusing to date outside their race. According to the 2000 census, black men enter interracial marriages at a higher rate—9.7 percent—than any other racial or gender group except Asian women. That's twice the rate that black women marry interracially. In fact, the census further revealed that 73 percent of black/white couples consist of a black man and a white woman.[14] Simply put, in the fifty-five years since Emmett Till's murder, black men have forgiven and forgotten. They've gotten over it.

In her book *Black Men in Interracial Relationships*, Kellina Craig-Henderson offers several theories for why black men pursue interracial intimacies at a greater rate than black women, including the fact that, thanks to the loosening of cultural prohibitions, there is a greater acceptance of these relationships. It also helps that the media portray black men in favorable ways.

> To the extent that images of Black male masculinity and sexuality have been widely distributed to mainstream American consumers in recent years, Black men have now been deemed desirable and attractive, potential mates for heterosexual females. Consequently, Black male sexuality is sought after by females of all races and copied by other males in a way unlike ever before.[15]

"Athletes, entertainers, and now the president of the United States—black men are presented in ways that young white people want to emulate. That enhances their image in ways that, until very recently, black women have not enjoyed," added Craig-Henderson in an interview. "As images of black women in our media change, so might their dating terrain. Still, there's very much of a double standard for black women dating interracially that they are very much aware of."

I love the way Lisa Vazquez breaks it down in her popular essay "Who Even Cares If Brothas Want White Women?" Using the data from the 2007 Population Survey of the U.S. Census, which determined that blacks are approximately 13 percent of the population, she writes:

> Black women who will *only* marry black men have chosen to have a pool of 3.5% of the population [of the United States] as potential mates. (Even though black men represent about 5% of the population, I am taking into

account the brothas who are homosexual, on the down-low, medically unsuitable, incarcerated or in a criminal lifestyle, mentally unstable, or otherwise not eligible to be fully participatory in the home as a marital partner.)

Let us assume that 3.5% of the [U.S.] population constitutes the pool of marriageable black men. About 40% to 50% of marriageable black men will not choose marriage. This leaves black women with less than 2% of the population that *could be* potential husbands. In this 2% segment, we know that not every one of these black men *will* choose to marry black women, but let's assume that 90% of them will.

Black women who only want to marry a black man have a pool of 1.8% of the U.S. population. If the population of marriageable black women is approximately 6% of the entire U.S. population (8% total, minus those who are gay, medically unsuitable, in prison, etc.—as we did for black men), it is *mathematically impossible* for all marriageable black women who want to marry a black man to have that desire become reality.[16]

If indeed, nearly twice as many black women are college educated as black men—and if education and income are important criteria to black women—in order to beat the numbers, black women interested in being married *must* look beyond the pool of black men.

When black women complain about black men dating out, they are labeled as "haters." But some black men also admit to feelings of anger and resentment when they see a black woman out with a white man. And occasionally that resentment has ended in violence.

THE DOUBLE STANDARD GETS UGLY: BLACK MALE RESENTMENT

On October 15, 2008, in Riverside, California, Jan Pawal Pietrzak and his wife, Quiana Jenkins-Pietrzak, were murdered by four men who entered their home by force. The killers first tortured and humiliated them, cutting the young woman's clothes off her body, raping her while the husband, beaten and helpless, could do nothing. Then, with their hands tied and their mouths gagged, the twenty-four-year-old husband and his twenty-six-year-old wife were shot in the head, execution style; their home was ransacked, robbed, and then set on fire.

Sadly, in these violent and uncertain times, this story reads like a terrible crime that might have happened anywhere, to any unfortunate pair unlucky enough to be in the wrong place at the wrong time. But what makes this case distinctive is race: the young couple was a white man and a black woman, and the suspects were four black men who served under the white husband in the United States Marine Corps.[17]

Initially in their confessions, the men stated robbery as their motive, even though the murdered couple were far from wealthy. They had purchased their five-bedroom home in suburban San Diego at a recent foreclosure auction. As the details of the crime became more clear, the suspects appeared to have had a more heinous motive involving resentment of Pietrzak for marrying an attractive black woman, and fury with her for choosing a Polish immigrant as her mate.[18] None of the men had known Mrs. Jenkins-Pietrzak before her marriage or had had any relationship with her. Their brutality toward her wasn't personal in the sense that she had personally rejected them, but general based on her standing as a black woman in a relationship with a white man.

A hate crime of this level of depravity and outrageousness often becomes a national media event: a rallying cry to confront the racism of our past and our shared national shame. But as is often the case when black men victimize black women, the crime has been met with relative silence by the mainstream media and similar quiet in most of the black press. As blogger Phillip Cohen notes:

> If the victims had been a gay couple, married or not, and the four killers heterosexual . . . this would be prosecuted as a hate crime. If the Pietrzaks had both been black or Hispanic, and the killers white, this would be prosecuted as a hate crime . . . and would be the subject of discussion on 85% of the broadcast and print media in the United States and Europe. Sad to say, if the Pietrzaks had been Asian, no matter who the perpetrators were, no one would talk about it. What is truly bizarre, hypocritical, and in the end utterly disgusting is that because the Pietrzaks were an interracial couple and their killers black, there has been and will be a rush to declare the motive purely robbery and to silence any discus-

sion as to the brutality of the crime being due to racial hatred on the part of the killers.[19]

While the Pietrzak murders represent an extreme, lesser levels of black male hostility toward black women's relationships with white men are not uncommon. In fact, many black women interviewed for this book recounted negative experiences with black men over their interracial relationships, or listed fear of that reaction as one of the reasons for their hesitance to consider dating a man outside their race.

"She's just with you for your money!" a brother shouted at one woman and her husband as they walked hand in hand down a city street.

"Come back, sister! Come back!" was yelled from a car at another woman, walking with her husband.

And there's this story from a white man:

> *One of my first run-ins with that was in high school when some black dudes tried to jump me and my brother because my older brother was dating the really, really smoking hot black female cousin of one of the guys. One of these guys [who jumped us] had gotten a white girl pregnant and two of the other ones were dating [interracially] a Puerto Rican and a Russian girl, respectively.*
>
> *These black guys wanted to [date] all the non-black girls but there had to be "action" if even one white guy dated a black girl. That's the hypocrisy of [some] black American men. It's tribalism, just like all humans are programmed for, but AA guys are the worst for it right now.[20]*

Few black men willingly discuss their discomfort with black woman/ white man couples. One spoke candidly with me about his mixed feelings about such couples on the condition of anonymity. "I admit, I always do a double take," he said. "But then I'll do a double take when I see a brother with a white woman too. But the black woman with a white man, it bothers me more. I pray about it, because I'm pretty sure it's a shortcoming, but there it is."

Seeing black women with white men bothers me for three reasons. First, it's my own personal background. I grew up in segregation, in Bluefield, West Virginia. I went to a segregated elementary school, but by the time I was in junior high, schools had begun to integrate. I was in high school in the height of the Black Power movement, and there was some interracial dating. No, I think dating is the wrong word. Sex would be the right word. It was really down low, mostly brothers with white women. But the sisters, they weren't having anything to do with the white boys. Or if they did, I didn't ever hear anything about it. But I suspect there wasn't much of that going on. I'm a part of that time period when black women had no protections from white men . . . and black men had no power to stop them.

The second reason is the things white men say about black women. It's always sexual. "Let's go chase some black ass." Things like that . . . but of course, I've heard black men say that about black women too. And I've heard black men make comments about seeking out white women for sexual reasons. I guess it's a double standard, but that's how I feel. It just bothers me more when I hear white men talk about black women that way. When brothers do it, I just chalk it up to, you know, trash-talking. Trying to sound manly or cool.

The last reason I don't like it is harder to admit to. But if the sister is smart and attractive and really has it on the ball, I feel disappointed that she couldn't find what she was looking for in a black man. It's a bit of envy or jealousy or something. And it's even worse if she's acting like that white guy is the be-all and the end-all. Like she's hit the relationship jackpot or something. Then it's really, really grating to me. It makes me angry. But if I'm going to be totally honest, I have to admit that I only feel that way when the sister is attractive to me. If I don't find her attractive, then I'm like "Whatever. He can have her."

Another man, who declined to be interviewed for this book but who has made his feelings known in various forums online and on YouTube, intimated that black women involved with white men are blind to a conspiracy aimed at the ultimate extinction of the black race.[21] His comments echo the writings of Black Power leader Eldridge Cleaver, who wrote that the black woman was "the silent ally . . . of the white man," who used her to destroy black manhood.[22]

Hogwash, responds Evia Moore of www.blackfemaleinterracialmar riage.com. "The truth is Black men have learned to *expect* the support and protection from Black women [in everything, including relationships]. Whenever someone does not get what they have *learned* to *expect* to get, there is disappointment, anger, and sometimes rage." Like a mother when her children are throwing a tantrum, black women must remain firm in spite of the pressure and make those decisions that are ultimately in their best interest. "I also always advise Black women to be safe," Evia cautions on her website. "These attitudes are real and they can be dangerous."

Craig-Henderson agrees. "It's an interesting phenomenon that several of the women I interviewed in my book reported. Black men felt perfectly within their rights to give black women with partners of a different race lectures about their choices—even when those black men were perfect strangers to the women. One woman told me about an older black man on a subway who felt it was his place to proclaim his objections to her boyfriend's race."

"Yes, I noticed black men with white women, and when I was single, I might have stared—or even glared at them. But it never went any further. . . . But it's different for me as a black woman now married to a white man. Some black men feel like they have the right to get in your face or say the rudest things," says a woman who prefers to remain anonymous. "And others feel they have the right to give me lectures about why my marriage is wrong."

Another woman confesses that the fear of similar reactions from black men keeps her from dating interracially, saying, "I'm not one hundred percent comfortable being seen as a couple [with a white guy] in public . . . I'm actually more fearful of how brothas will react."

Fear, of course, is the ultimate limitation for black women—fear of how the brothers will react, fear of being isolated and ostracized from the black community, fear of the unfamiliar experiences that interracial relationships might bring. But to be fair, there's a good deal of fear and uncertainty involved with the limitations of black-only dating: the fear that you might never find your good black man, the fear that you might remain unhappily single all your life. Fear is unavoidable in this life. The question is, who is living in your skin: you or the brothas? You or the entire black community? You or the fears of the resentments of others?

Of course, not all black men seek to apply to black women a double standard on dating:

> I am a black man who dates interracially. . . . I actually like seeing black
> women with white men, especially since it is perceived [in our culture]
> that white men are racist. To me [seeing a white man with a black woman]
> shows the progress that our country has made.
>
> —From an email to the author, June 2008

This man is right: while far from perfect, things are changing fast in America, especially for black women. It's our success, educational and material, along with social and historical factors that depress the numbers of eligible black men, that has increased the percentage of black women who are single. Another factor, however, may be our own attitudes—and our own prejudices. Finding the happiness we seek— with a man of any race—begins with comparing our real list of expectations for a mate with our "real deal" list of what we believe about ourselves. We must also be prepared for resistance from black men who may operate on the double standard that it's fine for men to explore partners beyond their own race but inappropriate for black women to do so—even if the result of our not doing so is that more and more black women remain single and lonely for the rest of their lives. Sometimes, however, the resistance a black woman encounters to seeking love from a good man regardless of his race comes from sources even closer to home, and that is the subject of the next notion we must dispel.

NOTION 3

My Family Would Never Accept Him—
and His Would Never Accept Me

I received this email from a young woman named Chaka in June 2008:

> *I'm a 21-year-old African American female; my boyfriend is 20 and is*
> *white. I met my boyfriend of three years while we were still in high school.*
> *He often says he "met his match" in me, because while his tendency to*
> *kind of jokingly pick on people perplexed most of our classmates, it didn't*
> *work with me. I thought he was sort of a jerk, but there was something*
> *about how honest he was that struck a chord with me. He had (and still*
> *has) a deep passion for politics, which I admired. Our many differences*
> *(he'll wear the same shirt for days while I have a passion for fashion, he's*
> *into classic rock while I'll listen to top 40 radio, etc.) didn't outweigh our*
> *attraction to each other. We began dating during the second part of my*
> *senior, his junior year.*
>
> *Our classmates and friends, for the most part, were supportive. We went*
> *to an arts school, so differences were accepted and embraced. Off campus,*
> *however, things were different. My parents found out we were dating*

when, after witnessing me give Dustin a goodbye hug one day, a church member told my mother that I was "all over some white boy in the parking lot after school." After passing a pair of black men on the way to his car one day, we were heckled with comments such as "Such a shame to see a fine black woman go to waste." We get stared at everywhere we go by people young and old. (I should probably mention that we live in the South, in Little Rock, AR.) While the older people raising eyebrows doesn't bother me as much (I can understand the long-lasting effects of growing up during the Civil Rights movement), it hurts to see it coming from someone my age. Our generation shouldn't have a problem with this. We've been integrated our entire lives, we've been taught to embrace diversity. Why is this still a problem, with blacks especially? [His] parents are fine with it and have never been anything other than incredibly sweet and inviting to me. While my father is totally accepting of [him], my mother refuses to even meet him or even acknowledge his existence. I have asked her why again and again but she says angrily, "I can't believe you brought home a white boy," and I feel like I've done something very, very wrong.

Chaka was born in 1987: Ronald Reagan was president and the top movies were *Moonstruck* and *Wall Street*. It was the year of the Iran-Contra investigations and of the publication of Toni Morrison's novel *Beloved*. The first episode of *The Cosby Show* spinoff *A Different World* aired on September 24, 1987, and the one-year-old nationally syndicated *Oprah Winfrey Show* won the 1987 Emmy for best talk show.

Chaka grew up with computers, television, the internet, and a limitless sense of her own potential; society for her has placed far less emphasis on "segregation" and "integration" than in prior decades. Going to school with kids of all races was normal for Chaka. She and her boyfriend grew up during a period in which interracial marriages between blacks and whites climbed from 65,000 in 1970 to nearly 500,000 in 2005.[1] In 1995, when Chaka was eight years old, 50 percent of Americans told the Gallup organization they approved of relationships between blacks and whites. In June 2007, when Gallup conducted the poll again, 77 percent of Americans said they approved, with African Americans responding favorably to black-white unions 80 percent of the time.[2]

But Americans over the age of fifty, both black and white, tend to have a higher rate of disapproval of interracial relationships than their younger counterparts, and other studies have shown that women are significantly less accepting of interracial relationships than men.[3] Furthermore, in the black community, there seems to be a disconnect between the progressive attitudes we project in national polling and what we say to our daughters in the home.

This is the case for Chaka, who told me in an interview that her parents work with whites, live in an integrated community, have white acquaintances and friends. But when it comes to romantic relationships, her mother in particular has drawn a firm line against the ultimate integration.

"I know they want me to be proud of my heritage, and I am," she added. "I wouldn't have expected my mother to react like this; she was always the one teaching tolerance and diversity. I don't understand it. I know what it means to be African American in this country. I know our history, I understand there's a lot of pain and suffering there. But I've also been taught to embrace the progress that we've made and to move forward. So which is it: am I supposed to be color-blind about men or not? Am I supposed to deal with white people, but only up to a point? What am I supposed to do?"

GENERATIONS

Chaka's story speaks volumes about just how much progress black Americans in general, and black American women in particular, have made in a very short time. In less than a generation, our spheres of possibility have widened substantially, so much so that sometimes our elders don't understand us.

Although I haven't met Chaka's mother, she is probably in her late forties or early fifties, which means she was born in the late 1950s or early in the 1960s. She might remember segregation or have some recollection of the civil rights movement as it reached its most violent and feverish pitch. And since Chaka's family lives in Little Rock, Arkansas, her mother either remembers or was told from an early age about the "Little Rock Nine": the nine African American youngsters who, in 1957, enrolled in Central High School—an all-white school—integrating it under armed federal escort, while the nation watched white parents scream racial epithets and riot in ugly, bigoted protest. When one sees the world as Chaka's mother might have—as a young black girl growing up amid some of the most violent and hate-filled moments of the civil rights movement—it's easy to understand that those images left deep and vivid memories.

I know my mother feels that way. Now in her seventies, she is more than likely older than Chaka's mom, but her memories give voice to what many children of the 1940s, '50s, and '60s feel: "If you grew up in segregation or during that angry, angry time of the late fifties and the nineteen sixties, you can't forget it," she told me. "I can remember here in Washington, D.C., how whites treated my father. He was a great big man—a construction worker—and they called him 'boy' like he was a child. I remember Whites Only signs. I remember my first teaching jobs in segregated schools, how inadequate the materials were and how, because they were for black children to learn in, the buildings were left in disrepair. It's hard to erase some of the ugliness you saw in segregation. I know things have changed; I see those changes in the opportunities your father and I had and even more in the opportunities you kids have had in your lives, and I'm happy about that. But I can't forget how the white people treated blacks in that time. I just can't."

Most grandparents today remember segregation, and there are elderly people who still remember knowing people who had been slaves. For many of us, the pain of Jim Crow and slavery are part of an oral history that connects many families to their heritage as survivors. But that heritage is a double-edged sword. It reminds us of our remarkable ability to triumph and overcome, but it also can be used to discourage black women from the ultimate assimilation—dating and marrying outside the race. As one woman I spoke with put it,

That [a black woman] would willingly date someone who has a history of devaluing your worth was unheard of [for black women]. It was a lesson that was passed on from mothers to their daughters. My mother, for example, always warned me before I was even of dating age that it was unacceptable [to date white men] and just not allowed. It wasn't until I was much older that my mother was okay with the multiracial thing. But even now she would prefer any other race to the white race, and black is always the preference.

There's nothing wrong with preferring to "date black." But I wonder, would this woman's mother prefer her daughter to remain unhappily alone rather than welcome a white son-in-law? Would she rather a child like Tiger Woods or Halle Berry or President Obama never be born than see her daughter build a family with a white man?

"Numerous court cases were launched to give blacks the opportunities to live wherever they wanted," says Washington School of Law professor Kimberly Jade Norwood. "And I think black parents of the 1960s and '70s struggled to move their children to neighborhoods where they'd have the advantages of white children. As a result, their children go to school with white children and become more comfortable in white environments. Still, when their daughters bring home white boyfriends, the black parents are surprised. As one of my friends said to her father, 'Hey, I'm living in an all-white neighborhood. What did you expect?' "

Cynthia, a black woman in her second marriage to a white man, can relate:

> I was born in 1969 in Alderson, West Virginia. It's a very small town, and a mostly white one: there were only a few other black families, and in school I was often the only black girl in my class. So I grew up with white people, having white friends both male and female. My parents were fine with that . . . until high school when I was asked to go to the prom by a white classmate. That would have been 1987, I guess. My parents forbade it, as did his. It was fine for us to go to school together, to hang out together. But the line was drawn when it came to dating: white with white, black with black. I went to the prom with a black guy I was friends with instead of the boy I really, really liked.

> I went to college near Lexington, Kentucky—a much larger town than where I grew up. My college was predominantly white. Tracy was my first serious boyfriend in college. I had dated one other guy—a black guy— who turned out to be really possessive and I didn't like that. Tracy was just fun and relaxed. We were friends for years and then it turned to

romance. When I told my parents about him, the first question my mother asked was "Is he white or black?" When I told her he was white, she said, "You need to quit messing with those white boys." That was probably 1990 or 1991.

The mother-daughter relationship isn't the only place where tensions can be felt. One young white man recounted difficulties with his black girlfriend's father:

> Before I met her parents, my girlfriend told me that her dad wanted her to "go back to dating black men." I knew right then and there I was in for more than I had expected by getting so serious with this girl. We're still together (we are the best of friends and we agree on almost everything in life except for her father). When I was out [in Memphis] for two weeks visiting them, I did my best to respect him. I probably said less than twenty words to him, all of which were ignored. It was obvious his attitude was "Ignore him, and maybe he'll go away." I just took [it]. I hope he and his wife will accept me in time and respect my patience. I understand he grew up in Memphis and is sixty, so he probably went through some stuff during the civil rights movement. I know he's experienced racism. But damn! How long do white males have to be shunned for our forefathers' mistakes? I love my girlfriend and I see us together for the long term. Isn't that worth something to a father—to see his daughter well treated and happy?

Forever might be this father's answer to the question of how long white males must pay for their grandfathers' sins, and in certain ways, his resentment is justified. While his daughter's boyfriend may not have personally participated in any overt racism, his white skin automatically confers a degree of privilege on him that this father is fully aware of, even if the boyfriend is not.

But difficult as that may be to accept, should it prevent the father from acknowledging his daughter's choice? Which is worse: to suggest a child forgo her happiness because her choice reminds a parent of injustices or to swallow decades of resentments and clasp a young white man's outstretched hand?

"None of us can help who are parents are," one woman said to me. "In the end that's something we have to live up to or, in other cases, live down."

But my friend Angela Shaw, who holds the distinction of being one of the first black women to graduate from Harvard Law School, has a different point of view on this father's anger. Having lived the last thirty years abroad, she sees the issue as a part of the United States'—and the world's—failure to take the integration of black people seriously:

> Living in post–Cold War Europe, I've had a front row seat on the subject of "integration." I know that little children of Slovenia (from the former "Evil Empire") have grown up as [European Union] nationals and holders of the euro currency with all that this entails, while black American children born during the same era don't have a similar assurance of this self-importance and entitlement. Can you imagine that a little kid from Slovenia can travel the world with "his" currency, which is stronger than the U.S. dollar? When I was 16 and I started traveling to Europe, the U.S. dollar was the strongest currency in the world. Believe me, that had an impact on the way I saw myself in the world and the way others saw me as well.
>
> I am not merely talking about socioeconomics here. I am talking about culture. There is a culture that does not take the status of black Americans "seriously." When the U.S. and Europe wanted to "integrate" Slovenia into the first world, they took realistic and meaningful steps to do so, something many blacks still feel the United States has failed to do. . . . The segregated signs in the South didn't say "rich only" and "poor only" but rather said "white only" and "colored only." Economic matters do not foreclose racial ones. The two are integrally connected, in Europe as well as in the U.S.

When a black father is unable to accept his daughter's white boyfriend, his reaction speaks to the economic and racial frustration many black Americans feel. The white boyfriend may not be "guilty," but he does benefit—socially and economically—by virtue of being white.

Yet the father's feelings fail to take into account an economic truth that might help his daughter, especially if the couple marry. According to Department of Labor and 2006 Census Bureau Statistics, white men earn an average of $10,000 per year more than black men with similar education. Before you accuse black women who marry interracially of "gold digging," consider this as well: she'll bring as much to the table as she gets, since college-educated black women make more than their Latin, Asian, and white counterparts. All else being equal, economically at least, this match might have benefits for both partners.

Of course, parental concerns go far beyond financial value to whether the white partner truly values the black daughter for all her qualities, or whether he is simply taking advantage of her for an "exotic" sexual experience. For parents who grew up in times when black women's rights, economic power, and social place were extremely limited, accepting the possibility of changed attitudes—even from young men who were born in the 1970s and '80s—is hard.

Cynthia recalls how her mother enunciated this exact concern. After graduating from Berea College in Kentucky, Cynthia and the white man she had been dating lived together. "I was talking to my mother about him one day and she said to me, 'You know he's never going to marry you, don't you?' While I don't think she was crazy about us living together, she was more concerned about it because of our racial difference. She basically felt that, in my boyfriend's eyes, because I was a black woman, I was fine to live with, to have sex with, but not worthy of a wedding vow. I told him what my mother had said, and his response was, 'Well, I guess we should just get married then.' And we did."

Black female/white male relationships also raise deep questions about assimilation and how far black people should go to fully integrate into the mainstream. "Black people have the idea that we should assimilate, but only to a point. We want full access in all levels of society—from the White House to the boardroom and everywhere else—but then we tell people to 'stay black' and 'not forget where you came from.' It's like we're walking around with a split personality," a woman who asked for anonymity fumes.

Norwood agrees, but only up to a point. "I think there's a lot of pressure on black women, from all sides. Racism and sexism are very much alive and they are real in black women's lives. But there is pressure from the black community too. It's extremely stressful . . . and unnecessary. But I'm not sure about the word 'assimilation' because to me it automatically connotes 'white.' I think there's good in 'difference.' I don't want us to give that up."

GEOGRAPHY AND GENERATION

In addition to generational concerns, geography also plays a role. Black parents with roots in southern states seem to have stronger views against their daughters' dating out.

Like Chaka's parents, Cynthia's parents lived in a southern community, and her parents were very much aware of racial tensions, in spite of the passage of several comparatively harmonious decades in which racial progress was made in education, employment, and opportunity.

Mona R. Washington, a New Jersey playwright who explores the lingering questions of race and racism in her work, grew up in the "black section" of a mostly white Philadelphia suburb. "It was the late 1960s and my parents were looking to leave the city, and there was a lot of construction going on in the New Jersey suburbs. They were one of the many black families who would call to make an appointment to see a new house . . . and when they got there, they'd be told, 'Oh, they're all sold.' They didn't want to sell to blacks, and my parents didn't want to live where they weren't wanted, so they moved to a black neighborhood outside Philadelphia instead. What's funny is all of us white and black kids ended up at the same schools anyway. I played with the same kids whose parents didn't want to live next to my parents. I was a late bloomer and didn't date much in high school, but I could have. And some of my dates might have been the sons of those same white people. The point is, when things start to change, they start to change. If your mind is stuck in another time, that's your choice. But times will just change around you anyway."

Lorraine recalls growing up in Indianapolis in the late sixties and early seventies. "My parents had migrated from the Deep South and our extended family is still in Alabama and Mississippi. Growing up, I went to integrated schools, and my family is deeply religious, so we weren't taught to hate anyone. My immediate family had no trouble with my interracial marriage. My parents never said, 'Don't bring home a white boy'; they really accepted people based on their actions, not on the basis of their color. But I knew there was some resentment from my cousins and some talk along the lines of 'You think you're white' and 'How could you be with one of *them*?' What's funny about that is one of those cousins, after a number of years alone, ended up marrying a white guy herself!"

Jacquetta, who grew up on Maryland's pastoral Eastern Shore, had an equally accepting family reaction.

> I was raised by my mother, who was very liberal, very well educated. She was a single mom, had a master's degree, and she dated interracially herself. But we didn't integrate well in that area: the small-town setting was difficult for both of us, I think. I know I had trouble with the other black students at school because I was smart and interested in education. The school district's gifted and talented program saved me from a certain degree of ostracism from my peers. Participating in it gave me a mixed group of liberal-thinking friends. But for me, the small-town environment was really hard. I didn't fit in until I was able to get away—and I did. I went to a boarding school in Philadelphia for high school, then on to Sarah Lawrence College in New York. I met my first husband in London and my second husband in Manhattan. My mom is fine with it, but I'm sure there would be some reaction from extended family and from some of the kids who made fun of me in elementary school. I really don't care.

Teresa grew up on the predominantly black Southside of Chicago, but both her parents had southern roots. Her father was from Mississippi and her mother from Alabama.

> I remember my father saying specifically, "Don't bring home a white boy." He and my mother were separated and he owned a record store in the suburbs, in a predominantly white neighborhood, while we lived with my mother on the Southside in an all-black neighborhood, going to all-black schools. He had lots of different kinds of music in the store and customers of all races, but I do recall him saying he didn't want to see me date white guys. By the time I was about thirteen, it was the *black* guys who I didn't want to date. I was afraid of them: strange guys would just say the most awful, rude, nasty things to me just for walking down the street!

I was really attracted to white guys in high school. I liked rock bands like Duran Duran; it was the early 1980s. Everyone at my all-black school thought I was weird. I was into white boys/white music. But the older I got, though I still liked that music, I really felt like I should become more involved with the black community, that I should really be a part of the struggle to make things better for the community I lived in.

I ended up becoming part of a black nationalist religious organization. I was friends with a girl in high school who was a member, and it sounded like something that would help the black community. Living in Southside, I knew my people were downtrodden and oppressed; I wanted to help. But the men in that group were even worse in a way than the guys who yelled and groped girls on the street. Very sexist, very abusive toward the women. I met my husband in that church, but he seemed different from most of the other men: respectful, opening doors for me and acting like a gentleman. He had ambitions. He was in college, and he wanted to be a teacher. He had his stuff together, and I remember thinking, "I can work with this." I was twenty years old when we married.

He changed after less than a year. He became verbally abusive, had outbursts over the smallest of things. "You use too much dishwashing liquid!" he'd scream and start on a rampage. The verbal abuse escalated to physical abuse. Then a woman called my house, intimating that he was cheating on me with her. When I confronted him and he got violent with me, I'd had it. I took our baby and left the state. That was thirteen years ago.

My father was fully aware of my situation. And while I never discussed my dating preferences with my father since splitting with my ex-husband, I don't think he's ever changed his mind. My father is set in his ways, same as my mom, who is still waiting anxiously for me to bring a black man home. She discourages me from dating interracially to this day, even knowing that I have not been involved with black men in the last thirteen years.

Once, my mom looked over my shoulder at my computer screen and saw my personal ad that said I was interested in meeting nonblack men. She scoffed at it. She says things to me like, "Oh please! You need to let that go!" Or she tells me that no man of another race would ever want me because I am black, I have a child, and I haven't finished my degree.

My mom never has any ideas about where to meet decent black men, only that I need to find a black man. My mom has had the opportunity to marry or date men of other races who were doctors, and she turned them down to be with black men who were no good, who had problems with abuse or drugs, and who were financially dependent on her.

I guess we've been made to feel that being black is the only qualifier a man needs to be with us. It doesn't matter if he's an abuser or a loser. When my mom told me that no nonblack man would want me because I'm black, I told her that that is how she feels about herself and that my situation or my race hadn't stopped me from meeting educated, professional nonblack men who find me attractive. Right now, I'm dating a man who is of Indian descent, and he's in his residency to become a physician.

Like Teresa, Tori grew up in an urban setting, in a racially mixed housing project in Woonsocket, Rhode Island. Her mother had a relationship with a white man, and Tori's younger sister is biracial. "I'd say that interracial dating was pretty much accepted in my household, but I definitely remember being told to keep my eyes out for my 'good black man.'"

Alisa grew up a world away.

I was born in Lynwood and lived in South Central L.A. until I was three or four. Then my parents moved to Culver City, California, which at the time was a predominantly white community. I lived there for about five years, but those five years made a *huge* impact on the woman I grew up to be. As a matter of fact, my first crush was a blond-haired, blue-eyed boy who wore OP clothing and Vans tennis shoes. Once my parents separated, my mother and I moved to a predominantly black community, Inglewood. Talk about extreme culture shock! I entered the fourth grade, and although I made friends, I really never fit in and it was pretty miserable. These were my peers racially, culturally, and scholastically, but I was from a completely different world. I was constantly teased for talking "white" or being smart.

My comfort level about sharing my dating preference grew as I got older. I just in my late thirties came to my own terms about it. My friends and family are completely okay and my parents (including my mom, dad, and stepfather) are excited that their son-in-law will be a nonblack man. I have aunts who either married or dated white men as well.

Interestingly, my family told me, "We *knew* you preferred men outside your race." Apparently, I wasn't fooling anyone.

Marvine is a first-generation American; her parents were both Haitian immigrants, and during her childhood, she spent summers in Canada, where her father's relatives had settled. "The whole issue around interracial dating is very different there. It's far less of a big deal. I went to my uncle's house during the summers and he was married to a white woman. My cousins were biracial. I think my parents might have preferred I marry a Haitian doctor or lawyer, but because of their background in Haiti, they were not as steeped in the whole black/white thing as American blacks are either."

GENDER

Generations and geography aren't the only factors at play when a black woman dates interracially and her family reacts. Dr. Rachel Sullivan, a sociologist who studies interracial marriage, explores how gender affects family reactions.

Family approval of interracial relationships is most likely lower for Black women than it is for Black men. Black women's families had more objections to interracial relationships than their Black male counterparts. Many relatives of Black women (especially male relatives) tried to protect their daughters/sisters/cousins from White men who they felt would sexually exploit Black women. Given the history of White male sexual violence against Black women, this is not surprising. However, family opposition also has the effect of denying Black women's agency because their judgment is held up to much more scrutiny than Black men's in interracial relationships.[4]

Nikki Doughty, founder of Black Women Who Date Interracially (www.bwwdi.org) and Multimixx, an organization that plans events for singles to meet cross-culturally, puts it more bluntly.

> Black women are raised with extremes. In many black families, girls are taught that there are "good girls" and there are "sluts," with nothing in between. Being a "good girl" has a narrow definition that includes following along with expectations. We're taught to be good servants to the family and to do what we're told to do, in many ways. Those rules usually allow for us to get an education and a good job and to make money to share with the family, the church, and the black community at large. Everything else falls in the "bad girl/slut" category. Which means what isn't taught is how to make the best life for ourselves. Black women are not taught how to achieve loving romantic relationships and marriages, or to select the right kind of man for a partner or to pick any man we choose to love. Instead we have to endure and do "what's right." A good girl takes care of everyone else, the family, and the community. But not herself.

While it is certainly understandable that male relatives feel protective, sometimes their "protection" comes across as "Do as I say, not as I do." Interestingly, several of the women I spoke with reported a double standard on dating out within their family that allowed male family members to pursue women of different races, while female family members were expected to date black men exclusively. Tori, for example, experienced this double standard without any sugarcoating.

"My mother had a relationship with a white man and my sister is biracial," she explains. "Also my uncles—who were in their twenties and thirties when I was a teenager—dated white women. One of them was even married to a white woman." But when a white classmate asked her to her prom in 1992, her uncles—and not her grandmother, who grew up in deeply segregated South Carolina—were the ones to react negatively. "They were like all he wants to do is sleep with you because you're black. But I kept saying that this guy wasn't that kind. He was a friend of mine and had always been very nice, very respectful towards me. They knew this guy too, because he and some of my other white friends had been to our house to eat my grandmother's great cooking. The fact that he and some of my other white guy friends came around a lot made my uncles even madder. 'Why are they here?' they would ask. Even though they were involved with white women, they were just furious about my white guy friends."

Other black women have discovered that in their families, interracial relationships are fine in the abstract but troubling when the family's own daughter/sister/niece is the one bringing a white man home. "In many ways, I think black families are more conservative," says Mona Washington. "At least about the expectations they hold for members of their own families. I remember when I was a young woman and I'd talk critically about patriarchy and black identity and gender roles, my mother would get upset and say things like, 'You must be getting those ideas from those white kids.' She, like a lot of people, got uncomfortable when something or someone was new or unfamiliar . . . and that's when the racial comments would come out. Ultimately, though, I think both my parents were guided by their faith."

Kellina Craig-Henderson adds the social psychologist's perspective. "In various studies it's been shown that men are socialized to venture further than women are," she told me in a telephone interview. "Even little boys at play go further from home than little girls do. Little girls are taught to 'stay close' and that's what they do, physically and socially, even now."

Socialization that keeps black women "close to home" emotionally can proscribe certain dating behavior or at least place in a young woman's mind the strong suggestion of who the appropriate men are. At her mother and sisters' suggestion, Tori stopped bringing home white boys and instead chose dates with black men. "I had gone to this really liberal, artsy college and I had a master's degree in fiction. My conversations [with these black men] were weird. They just weren't interested in any of the things I was interested in," she said. "I love my family, but . . . they are not living my life. Your family are not the ones who share your life. You can't live your life wondering if others are going to approve of something."

WHEN HIS RELATIVES REACT

The flip side to a woman's concern about her black family's resistance is her concern about the reactions from family members on the other, non-black side. This too cuts both ways, with approval and disapproval sometimes correlating with geography and generation.

Wendy Coakley Thompson, who based her novel *Back to Life* on her own personal experience, broke up with her fiancé over his family's lack of acceptance:

> He didn't think it would be an issue, but of course it was. He proposed to me, but he waited a year before he told them. I was hiding the ring from them when everyone else in our lives knew. When he finally told them, there were these games. They would call and ask him to dinner, and make it a point to tell him that I was excluded. They would be really kind one minute and then start screaming at him the next. He seemed unable to really just break free of them and stand on his own. My family lived in the Bahamas, and I really hoped that his family could be mine too. I wanted that embrace, but I never got it. I couldn't imagine how we could be happy. After these intense hateful moments with his family, I'd see this look on his face, like a whipped puppy. If they weren't happy with his choice, I didn't see how we'd make it. I broke it off with him.

"I regret it now," she says, almost twenty years later. "I'm in my forties and I've never married. I think if I had it to do over again, I would have at least tried to make it work. Maybe his family would have come around."

The success of a relationship may depend on the man—on his strength of commitment to it and his independence from his family. Greg lost his relationship with his father, a Cypriot Greek immigrant, over his choice to marry Jacquetta:

> My father emigrated from Cyprus when he was sixteen; my mother was born in the United States but her parents were Cypriots too. There's a whole history of Cyprus that is very exclusive and separate—from Greece and from the rest of the world. The island of Cyprus was once enslaved

by the Turks and that bad blood lingers to this day; there were demarcation lines between Turkish sections and Greek sections as recently as 2003. You would think that being aware of that history would make my parents—my father in particular—more understanding of African Americans, given the shared history of slavery. That wasn't the case. In fact, I think the only thing I could have done that would have been more disappointing to him was marry a Turkish woman.

My parents have never met my wife. I was in Manhattan, working for the district attorney's office, when Jacquetta and I met. After about three years of dating, we made the decision to marry. I asked them to come meet her many times, and finally they drove from their home in Webster, Massachusetts, down to New York. But they didn't meet her. They parked outside my apartment and asked me to come down. I thought they just wanted a minute alone with me before coming in or that they needed some help, so I went. Instead, they begged me to break it off with her, and when I refused, my father shook my hand and they got in the car and left. I haven't spoken to him since.

My mother is in a tough spot. She is American-born and grew up in New York City living around all kinds of people. She is a special education teacher—just like my wife—and works with people from all races and nationalities. I'm sure my mother and my wife would get along. She calls me from time to time, and I get the sense she would like to reengage with us. She tells me that they love me and then she tells me she wants us to apologize: she feels that I "just sprung this on them" and my approach was wrong. They feel my behavior indicated a lack of respect. From where I'm standing, that's just ridiculous. There is no greater "lack of respect" than the kind of bigotry they are showing. They owe us an apology, not the other way around.

No one from my family came to the wedding. My brother and other relatives say that my father is so angry, he will be angry with anyone who befriends us, and until things cool down they felt it was best not to get involved. One of my best friends actually went to my parents and told them, "This is crazy!" My father just got up and left.

I do think they'll come around in time, though in many ways the damage is done. I don't know that I'll ever view them the same way and I doubt Jacquetta will ever fully trust them, no matter what they say or do in the future. In the meantime, Jacquetta and I just live our lives. I have a busy law practice and I teach martial arts. Jacquetta is teaching and working on her comedy. We barely have time for our good friends, let alone time to worry about this. We just live our lives.

If I had to do it over again, I'd change nothing. Jacquetta and I are happy and that's the most important thing.

Greg expects that when he and Jacquetta have children—something they plan to do—his parents will want to become involved in their lives again, and for many interracial couples, the birth of a child improves extended family relationships. Religion and faith have healed other tense family dynamics. Some couples have experienced a re-engagement after family members have done some serious soul searching, as Cynthia found with her ex-husband's extended family:

I'd met his parents of course and that had gone okay, but he'd told me the one to worry about was his grandfather. I'd never met him, and although we invited him, he didn't come to our wedding. So one day we were at a gas station in Richmond, Kentucky, near where his family lived, when his granddad pulls his truck into the same station. Tracey [her husband at the time] said to me, "I want you to meet him." I was nervous; this old man clearly didn't want to meet me and he'd made his feelings about us as an interracial couple pretty clear. And sure enough, when we walked over to speak to him, the old man wouldn't look at either of us or speak. He just turned his back and kept pumping his gas. I remember Tracey said, "If this is the decision you've made, Granddad, I'm sorry for it. But I want you to know if you're not going to talk to her, you're not going to be talking to me either, and that's just the way it's going to be."

A year went by and we didn't hear from his grandfather or see him at any of the family events we went to. Then that Christmas we were invited to a big family Christmas gathering at his grandfather's house. As soon as I walked in, the old man pulled me aside and said, "I was wrong in the way I treated you. I've asked God to forgive me and I hope you will too."

Faith seems to be a recurrent factor for many parents of children in interracial relationships. Jarrod, a thirty-three-year-old software salesman, has been dating a black woman for five years. His parents grew up in Cicero, Illinois, a predominantly white enclave south and west of Chicago with a history of segregation that attracted marchers during the civil rights movement. "My grandmother was definitely a racist and was dead set against any blacks moving into Cicero," Jarrod says. "Even now, in my parents' hometown, neighbors worry about whether a home will be sold to blacks, even though the largest ethnic group is now Hispanics, mostly Mexican immigrants." Jarrod had dated only white women through his entire dating career—until he met his current girlfriend. "When I told my mom that my girlfriend was a black woman, she was a little worried. She's had a very limited exposure to blacks and most of that was based on either things her mother, my grandmother, had said when she was a child, or what she sees on television. She just doesn't know that many black people." Ultimately, what made Jarrod's mother relax was his girlfriend herself. "Jamie is a very sweet, kind person. She's intelligent and thoughtful and put my mom at ease. But even more than that, it was religion that bonded her to both my parents." His parents are both fundamentalist Christians, and the fact that Jamie grew up attending a small, Bible-centered Baptist church in small-town Virginia helped immensely. "Once they understood that she shared their religious beliefs, they were more than willing to accept her. They get along well."

Some black women take a direct approach with any latent racism in their white spouse's family. Joan, an outspoken black attorney of Caribbean descent, married her husband in 1992.

When I met his family, I got this sense that there might be something there, a little bit of a reaction, although no one ever said anything. I felt it partly because I could tell David was nervous about it. I had met his brother first, and I met his mother and sisters in 1990. I felt a little like they looked at me like I was something they had never seen before: like an exotic animal roaming free around his mother's living room. I told David afterwards that if we were going to have a serious relationship, he needed to make sure his family understood that I wasn't going to be made to feel small because of my race. I said to him, "None of your ·

sisters could have walked in my shoes [growing up very poor in St. Vincent, working their way to the United States, graduating from law school, passing the New York bar]. I won't put up with bigotry from them." I don't know if he told them that or not, but we've had very little trouble from his family.

MODERN FAMILIES, NEW WRINKLES

For contemporary interracial couples, concerns about family reach beyond looking backward to parents and grandparents. They also must look forward to how those relationships may impact the children they already have. Mike and Cynthia's relationship took "family" to a new level, since it was a second marriage for both and both had children with their former spouses.

"I had some slight concerns in the back of my mind," says Mike. "When we both started to realize that there was potential there [for us as a couple], there were new issues. Not just because of race, but for all kinds of reasons involving our children. I have a daughter (age eleven) and a son (age nine) from my first marriage, and Cynthia has a daughter from her first marriage who is eleven as well. We made a conscious effort to get everyone together and to make sure the children were comfortable. In the end, there were very few problems and the problems we have encountered came not from the children themselves, but from their friends."

> My children live with their mother and stepfather in a rural county a few hours from where Cynthia and I lived before we got married. We'd been dating several months when my daughter told me one of her friends had said, "You know your daddy and his girlfriend can't get married. It's in the Bible." I explained to her that her friend was wrong, and we got the Bible out and read and talked about the various verses. I'm pretty sure that my daughter went back and gave the little girl a lesson in theology . . . and I hope the little girl went to her parents and gave them that lesson too.

But Cynthia had different concerns for her daughter, who is biracial. "I made a conscious decision to date only white men after her father and

I divorced. I just felt that, because she is biracial, there might be less difficulty for her in accepting a stepfather who looked like her real father. I guess I was also worried that a black man might have resentments toward her [because her father is white]. I'm sure there would have been black men who would have loved her no matter what, but I decided that, given what I know about color-consciousness in the black community, there might be problems." Cynthia's daughter accepted Mike, her new stepfather—as well as his children from his prior marriage—with enthusiasm. "We all go out together sometimes," said Mike of his two white children, his ex-wife and her new husband, his black wife and biracial stepdaughter. "Here we all are in some restaurant together in Lexington, Kentucky, and you can see all the people around us staring, trying to figure out which kids go with which couple, while all of them are calling all of us Mama and Daddy. It's too funny."

When my husband, Kevin, and I got married, my daughter was nine. "He's very white," she remarked to me on one occasion, noting his skin color like a scientist. "But you guys love each other, so it's okay with me." Indeed, that's the best response any woman could hope for, from any member of the family, young or old.

FAMILY ACCEPTANCE: WHAT THE EXPERTS SAY

Fear of family reaction is definitely a consideration that keeps some black women from expanding their dating pool. But as several women noted in the stories they told me, families can't—and shouldn't—dictate how an adult woman lives her life. Still, most people want harmony between their significant others and their families. Is there hope when the initial reaction is hesitancy, distrust, or outright dislike?

"The black community tends to have a more negative reaction to interracial dating in general," says Dr. Rachel Sullivan, speaking of her research on why black women are less likely to date interracially. "If you just ask someone who is African American on the street, 'What do you think of a black woman dating outside her race?' you're more likely to get a response that includes some negative feedback." Faced with a specific case—"What do you think of my cousin's (white) husband, Paul?" for instance—Sullivan observes that "African Americans are more likely to reach acceptance. A person can be dubious about white people and interracial relationships in general but be able to deal with Paul as an individual. So African American families can ultimately become more accepting as they deal with the white family member. White families, however, tend to be the opposite. In general, they will say that they are accepting of interracial relationships, but there's a definite feeling of 'No, I don't want my son or daughter involved with that black woman or man.' Once again, however, exposure does tend to blunt the negative impact."

Dr. Kellina Craig-Henderson, author of *Black Men in Interracial Relationships* and the upcoming *Black Women in Interracial Relationships*, agrees. "What I found in my research is that black men in interracial relationships received one hundred percent support from their families toward them and their white female partners, while the families of white women they dated or married might have any reaction from total disowning to enthusiastic support and everything in between. With black women in interracial relationships, however, I didn't find that one hundred percent support for the relationship from her family that we found for black men. Usually one of the parents had some feelings of dislike or resentment. But for most of the black women I interviewed, over time, her family did come around to a level of acceptance of her white partner."

In other words, experts assure us, for most couples time usually heals all wounds. As nervous relatives become more comfortable with the nonblack family member, tensions often ease, and as his nonblack family gets to know you, they too become more comfortable. In my own story, after some months of awkwardness, my parents thawed considerably toward my husband with the passage of time. And, blessedly, there was another incentive for them to come to know him better: the birth of our daughter. My experience was hardly unique, according to the experts. The birth of children has also been known to help thaw chilly relationships.

Although concerns about children are cited as the primary reason for opposition to interracial relationships, ironically, most couples who had children reported that the birth of a child made their families more accepting of the relationship (which is consistent with Rosenblatt et al.,

1995). Several couples talked about how happy their family was when they had children. This was especially true if the child was the first grand-child, and this phenomenon was particularly dramatic in White families who had strongly opposed the interracial relationship. Grandparents wanted to develop relationships with their grandchildren, and in some cases, grandparents began to understand more about racism by gaug-ing others' reactions to their grandchildren. The birth of a child may lead to greater approval because relatives see the couple following some elements of the traditional family script; moreover, it is much easier for relatives to be upset with adults than it is for them to be upset with children.[5]

While having children tended to make families more approving, it did not necessarily mean that the relationship was completely accepted or that there was peace in the family. Indeed, sometimes children can raise new issues.

"My wife and I would like to have children and I'm sure that my parents will want to see their grandchild," said Greg. "But after all we've been through, I don't know how I will feel about that. Knowing that they've been so bigoted in their reception to my child's mother will make it hard for me to believe that they can completely accept our child. And we worry that, if they haven't completely reformed, will we be exposing our child to their bigoted ideas? We aren't pregnant yet, but I think about these things. I can't help but wonder how much the birth of our child will heal the relationship." He added, after a thoughtful pause, "I guess time will tell."

FAMILY APPROVAL ISN'T BLACK AND WHITE

Sullivan's analysis includes some thoughts that help turn the discussion of family approval of interracial relationships completely on its head. "Let's be real," she writes. "Family doesn't just influence interracial rela-tionships, it also heavily influences *intraracial* relationships. In order to challenge the mythologies of interracial relationships, it's useful to first explore the mythologies of intraracial relationships," for instance, the notion that "marrying someone of the same race guarantees that friends and family will approve of the relationship: Not so. There are a host of reasons why a family can oppose a relationship, and marrying someone of the same race is no guarantee that families will be happy. They may find other reasons to object—religious differences, age differences, personality clashes, and many other issues."[6]

And of course, she's right. Families can have all kinds of reasons for disapproving of a potential partner; race is just an obvious one. In the end, however, there are no guarantees: a couple can succeed wildly without family approval or fail miserably even when there's nothing but unconditional support. As has been noted time and time again, your family can't live your life—or make your relationship work. In the end, it's always a question of the two individuals involved.

Letting your family's reactions govern your decision making can come at a high cost. Consider this letter of love and acceptance lost, which I received by email in June 2008:

My wife and I are white. But my son fell in love with a black woman in college. They were together for most of his college life. Though she was from North Carolina and we live in Maryland, she visited us frequently and even spent several months with us in our home while pursuing an internship for her college program. She called me "Dad" and we related so very well together. She became the daughter I never had. My son and she began talking marriage, and we were delighted to offer our blessing.

However, things didn't go so smoothly for her with her family. She met resistance. She began expressing ambivalence to our son, then unexpectedly and abruptly, she cut off the relationship via email. My son pursued her for several months trying to mend the relationship. She ran hot and cold. We ached for him, and while we surmised that the relationship probably shouldn't move forward if her family was against it, we ached for ourselves too.

My son moved on and found love again. While it was probably for the best that he and his college sweetheart did not marry, I do miss her and the father-daughter relationship that was forming between us. I've wondered what stresses, what questions, what conflicts she encountered that ulti-

mately sabotaged her love for my son. Before this experience I never realized how uniquely stressful a relationship with a white man can be for a black woman.

I hope this young black woman found what she was looking for; it sounds like she lost out on not *one* man who loved her, but *two*.

Other women have vowed not to make the same mistake, even if it causes family members some discomfort. "My mother," one woman writes, "always warned me before I was even of dating age that it was unacceptable and not allowed [to date white men] since they had a history of [devaluing black women]. That was a lesson that was passed from mother to daughter in our family—you just didn't do it. But the thing is, you have to do what makes you happy. You can't live your life for your family or you end up miserable and alone."

Well said. Good luck, Chaka. Here's hoping your mom comes around, but even if she doesn't, you have to live your life your way. Happiness can be hard enough to come by in life. Don't throw it away for the sake of other people's prejudices.

NOTION 4

I Don't Find White Men Attractive

In a recent comedy special, comedian Chris Rock pokes fun at how willingly black men will sleep with white women and how hesitant black women are about sleeping with white men. "The reason is," he declares, mugging for his audience, "black women aren't attracted to white men." There are groans throughout the audience—crowds in New York, London, and Johannesburg, South Africa, spliced together for this HBO special—as this "joke" struggles to find purchase. Rock gets adamant. "Sure, you'll give some to a handsome white boy, but after that..."[1] And he goes on to suggest that, in the absence of good looks, the only reason black women might forge a relationship with a white man is money (an idea that will be discussed in depth in Notion 7). Rock further theorizes that black women are angry with black men because they are attracted to women of all ethnic backgrounds, while black women are only attracted to black men.

Whether Rock is being funny or whether he's offering a valid social commentary depends on your sense of humor and your point of view. Many black women, however, echo Chris Rock's sentiments in sister-friend conversations daily. "I'm just not attracted to white men," writes one woman in an email. "I've gone out with a couple," says another. "But there's just nothing there." Says a third, "I could imagine dating a guy with some color to him—a Greek guy or an Italian. But those really, really white-looking guys just don't cut it." And finally, "My personality is too strong to attract a white man."

Books have been written about the images and standards of beauty that bind black women and white women. And the images that portray black men as either "cool" or "criminal" have been written about at great length. But what about white men and their image? Does a "pretty boy" have a better shot with a black woman than an average-looking white man? Is "handsome" a prerequisite for a relationship? What role should physical attractiveness play in any relationship?

With her years of running interracial dating events through Multi-mixx, Nikki Doughty knows it's important to keep it real about the role good looks play for white men seeking to date black women and vice versa. "What we found at Multimixx is that attractiveness is universally appreciated. It doesn't matter what race you are. Good-looking is good-looking: all the same rules apply. It doesn't have to be in the Hollywood way. Men typecast about what they find attractive, but women do too. When you do interracial mixers, it's obvious. When the women are attractive—and by that I mean physically fit, pretty, stylish—the men gravitate toward them. And when the men are a catch—good-looking, tall, smartly dressed—the women tend to float in their direction. That may not be fair, as not-so-good-looking (or -acting) people will get left out of the selection, but it is true."

For many black women, it's not just about Hollywood good looks or financial success. There's a more visceral physical discomfort with straight hair, pink skin (especially private parts), and the perception that white men will be either too "weak" or too "feminine" to handle their strong personalities and cultural experiences.

While individual women are entitled to their preferences, these comments actually may be shorthand for ideas that exclude potential partners on the basis of race without much consideration for the real qualities and characteristics that build successful relationships. Identifying which stated preferences are genuine and which are shaped by erroneous notions may help black women to become more willing to explore all the options in the global village more fully.

PINK PRIVATE PARTS

When it comes to dating white men—and sometimes men of any race—
skin color seems to be a major issue for black women. Here are some
typical comments I heard and received in the researching of this book:

> *I can't imagine making love with a white man. I can't imagine dealing
> with . . . you know . . . his pink private parts.*

> *I don't see many white men . . . as being attractive either. It's that milky
> white skin color. The skin, the hair, the smell . . . ugh. Gross!*

> *Yes, white men approach me. I would date one if he swept me off my feet. I
> wouldn't be totally comfortable right now. . . . I really love a brown-skin
> brother, but a big heart, lots of love and attention may erase some color
> lines. As of right now, I need Brown!*

Of course, black women are as entitled to their preferences in choosing a mate as any other group. But often, for black women, it's not a
matter of preferring a certain texture of hair or color of eyes. It's a preference based on more subtle cultural beliefs and, worse, in some notions
perpetrated by white racism. As Mona Washington observes, "At the
end of the day, all this emphasis on color gets to be foolish. Can anyone
really tell the difference between a white guy and a really, really light-
skinned black guy?"

"It's all the same in the dark," agrees Cynthia.

"All cats are gray at night," adds another woman.

But for some black women, it's tough to get that far. Considering a
"pale male" gives them shudders of revulsion, especially when it comes
to imagining any kind of sexual relationship. What's the deal?

> *Why do I want a black man? Because I want a BIG DI@K!! LOL! I'm
> actually kind of serious! The thought of pink "junk"—Yuck!*

This email echoes what has been common girl talk among women for
over a century. You know what I'm talking about. It's not just the "pink-

ness," although, as the correspondent above indicates, many women do have objections to the color of a white man's genitals. But usually, it's about the size.

"You wouldn't believe how many of my black girlfriends have asked me this," said Marvine, whose husband of eight years is white. "I have to set them straight. There's just no difference!"

"The first time I saw my husband's penis," Joan says, laughing, "I said, 'Nice size!' And he was like, 'Don't tell me you believed that white-guys-have-little-dicks stuff!' I was teasing him, of course."

For centuries it's been said, as though it were an indisputable fact, that white men have smaller penises than black men. If you're like me, you may have wondered if indeed there has ever been a study—some kind of objective scientific test that measured the penises of men of all races—and just who in the world had gotten *that* particular job. Turns out, in this modern age, there's no hypothesis that science hasn't tested. There have *indeed* been studies—not just one, but several—of penis size as it relates to a man's race.

Ladies, the results may surprise you.

For sixty years, British researchers Kevan Wylie and Ian Eardley have studied, measured, and asked both men and women about the male sexual organ. After more than fifty different research projects conducted all over the world, measuring the penises of men of all races and nationalities, they published their findings in the *British Journal of Urology* in 2007. They concluded that the average erect penis—regardless of a man's race or nationality—was 5.5 to 6.2 inches long and 4.7 to 5.1 inches in circumference.[2] Similarly, a United Nations study of penis size published in 2008 found the average man's penis size to be 14 centimeters (around 5.25 inches for those of us who are nonmetric). Finally, the respected Kinsey Institute weighed in on the issue, announcing that in their studies, the length of the average penis is 5 to 7 inches, regardless of race. Some studies did find some very slight differences in length among white, black, Hispanic, and Asian men, but the rankings of "who's the biggest" varied from study to study and were statistically insignificant. Of course, some men of all races had penises larger and smaller than the measured average, but height and body type, as well as more complex issues like poverty and childhood malnourishment, account for those differences in size. Interestingly (though not really surprisingly), in another study, when asked to estimate the size of their erect penis, most men exaggerated by more than a full inch![3]

Add to this tendency toward exaggeration the ubiquitous images of pornography of black men with unusually large penises and the population's seemingly endless appetite for Long Dong Silver/Mandingo stereotypes, and this myth of the black man's larger endowment remains alive and well.

But, sorry, guys and ladies. The bottom line is this: all men lie about the size of their penises, and the lie that black men's penises are substantially larger than those of other men is the biggest one of all. In fact, the whole story began not out of any actual perception of truth (however misguided or misinformed) but out of the ugly, racist rhetoric that permeated the South after the end of the Civil War.

THE "BLACK BEAST"

After the end of the Civil War, during the Reconstruction years, black people—black men, in particular—enjoyed a host of new freedoms. In the first couple of decades after the Civil War, black men ran for public office, opened businesses, and pursued education, all under the auspices of the federal government. New programs for freed slaves aimed at rectifying the harms of slavery proliferated, at least briefly, and many white southerners were worried. The rise of these formerly enslaved people put at risk their own livelihoods and way of living. Something had to be done, and fear was one of the best ways to corral support for ending Reconstruction and returning the black man to near-slave status.

> The abolition of slavery and the elevation of blacks to formal racial equality moved whites ferociously to reassert their racial hegemony. During this period, fear and loathing of black advancements ignited an intensified effort to vilify and contain expression of black "manhood." The argument was that only slavery had tamed the black man's latent sexual savagery. With slavery ended, the "black beast" was loosed to visit its depravity on white womanhood.[4]

Reconstruction-era physicians distorted science to explain their racist political agenda. In 1903, for example, Dr. William Lee Howard wrote that, in his medical opinion, "the large size of the Negro's penis" and the lack of "sensitiveness of the terminal fibers which exist in the Caucasian"[5] made the black man a sexual demon that had to be suppressed. The result of these wrong and racist ideas about the size of black men's genitalia was decades of violence. Beatings, intimidation, and most notably lynchings—an estimated four to five thousand of them between the 1880s and 1960s—were the tactics used against black men for even the slightest suggested affront to a white woman.[6]

In light of this history, it's downright bizarre that this southern racist myth about a black man's penis size is still embraced by black men and black women with pride. Why are we celebrating something that is completely and resoundingly false, and why on earth would we as African Americans want to reduce manhood to something so limited and so crude?

THE POWER IN HIS PANTS

Black men hold on to the "big dick" image because it gives them power in a society that can often leave them relatively powerless. In their book *Gender Talk*, Johnnetta Betsch Cole and Beverly Guy-Sheftall explore the development of sex as the black male's last frontier of power and dominance. "When black males are unable to be men in traditional ways . . . they compensate by exaggerating what's left of normative gender roles. . . . The result is exaggerated sexuality."[7]

For some years, black men have been identified as "endangered" because of high rates of incarceration and homicide and low rates of education. According to sociologist Robert Staples, it is more difficult in this culture for black men to achieve appropriate gender roles—as providers and protectors—than it is for black women. This "role failure" results in conceptions of manhood that rely upon the power in a man's pants: having a large penis, impregnating females, fathering children, having many sexual relationships and many sexual conquests. While these behaviors have been studied primarily in terms of black men in lower socioeconomic groups, it does appear that, as playwright Mona Washington says, "we're all sipping the same Kool-Aid," and the association of black masculinity with what we might call "penis power" is something that some black men and black women across socioeconomic groups have absorbed as part of what it means to be black and male in America.

Unfortunately, penis power brings with it a host of problems that do more harm to black men as a group than they help—whether an individual black man engages in the behaviors associated with the big dick image or not. And believing in penis power doesn't do black women any good either, since it presents an image of masculinity that supports infidelity and may discourage the kind of behaviors that produce the "good black man" so many black women seek.

On some level, most black women know that penis power is a myth and that rejecting or accepting men of any race solely on the basis of anatomy is a recipe for an extremely limited, primarily sexual relationship. But often penis power isn't really about the male anatomy: it's a shorthand for a whole raft of images and beliefs about masculinity. What we believe about "what makes a man a *man*" can be just as limiting— and potentially damaging—to our choice in mates as running around sticking rulers down men's pants and using the resulting measure to determine their desirability.

COOL, SWAGGER, AND LIMITED DEFINITIONS OF MASCULINITY

I have seen white men who I think are attractive but I could never see myself in a relationship with one. During graduate school, I was attracted to a white guy, he was very handsome and cool to hang out with but it never went beyond that. I just couldn't do it. Something was missing. I have had several white men come on to me but it never got beyond the introduction. I personally don't feel comfortable in a relationship situation with a white man. It is just something about black men that I love. When I settle down and get married, I definitely plan on it being with a black man.[8]

While this woman couldn't identify the missing something that turned her off men of other races, other women have been much more specific.

"White men seem feminine and weak to me," one woman I interviewed said when asked whether she would date outside the race. She admitted that she'd noticed white men "looking" at her with interest, but consciously or unconsciously, she never encouraged them out of a certainty that they would be inadequate partners. Other black women define the appeal of black men on a much more basic level. Writes one, "For me, there's something about a black man that defines strength. You know you are going to be taken care of no matter what. When he says, 'I got you,' you believe it. And even the most independent black woman wants to feel that her man can take care of her." As another woman puts it, "For me a black man is the shit! It's the swagger and everything else! I can't imagine being [attracted] to anything less."

Women of all races are often attracted to men who have a certain "edge" to them. You know what I'm talking about: a certain bad-boy quality that some call "swagger," some call acting "hard," and still others call "cool." As Craig-Henderson observes, "Black men are portrayed in our society as sexy. Black male athletes, entertainers—even the president of the United States—these are mainstream images of masculinity in America. Even young white men want to emulate them. It's hip to be a black man."

Black men—and by extension, black women—are in a long-running love affair with what psychologist Richard Majors, cofounder of the National Council of African American Men, calls the "cool pose." The "cool pose" comprises an array of "coping behaviors and psychological defenses, both positive and negative, that some black males employ to deal with the persistent stressor of an oppressive society: being tough, violent, and exerting control of others."[9] Any male who fails to exhibit the requisite "toughness" is considered "weak." Being weak makes one prey to abuse and violence from other men.

And while "swagger" seems tough and masculine on the surface, most women who become involved with masters of the cool pose quickly find out that it has its price in emotional intimacy, physical safety, and fidelity. In *Cool Pose: The Dilemmas of Black Manhood in America*, Majors and coauthor Janet Mancini Billson identify a multitude of problems that can accompany "swagger," including stormy male-female relationships.

Donning of the cool pose may condition the black man to suppress and lose touch with all his feelings, including those that might facilitate nurtur[ing] relations with others. . . . A black man who experiences economic role failure may compensate by defining masculinity in terms of being able to impregnate women and produce children. . . . Or he can define manhood in terms of multiple relationships and sexual partners. For some black males there is an inseparable link between self-esteem and the ability to have affairs with women who produce their children.[10]

Certainly not every black man fits this description, but most black women know at least one who does. Most of us have dated a few men who seemed to define themselves not by fidelity to one woman but by their ability to "play" as many women as possible. Allison, a successful attorney who has been married to a white man for seventeen years, recalls her experience:

He was athletic, good-looking, and in the military. We dated while I was in law school. I had an immediate physical attraction to him. It was hot, hot sex. Wild. Animal, you know? The kind of thing that would have you screaming. But when it was over, he was jumping up to leave. And more than once, when we were out together, he'd be on the phone in these whispered conversations. Ultimately, I got tired of wondering where he was and who else he was seeing. I decided to give Jacob [her current husband] a chance, and the more I got to know him, the more I realized that I liked not having to worry about who else he was seeing. I knew I could trust Jacob. I knew I was his only woman. I found out years later that [the cool black man] actually had gotten two other women pregnant while we were dating. Sure, the sex was great, but I'm glad I didn't make my life decisions just on that.

Allison's experience is hardly unique. Another woman who preferred anonymity but who has been in a long-term relationship with her white boyfriend for five years, experienced something similar:

The black guys I was sexually involved with were aggressive. It was always clear that they had experience. They knew what they wanted [sexually]. They told me what to do, and if I didn't want to, they knew they had other options. They'd just move on to another woman who was willing to do more for them and ask for less.

"Players"—black men involved with multiple women—don't always let marriage stop their game, and infidelity may play a role in the divorce rate for black couples. While there have been studies on the issue, the jury is still out on whether African American men are any less faithful than men of other races. Some researchers report a positive correlation between being African American and engaging in infidelity, while others conclude that it's the level of a man's education that impacts his propensity to cheat. Other surveys suggest that for African American men, education doesn't have a thing to do with it and the likelihood of "stepping out" on a committed relationship remains high, regardless of educational attainment. Still other studies find that African Americans and whites do not differ in terms of lifetime incidence of infidelity. Black men are better positioned than whites to take advantage of the shortage of single men in the black community, which means increased opportunities for married black men to engage in infidelity with single black women.[11]

Regardless of the reasons, no woman with self-respect wants to be one of a harem for any man, regardless of his race. Good women want to be cherished and respected by men whom they know they can trust. But for far too many black women, because of their limited notions of what manhood means, being a "good woman" means putting up with a not-so-good man. For some, it's important to have a man who has that swagger—important enough to accept infidelity, conflict, drama, and, worse, the potential for violence rather than consider men who on the surface may to them appear soft or feminine. As many a good man has said, "Women don't want nice guys." Unfortunately, many women who search for swagger, who like men with edge and cool, prove that axiom to be true. Indeed, many "nice" black men complain that the same women who assert there aren't any "good black men" refuse to give them any love.

Many of the most eligible black men . . . were not necessarily the "coolest" in school. In high school and college, the most desired black women went for the "hard" guys [with the most swagger] who treated them badly. The most popular men were not the ones who studied the hardest or treated women with respect. Black men pay a penalty for being quiet, thoughtful, and bookish. Black women don't want us.

Yet another man—this time a white man—recounted a similar experience in an email to me:

I work in an office where I am surrounded by beautiful, fun, smart black women. We go to lunch, sometimes drinks after work, and in general they make it a joy to go to work. I have found myself attracted to one of the ladies and more than once tried to take our relationship from "work mates" to something more. But I keep getting shot down for being "too nice" and "just a friend." She keeps telling her friends she's looking for a good black man, whatever that means. The black guys she talks about don't sound that good to me. In fact I think they treat her very badly. It makes me wonder if she's really looking for a "good" guy at all.

While these men's comments may not be entirely fair to black women, they do speak to the larger point: that it's time for all women to embrace a new definition of manhood—one that allows for kindness, intelligence, faithfulness, and caring.

Black women certainly aren't alone in their preference for bad-boy swagger. All women are susceptible to it to some degree. In fact, it's so common that scientists have attempted to explain why women seem to be attracted to men who exhibit bad-boy tendencies. In a study conducted by researchers at New Mexico State University, Las Cruces, two hundred college students were given personality tests to see how many of what psychologists call "dark triad traits"—callousness, impulsive behavior, extroversion, narcissism, and various antisocial traits for which "bad boys" are known—they possessed. The researchers also asked about the students' sex lives, their feelings about sexual relationships, their number of sexual partners, and what they were seeking in sexual or romantic relationships. In an interview with ABC News reporter Audrey Grayson, Peter Jonason, lead study investigator, said that although society tends to look down upon these "negative" dark triad personality traits, there seems to be quite an upside to being a bad boy.

"We would traditionally consider these dark triad traits to be adverse personality traits, and we think women would avoid these kinds of men, but what we show is counterintuitive—that women are attracted to these bad boys and they do pretty well in terms of sheer numbers of sexual partners," Jonason explained in the interview. "They're taking quantity over quality as their sexual agenda, being serially monogamous and having multiple partners or one-night stands. . . . If you like someone and want to meet them and date them, people who have the dark triad traits appear to be more successful at facilitating short-term mating." The researchers theorize that it's the presence of higher levels of testosterone in some men that makes them more aggressive, more manipulative, and more willing to tell women what they want to hear to get sex.[12]

This is nothing that most women don't already know. These traits are the edge, the swagger, the cool, translated to include all men who fall into the "bad boy" set, regardless of race. These are the mannerisms and behaviors that get our phone numbers, talk us into bed, and then never call. It doesn't take a study to introduce most women to these guys; we've already met them.

We may be attracted to these men, but these *are not* the men we ultimately want to marry, and understanding this is critical to any woman looking for a good man, regardless of race. Callous, impulsive, self-centered, aggressive, cool, hard—call it what you want, this quality spells devotion to one person's needs. It has little to do with building a relationship for two. Women who want to be in committed relationships must surrender their infatuation with bad-boy traits. Not surprisingly, the New Mexico State University study concluded the same thing. A nicer guy may not hit you over the head with his charms, but he will invest the time in getting to know you, building trust, and developing a mutually satisfying relationship.

Both Allison and Jamie ultimately found serious and committed relationships with white men, but after some difficulties in reconciling their notions of masculinity with their core needs.

WEAK MEN OR A DIFFERENT STRENGTH?

Before we go any further, we have to acknowledge the obvious: that this whole "me strong man, you weak woman" thing is a male creation—a construct devised for the purposes of male domination to place a higher value on "maleness" than "femaleness." The whole weak/strong dichotomy fails to recognize what we all know to be true: that men and women are different. Their strengths and weaknesses vary by situation, by individual, and by the way in which we choose to examine them. For centuries, men have defined "strength" in their own image, basing it on physical abilities and aggressiveness. But as our world requires less and less physical strength for achieving success, the same definitions men created are coming back to bite them.

The notions of what is masculine versus what is feminine have already taken a big chunk out of black women's identities. Thanks to a history of holding families together in the face of overwhelming odds, black women have garnered a reputation for resilience—a traditionally masculine quality. Thanks to negative media portrayals of snappish, emasculating, and harshly critical black women (often called "Sapphires" after the eponymous character in the 1950s *Amos 'n Andy* television show), we are perceived as direct and outspoken—other traditionally masculine traits. And finally, our abilities as wage earners and matriarchs who provide for families—another traditionally male role—seal our fate, even though many black women take on that obligation out of necessity, not choice. Instead of being celebrated for our ability to not just survive but *thrive* in a system that we didn't create, many black women are cast as "too masculine." The translation of "too masculine" for many men is "unmarriageable."

"Black girls are perceived as scary, hence Scary Spice," says Nikki Doughty, who in addition to her work with Multimixx is the founder of Black Women Who Date Interracially (www.bwwdi.org). "Sometimes that's how men of other races feel about us—what they see of black women on television (sometimes their only way of getting to know us). Head rolling, sass, and diminutive supportive roles where the black female characters only suck their teeth are what people see in movies and television. It damns black women to being cast as scary. Our honesty and common sense have been miscast as negative and intimidating. All these negative perceptions of black women in America make us seem like there's an invisible force field around us. It's like we're encased in glass and completely unapproachable. It is *so* not true."

But while we hate the label of "masculine" and how it isolates us from potential partners, many black women have no trouble labeling men—particularly men of other races—as feminine when they approach us with gentleness, kindness, compassion, and sensitivity.

As Patricia Hill Collins points out in her essay "Telling the Difference," definitions of "weak and strong" ultimately spring from a power structure that values traditional notions of patriarchy, in which men are supposed to dominate and women are supposed to submit. But many black women have incorporated a kind of outspokenness and force of character that is typically considered masculine (and by some men emasculating). "I need a man strong enough to deal with me," one woman told me. "I don't want a man so weak that I can run him."

While these comments seem to reflect the strength of the woman's personality, they actually enforce a kind of superpatriarchy: a strong woman (that is, one who exhibits some of the traits traditionally considered to be more masculine) needs an even stronger man, escalating the traditional notions of patriarchy so that the woman can be both strong and submissive at the same time. Not surprisingly, these kinds of male-female power struggles can end in violence. As Joan says, "My husband and I have had the kinds of arguments that I know many a black man would have had me swallow my teeth. Being with David has helped me rethink traditional power dynamics. Sometimes the strongest thing a man can do is remember his kindness—his inner centeredness—even when the woman, in this case, me, can't find hers! I think him *more* of a man for that ability, not less."

While some white men express anger in violence against women too, Joan's experience suggests the kind of paradigm shift that can provide black women with a new way of examining potential partners— a shift away from the kind of man who can outyell us or do even worse. Instead of "strong men," what we need are men who are comfortable enough with themselves not to require the traditional man-on-top pecking order. Instead of strong women and stronger men, what we need is an appreciation of all the qualities that are necessary for successful long-term relationships: caring, commitment, kindness, compassion, a willingness to listen, and a sense of shared enterprise with one's partner. Stated differently, confident women need partners who bring out their gentleness and vulnerabilities, not partners who can yell even louder than they can.

Men and women are different, and no one wants to turn men into women or vice versa. But in our modern world, traditional patriarchal notions of what is "feminine" and what is "masculine" could stand some revision for the good of men and women of all races. The challenge is to come up with progressive definitions that allow us all to express all aspects of our identities, and that ain't easy. As M. Bahati Kuumba, director of the Women's Research and Resource Center at Spelman College, puts it,

> Although most agree that gender transformation is a necessary part of the struggle for liberation . . . black feminist perspectives on how to achieve this objective vary as widely as the spectrum of black masculinities. Further, even though most agree that men must play a substantial role in changing gender relationships, these women also differ about what role women should play in engaging black men about black men's own gendered roles and expectations, as well as about educating them about sexism and the achievement of women's human rights.[13]

And of course, this isn't a discussion for African Americans only. Gender definitions are an ongoing discussion for the entire human race.

How then does the individual black woman navigate these issues? The first key is to recognize that, to use Mona's words again, we're all drinking the Kool-Aid: to some extent, all of us are shaped by these long-held ideas of masculine and feminine, even though they are outdated and more than likely unfairly applied. Realizing that we may be rejecting men based on outdated and unfair definitions of masculine and feminine frees us to reconsider the definitions and expectations that have governed our choices. Recognizing and questioning our own belief system enables us to step back, take a second look, and perhaps make a different choice when confronted with a man who doesn't easily fit into our usual box. Remember the old adage: If you do what you've always done, you'll get what you've always got. Thinking differently about your needs leads to new possibilities—and new results.

Many of the black women interviewed for this book admit that they found their white male spouses "weak" or "feminine" upon first meeting. Joan describes how her future husband

> used to hang out in the library near where my friends and I would congregate. He went to another school, but he was taking a summer minicourse at my law school. I didn't like him. He was too quiet, too laid-back, too pale. I was this outspoken Caribbean woman with a huge afro and a criminal record! I couldn't imagine what I would do with this pale, quiet, unassuming man!

Lorraine also was less than wowed with her husband when they first met. "I didn't like him. I found him too forward with his intentions. He just came out and said he was interested in dating me. There was no dancing around the issue, no 'game' at all." She didn't like his approach. "It was so direct that it was weird."

Jamie, who has been in a relationship with Jarrod, who is white, for five years, reports a similar experience:

> We were training for a marathon in a running club; he and I ran about the same pace, so we were sort of thrown together. I liked him well enough, but I never considered him other than a white guy I ran with. When he called and asked me to go out with him, I was like "Yeah, okay." I was thinking we were just going to hang out, like we'd done many days after a long run. He actually had to say to me, "You understand I'm asking you out. On a date." Up until he said that, I had no idea. He was nice and all, but he just wasn't what I normally would have dated. And he completely confused me by being so up front. I was glad, because otherwise I totally would have missed out. I guess I just don't understand white game.

Some women avoid men of *any* race whom they perceive as "feminine," "quiet," or "weak." They do so to their detriment. These are the positive qualities that form the basis for solid relationships with long-term staying power, but it takes time to appreciate them. Allowing yourself time to really get to know a man—and for him to know you—gives you the best chance to determine whether the two of you have the stuff to go the distance.

So many black women, like Jamie, say that they aren't sure when men of other races are expressing romantic interest. Jamie saw only a slightly nerdy white guy she considered a running buddy until he spelled it out. As she aptly put it, she didn't understand "white game." In the absence of swagger, some women can't tell the difference between "How are you" and "How *you* doing?"

Time for a brief primer in "white game."

WHITE GAME?

I've had a few [white guys] just start random conversations but I don't know if it was general conversation or an attempt to lead to something. Hmmm . . . I'm a bit clueless to the "white game"! LOL!

—from an anonymous email to the author

White men, I've noticed, don't tend to openly *eyeball women and make moves on women the way a lot of black men in large urban areas do, and many white men are definitely hesitant about approaching a black woman because of cultural differences and the ongoing undercurrent of racial tension. Likewise, many black women don't give white men the green light, usually for the same or related reasons.*

—Evia Moore, www.blackfemaleinterracialmarriage.com

Pat and her husband have been married for more than forty years, but when I asked her about their earliest days, she confessed to being not just uncertain but *unaware* of Kevin's interest in her.

I chuckle about it now, but there was a [black woman] who flat out said to me, "Pat, that [white] boy really likes you and you need to stop being so stupid because he is a really nice young man." In the back of my mind, my South Carolina upbringing was weighing in heavily . . . but on the other hand, it was the 1960s and I think I was influenced by the "do your own thing" attitudes of the time. So I took [the woman's] advice and here we are, all these years later!

Halima Sal-Anderson, author of *Supposing I Wanted to Date a White Guy . . . ?* and founder of the popular blog dateawhiteguy.blogspot.com, analyzes why some black women confess to cluelessness rather than suspicion when white men express interest: "Black women and white men are coming out of a kind of 'cold war' situation with each other. At this point there is so much uncertainty and insecurity on both sides about whether we are attracted to each other or not. There has been so much encouraged fear and hostility between the two groups, and many white men believe that most black women would love nothing better than to cut them down with an axe!"[14]

The fear of rejection—on both sides—haunts the early stages of any relationship. "No one wants to show their hand first in case of a severe rebuff," Sal-Anderson adds. "Everyone is waiting for the other to be clear and apparent before they even show the slightest interest back. Add race and it becomes even more complicated: most white men know they can't use the same aggressive style minority men use and get away with it. Furthermore, the whole culture of fear for men about things like sexual harassment has a lot of men running scared about walking up to a woman and stating their case—especially in the workplace."

It helps to remember that different men express their confidence differently. "Sometimes black women get used to seeing confidence as appearing in one way—which doesn't leave room for them to appreciate it in a different style from another kind of man. Unless black women become more aware of it, this limitation can work to their detriment as they might not see the charms and good attributes of other men. I think as women grow older they zone in on the substance of a man and silly things don't matter," Sal-Anderson continues.

Fortunately, the cues of attraction are not that different between races. Eye contact and flirtation are universal languages that everyone speaks, and black women who are open to receive those signals can be pretty sure that, when both are there, there's interest too. In *Supposing I Wanted*

to Date a White Guy . . . ?, Sal-Anderson offers numerous tips on flirtation, for those of us who feel we may need a little help. "I call it 'How to
Get Brad from Angelina!' " she says.

"Take your time. Go slow. Get to know him. I think it's important for
black women to remain sexually cautious," Evia Moore advises. "There
are a lot of negative stereotypes about us out there, and just as there are
black men who might be predatory, there are white men who are as well.
Getting to know someone takes time, and we should *always* take that
time to determine if a man—of any race—is someone worth getting sexually intimate with."

Both women agree, however, that if a man keeps making an effort to
be around you, he's probably trying to tell you something. Novelist
Wendy Coakley-Thompson says, "More than once in a work situation,
I've found myself wondering, 'Why does this guy keep stopping by my
desk to chat?' Sometimes it really does take me a while to *get* it. Then
it's like 'Oh . . . he *likes* me. That's what it is!' " She laughs. "It's a shame!
But I'm glad to know it's not just me who walks around absolutely clueless about when men are interested in me. That makes me feel a little
better."

If you're like Wendy, for all you know, you've been approached by
nonblack men with interest time and time again but shrugged it off as
nothing. Widening your dating pool may be as easy as being willing to
let your guard down so that you can be seen for the woman you are. I
love this story from Evia:

> I went to the bank this morning to discuss a special type of account that
> is connected with my home business, so I had to speak with a bank of-
> ficer, who turned out to be a white male around my age. We started
> talking about the pros and cons of various types of business accounts
> and such, all quite formal and the usual stuff. He was reasonably attrac-
> tive and very well groomed, as you'd expect from a bank officer. Sud-
> denly, I thought about some of the sistas on my blog here who continue
> to say that white males don't show interest in black women, and I de-
> cided to do an experiment.
>
> I became chatty, friendly, threw in some wit, and smiled whenever it
> was appropriate. At a certain point, maybe 5 minutes into the discussion,
> I became aware that his manner had changed. He was now talkative,

warm, humorous, and began to dig for information for me on his computer. He went on and on explaining many features of various accounts and details to me, and suffice it to say that I knew he was going just a tad beyond the call of duty, so to speak. He was becoming more interested in me, as a person—not just a bank customer. He actually found a way for me to get an account without paying fees. Yippee! Anyway, he then asked me my name, whether I was local, etc. . . . He gave me his card and shook my hand. When I left the bank, I knew without any doubt that this guy was going to get into my account and get the whole scoop on me.

Now, I wasn't dressed up or anything—just had on jeans, a plaid shirt, windbreaker, and since it was windy, my hair was looking wild. I didn't have on makeup except for a little lipstick and the only thing that may have been a little unusual about me was that I was wearing some of my jazzy, long earrings that I made. As I drove off, I tried to see myself through his eyes. I guess I'm average-looking, on the slim side, well-spoken, and I'd been very friendly. I definitely knew that something about our interaction had perked his interest. I didn't have up any wall. I treated him exactly the way I'd treat a black man who I felt comfortable with because I *had* felt very comfortable with him. After all, white men are just men like any other men—they like to see themselves as interesting in a woman's eyes.

It helps to release your expectations and relax. Many black women who are now happily married to men of other races say their relationships began very slowly, allowing both parties time to really get to know each other. When the emphasis is on communication, there is no "game" to learn.

Both Jacquetta and Cynthia met their husbands online. "There was lots of emailing—long before we met," Jacquetta recalls. "I posted my ad on craigslist.com and I got lots of responses. His was just one of the responses I liked. But we just kept emailing. We went back and forth and back and forth. Right up until we met, I thought of Greg as just one of the men from the ad that I would go on a date with. But when we met, that was that. I was comfortable: because of all the emails, I felt like I already knew him well. We were married two years later."

Pat relates her experience a little differently. "Tom and I worked together, but I honestly hadn't paid much attention to him. Then one day, in the break room, we started chatting at the vending machine. He showed me a picture of his son and he asked me if I had a boyfriend. I said no and he said he didn't have one either, which was kind of funny and I laughed. I really didn't think much of it until after work, when he waited for me. 'I'm going to ask you out,' he said. He didn't ask me out, he just told me he was going to. I was a little surprised, so I just said, 'Oh, okay.' I was actually kind of hoping he wouldn't. But sure enough, a couple of weeks later he did." She admitted to some reluctance about dating Tom. "I kept ducking him . . . until finally he caught me on the phone. We had this long, good talk. And I suddenly felt like, 'Okay. I like him. I can do this.' "

Alisa is single but looking—and in the places where she has interests and feels excited and involved. "Within the past year I have been hanging out at events and places in neighborhoods where I am most apt to meet the type of men I am interested in. I live in Southern California, so it's mostly the South Bay beach cities like Manhattan and Hermosa Beach. I like surfing, so I have started to attend surfing competitions and events. I used to be pretty shy about making eye contact or just being friendly, but a very good friend gave me some great advice: 'Saying "Hi" is really very simple. Try it sometime!' I'm realizing that I am pretty and a fun person and that just by being myself and being willing to start a conversation, I'm getting to know the type of men I would like to know. I have also joined a church that is very integrated. I enjoy these things, so it doesn't feel like a manhunt. It feels like doing what I like to do!"

Black women should assume at least the *possibility* of a romantic interest when meeting men of any race. Evia Moore writes, "All men are interested in friendly, winnable women—and by that I mean women whom they perceive they are able to attract. Instead of blocking the possibilities, black women who exhibit openness to male attention—from any shade of man—might be surprised at the results."

Taking the time to talk, to get comfortable, and to get acquainted with what a man's values and qualities are seems to be particularly important in interracial relationships, which are fraught on both sides with deep subconscious perils thanks to America's racial history. In my own story—and in many of the stories that black women share about their interracial romances—time and patience were important in developing the relationship. Sex entered the equation very late in the game, allowing both the black woman and the nonblack man time to determine that the basis of the relationship reached beyond sexual fantasy or curiosity.

Our challenge as women is to more closely examine our notions about men, manliness, and masculinity—regardless of the color of the man in question. With a long-term relationship or marriage as the ultimate goal, our definition of what we want in a man must reach deeper than "pinkness" or penis size, club-style charisma or pretty-boy looks. If we hope to be cherished and adored, we must be willing to abandon the shallow concerns of the external and focus more deeply on the man inside. After all, isn't that exactly what we hope our partner will be able to do? As one woman said about any physical differences among men, "It's all the same in the dark."

She's right, of course. Sex matters, of course, but it also matters how well a man treats you in the full light of day.

NOTION 5

White Men Don't Find Black Women Attractive—
Unless They Look Like Beyoncé

As I started writing and publishing essays that eventually led to the notions discussed in this book, I received a lot of emails, including the following two from June 2008:

> *Some of us feel no obligation to exclusively date black men and are open to dating "others," but it's not as easy as deciding to keep your options open. Black women are not the American standard of beauty and it's not as though most black women have "other" men knocking down their doors but are turning them down left and right. Did you have a bunch of white men asking you out before you met your now husband? I doubt it.*

> *If black women are queens of the world, and I believe that they are, why do they not believe that most men, irrespective of ethnicity, find them attractive? All other women feel they may select from whatever arena of manhood is available, yet black women remain interestingly "racist" in their unwillingness to choose viable partners based on what really makes a relationship work? What makes a relationship work? Common ground . . . and common ground is not always rooted in color.*

What men and women find attractive in another person is as individual as people themselves, but the research—as well as the personal experiences of many of the women I talked to—suggests that race is less likely to be the determining factor of attractiveness than black women tend to think. The dozens of black women I interviewed for this book found this notion about looks to be flat-out funny, especially since I interviewed the vast majority of them over the phone. "Describe yourself," I'd say, and then I'd tell them about this notion that in order to be attractive to nonblack men, they were expected to meet a Hollywood standard of beauty.

"Really? You mean that light-skinned, long-haired, skinny look?" quipped Tori. "Forget it. I'm totally dark food!" She continued, laughing, "I'm not skinny, either. Fit, but curvy. Not skinny at all. I'm not in a relationship right now, but I certainly haven't had trouble attracting white guys."

Comedian Jacquetta Szathmari's comments were similar. "I'm in good shape, but I would describe myself as an average black woman. I'm brown-skinned and I'm not running in and out of the beauty salon: I have a short afro. Before I met my husband, I had no trouble attracting nonblack men. In fact, my craigslist.com personal ad got hundreds of responses from white men."

"L'Oréal calls me 'cappuccino,' " replied Cynthia. "I try to take care of myself but I don't think I have Hollywood looks. My husband thinks so, though, so I guess that's all that matters!"

"I have dark skin—the darkest in my family," added Lorraine. "It was something I was teased mercilessly about by black boys when I was a girl . . . but my husband loves the color of my skin. He finds it beautiful."

"I never thought of myself as light-skinned," commented Jamie. "Around my family, I'm more brown-skinned. But since everything is relative, some people might call me that. But I have a short natural and I certainly don't qualify for Hollywood glamour."

"He doesn't like skinny women. He said he liked my shape, but he loved my personality. I'm the warm, people-loving type of person. He's not, and he liked how comfortable I made him," says Marvine. "Chris would love it if I grew an afro. He prefers me without makeup. He says I'm naturally beautiful and that I don't need a thing! When I was at Virginia State, it seemed like that light-skinned, straight-haired look was what the *black* guys were into, not the white ones."

Kellina Craig-Henderson's research for her upcoming book *Black Women in Interracial Relationships* supports the idea that the black women in interracial couples represent a variety of physical types: "Women who are not in interracial relationships tend to expect that only a specific look appeals to white men. But the women I interviewed run the gamut. There is no 'type' as far as I observed."

"It's about working with what you've got," says Nikki Doughty. "At our events there isn't just one type of woman who is desirable. But she's always the one who takes care of herself, who has made an effort to present herself in the best light. It doesn't matter what that is: dreads, twists, a natural, relaxed hair, or a weave. And while thin isn't everything, being fit is important. Most people—male and female, black, white, Asian, or Latino—want partners who look healthy." She adds, "It's about confidence: it's a big smile that says 'I'm approachable.' "

In an article titled "Racial Preferences in Dating" published in the *Review of Economic Studies* in 2008, researchers confirmed that when age and educational backgrounds are equal, race tended not to be a factor in ranking a potential partner's physical attractiveness. "Our subjects do not find partners of the same race *more* attractive," the authors concluded. Men in particular ranked women of all races attractive. Furthermore, the older the respondent, the less likely they were to make racial distinctions, leading the researchers to conclude that when people of both genders are ready to settle down, race takes a backseat to other qualities in mate selection.[1]

Let's face it: if we were to be brutally honest, the truth would be that very few of us—male, female, black, white, Latin, or Asian—are anything close to the American standard of beauty or a Hollywood ideal. If that were the criterion for a happy relationship, then *most* of us would be alone.

Fortunately, most good men, of any race, don't really expect women to reach a Hollywood standard of beauty. Most men just want women who take care of themselves and who bring warmth, confidence, and approachability to the table. And for the most part, white men aren't fixated on a certain skin tone or body shape. Like men of any other race, their tastes are as individual as men themselves.

Sometimes, though, black women believe that our physical charms are primarily attractive to black men—and that when men of other races express interest in us, they have some lecherous interest in mind. Remember Teresa's story in the last chapter? Her mother insisted that as a black woman with a child, Teresa was unattractive to anyone but black men. Teresa, however, saw herself differently and is currently dating a successful nonblack man who mirrors her image of herself. Or Evia's story about her encounter with a bank manager? She thought she could transform how the man "saw" her by changing her manner, and it worked.

Clearly, there is power in the mirror of our own expectations of who we can attract and how. If you believe you are beautiful to a wide cross-section of men, chances are good that a wide cross section of men will find you appealing. Beauty begins in the mind and flows from there.

Thanks to some cultural programming, however, some of us believe that when nonblack men express interest in us, they're up to no good.

It's true that some nonblack men are interested in black women for sexual purposes only, but remember, some *black* men will be interested in us for sexual purposes only. That's a female fact of life. Other times a white man's appreciation of your physical assets can be a sincere compliment that can mature into something much more. With more and more black women unhappily single, being willing to accept and embrace the appeal of our beauty to a wider cross section of men is critical to our finding the men of our dreams. To make that leap, we must ask ourselves *why* we believe that our beauty only appeals to nonblack suitors when we are light-skinned, straight-haired, skinny, and sexually compliant.

THE HYPERSEXUALIZED BLACK FEMALE

Saartjie "Sarah" Baartman was born into the Khoikhoi tribe along the Eastern Coast of South Africa in 1789. Orphaned at a young age, she became the slave of Dutch farmers near Cape Town. In 1810, at the age of twenty-one, the brother of her owner suggested she travel to England for exhibition, promising her marriage and wealth. She obtained permission to go . . . and soon was a sideshow attraction in 19th-century Europe

under the name Hottentot Venus. For six years, Saartjie was exhibited
around Britain and France, gyrating nude and showing what, to Europe-
ans, were highly unusual bodily features: her very large buttocks and hips.
She died at age 27 from alcoholism, pleurisy and pneumonia, but her
genitals—which had elongated labia common to her tribe—were preserved
and displayed in Paris' Musée de l'Homme until 1974, when they were
removed under public pressure. In May 2002, her remains were returned
to South Africa and laid to rest.[2]

Saartjie Baartman's story sums up the kind of exploitation that is at the root of many black women's fears about white men's interest in our physical selves. We fear that when we are not otherwise invisible to them, the basis of their interest in us derives only from a perverse sexual curiosity. These beliefs date back to slavery days and certain racist images created to justify the sexual abuse and subjugation of black women, but they are still very much alive and well today in our American consciousness—even though they are completely false and have nothing to do with who we really are.

Sociologists and psychologists, among others, have written volumes about the three main stereotypical images of black women that, in various forms, pervade our media. You've probably heard of them: Mammy, Sapphire, and Jezebel. Mammy is, of course, the overweight, dark-skinned woman who offers comfort and security while seeming to require nothing in return. She's the image that has the least sex appeal and lives today in the "matriarch" image: the ceaseless caretaker who puts the needs of others above her own and seems never to require anything for herself. Sapphire, the sharp-tongued, tough-talking emasculator, is usually found in the stereotype of a black woman with a finger-wagging, neck-rolling swagger. Finally, there's Jezebel, the shapely, light-skinned, exotic seductress who can't get enough sex: anytime, anywhere.

Who *are* these women?

"I don't know any women like that," says Teresa.

"I guess I'm not your typical black woman," says Marvine.

"I think many black women's self-image has taken a real knock due to, among other things, how we are portrayed in the media," writes Halima Sal-Anderson. It's also damaged when "black men glorify 'near white' black females." Black women then "expect to find the same fascination with light skin in white men."[3]

"My life as a black woman would be so much easier if men stopped watching videos and porn," observes Nikki Doughty. "Don't tell me you watch TV and you know what a black woman is like. I've been a black woman all my life and I can tell you with absolute certainty, what you see on TV isn't real!"

She's right. Too much of what men of all races believe about who and what women are comes from the media images they consume, with music videos and pornography being the biggest offenders. And black women certainly aren't the only ones with this problem: all women are objectified and stereotyped in media.

But those images aren't real, and smart men of all races know that, just as smart women do.

"I think it's good that there are more and more television shows and films featuring black women than there were even ten years ago," Craig-Henderson says. "But there's still a lot of work to be done. Certainly most television shows and films trade in stereotypical images, but there are more 'types' for white men and white women. For black women we still see the same handful of types: you're a Mammy, a sharp-tongued Sapphire, or a slut. That's one of the reasons black women are so excited about Michelle Obama. She's like Oprah and Whoopi and Condoleezza Rice. She introduces the mainstream to what we as black women already know—the 'type' that is the attractive, smart black woman who isn't fat, isn't sharp-tongued and emasculating, isn't slutty."

The black woman stereotype in the media is under renovation. As we see ourselves take on wider roles in the wider world and see ourselves in different images in the mainstream media, we can expect to be seen differently by men of all backgrounds.

JEZEBEL LIVES, BUT SHE'S STILL NOT REAL

In a recent paper, Dionne P. Stephens and Layli D. Phillips define "Jezebel" as a "sexual script" or an image that is learned and acted out by black women through the wider culture. A Jezebel is

a young exotic, promiscuous, over-sexed woman who uses sexuality to
get attention, love and material goods. Portrayed as having light skin,
long hair and a shapely body, the Jezebel was sometimes referred to as
a mulatto or half-breed. Myths of their insatiable sexual appetite were
used to justify the rape of slave women by their masters.[4]

Jezebel was never real. The fantasy that we see replicated even today
in music videos and television shows was in reality a sexually abused
African American woman used to fulfill the master's sexual and economic needs, a woman with little or no power over her circumstances.
Stephens and Phillips analyze how Jezebel remains a "foundational image" that forms the basis for new stereotypes we see in music videos and
other programming where black women are objectified.

Fake as she is, Jezebel titillates many men—of all races. What man
doesn't love at least the idea of Jezebel: a physically appealing woman
who is easily sexually available to his every desire? Black men love Jezebel, white men love Jezebel, Asian men love Jezebel, and Latin men
love Jezebel. That's why she's still around in various forms. But she's a
myth all the same. She's a construct of racist imagination that has been
embraced by our society, but if you ask black women about Jezebel, they
are as clear as Nikki about how irrelevant Jezebel and her sisters are to
their lives. Men of any race who define black women by the Jezebel image are bound to be disappointed.

"Studies show black women to be very sexually conservative, compared to white women and to black men," says Rachel Sullivan. "But
these images of black women as rapacious sexual animals still persist. I
think that drives many black women to be very conscientious about their
sexuality because they don't want to be perceived as slutty."

Or to put it another way, fake as she is, Jezebel makes most of us as
black women particularly careful about our sexual behavior. Most of us
are more accurately the anti-Jezebel in our manners, our style, our approach to sex and intimacy. The more rap and hip-hop videos emphasize
the shapely young body of the Jezebel, spreading her legs and shaking
her rear suggestively, the less likely you and I are to actually do anything
that even *suggests* that behavior in our real life.

Still, Jezebel probably won't die anytime soon. She's a male fantasy—

along with dumb, leggy, buxom blondes, Playboy bunnies, and strippers. She's a hot babe who finds her fans to be the most fascinating studs on the planet! I wish all the men out there—of any race—good luck in finding a real woman who approaches what they imagine Jezebel to be like. Even if she works in the music video industry, dances topless, or lives with Hugh Hefner, a woman is still a woman and therefore has a depth of emotion that no media image can ever approach.

WHITE MEN AND BLACK SKIN

Jezebel's alleged appeal comes not only from her wanton sexuality but from her light skin as well. Light skin approximates white skin and, in racist language, makes her "closer to white" and therefore more desirable. Through the centuries of slavery, lighter skin signified closer kinship to the master—son or daughter, sister or brother. Lighter skin might mean kinder treatment because of those blood bonds. Lighter skin might have meant easier labors. And after slavery, lighter skin might have led to greater opportunities in education, in the work force, and in the marriage market—especially for women. Darker skin meant greater limitations, harsher treatment, and a greater remove from privilege. These "colorist" divisions are still very much alive. In a 1993 study conducted by Kathy Russell, Midge Wilson, and others at DePaul University, both black and white students reacted negatively to images of darker-skinned women, indicating that, even relatively recently, darker skin was seen as a disadvantage.[5]

As many black women know from painful experience, a premium is often placed on light skin and "good" (straight, long, or wavy) hair. And certainly, if Hollywood, politics, and corporate America are any indications, lighter skin eases the rise up the ladders of success.

But what about in interracial relationships?

"In my study," Kellina Craig-Henderson tells me, "I talked to seventeen black women who were in or had been in committed relationships with white men. Their skin tones ran the gamut from very fair to very dark."

"What I see here in Atlanta," says Teresa, "is that white men seem to be attracted to the Iman type: deep brown skin."

Jacquetta adds, "The whole skin tone issue matters less to them. I mean, we're all black to them. We're all darker than they are. They just don't care."

Lorraine writes candidly about her painful experiences with this internalized preference for lighter skin—and how little it mattered to her white husband when they met:

> My entire existence in the Indianapolis Public Schools was a dismal failure. I mostly remember being incessantly bullied, called names, beat up and picked on by both girls and boys. The black boys always called me names like "blackie," "dark shadow," "spook," "black Lorraine," "ghost." One girl even asked me why I was so dark. I didn't know what to tell her. This went on for years and I internalized every single insult . . . in essence, I was terrorized by my own people.
>
> Any boy I had a crush on was also doomed to ridicule by the other kids. Of course I only liked white boys because I knew the black boys would not be caught dead [with] me. . . . What I found ironic was that even the dark-skinned black boys had the audacity to criticize me even though they were just as dark as me, if not darker. Now what kind of message was I to take from that?
>
> I made it through those years without a boyfriend. Shortly after I graduated from high school, I married the first man to come along, a Mexican man. In my immature, inexperienced mind, I thought anyone who would show an interest in me had to be nice, sincere and good. I was wrong. I ran right into the arms of an abusive man. I did manage to escape with my life, but it was years before I understood: I was used to being beat up and bullied. I was used to being insulted and called names. I vowed to never again allow anyone—of any race—to make me feel bad for the color of my skin. I learned to love it, to embrace it and to thank God for it.
>
> My second husband is a white man who loves my dark skin. He finds it beautiful and says it was one of the things that drew him to me. Now I am a Christian wife and mother proud of my dark skin. Divine intervention placed me with a man who loves my skin just as much as I do.

Lorraine has learned to appreciate herself and her beauty—and found a man who appreciates it too—but her story is far from unique. Colorism may have originated in white supremacy, but it is perpetuated daily in the black community by black folks against other black folks. Perhaps you recall the recent casting call for models for a Ciroc advertisement featuring Sean "Diddy" Combs? The one that requested only "white, hispanic or light-skinned african american women" to represent the prestige liquor brand in advertisements intended to appeal to minorities?[6] While Mr. Combs, his advertising agency, and the talent agency hired to find women to appear in the advertisement all denied the intention to exclude, the casting call was worded exactly as quoted above. The point is this: it's very hard to argue that only *white* men have color preferences when it's patently obvious just how much color preference pervades the black community.

Lisa Vazquez argues that until black people come to terms with their own issues about beauty and color, we shouldn't be projecting those concerns onto other ethnic groups. In an essay called "Sistas, What Goes Around Comes Around," discussing the common complaint that men of other cultures devalue black women, she writes, "If we remain silent about bigotry and defend cultural hostilities *among ourselves*, then we set ourselves up for failure."

> There are many blog forums that I have visited where black women are bemoaning the Eurocentric standard of beauty that is being elevated in white publications and in Hollywood. While they are proud of Beyoncé and Halle's success, they are also resentful that a large part of their success is tied to their cross-over appeal. "Anything that isn't Eurocentric is delegitimized!" they sneer.

> *Their solution to confronting white supremacy is to validate their own bigotry against biracial women and black women with Eurocentric features? Their solution is to dismiss the worth of other races?* I don't believe that solution will reap *any* benefits for black women—politically or socially. . . .

> I believe that black women will have to utilize approaches that will impact our collective advancement. We often choose

approaches that produce *more* ostracism of black women, and validate approaches that serve to generate *more* negative perceptions about us.[7]

IF HE'S INTERESTED, IS THERE SOMETHING WRONG WITH HIM?

White men have found black women beautiful and desirable since the days of slavery. Of course, in the antebellum days through the civil rights movement, white men also exercised sufficient power over black women to "take" those bodies when they chose. Although those are no longer the norms in our society, we still often see a negative reaction when a white man admits to finding a black woman attractive. For many black women, what might have been meant as appreciation, as a compliment, is interpreted as the ultimate objectification. Some black women fear that a white man who is "into sisters" has some latent underlying fetish and that his interest amounts to seeking a participant in an "exotic fantasy" that, like the tragic story of Saartjie Baartman, can have no happy ending for the woman.

A black male friend who asked to remain anonymous says, "While you may have found a good man who is white, the majority still look at black women as sexual objects and participants in their fantasies. I've been approached on numerous occasions over the years by white male acquaintances who have requested that I take them to a black club so that they could chase some 'black tail.' The most recent of these solicitations was two weeks ago. I also hear how they talk in locker rooms, bars, and any other venue where male bonding occurs, and their attitude toward black women as a whole is consistently sexual."

And take a trip to YouTube.com, where the pulse of the extremes in the black community can be found in the videos of average people. You may find posts that reveal a frightening degree of ignorance and hate, like this one I stumbled across while researching this book:

Media think black women are so fucking stupid they tell women it's the style and they'll do it . . . watch TV, watch the movies, keep your eyes open. Any time you see a commercial or TV show with a black woman in it . . . watch how often they try to pair that woman up with a white man. . . . It's being pushed to y'all, it's a part of the new style. It's a part of a larger plot, you see. I know how these motherfuckers think. These white men who go after these black women, they don't look at you like a woman. You're just like a thing, a plaything, a toy. They're not looking at you like you can be a wife, like they're not going to put you on a pedestal, like you're a queen. No, you're a plaything.[8]

Not surprisingly, when I contacted the poster, he declined to be interviewed. He didn't actually want to put his name behind his comments, even though he felt perfectly comfortable posting them to the entire world on YouTube.com.

These are the views of two black men from very different generations on white men in pursuit of black women, but they amount to the same idea: a white man interested in a black woman more than likely sees her as a sex object and nothing more.

But the women I talked to—the women actually *in* interracial relationships and marriages—were having the opposite experience. As Marvine expresses it, black women "should never say never" about dating out. Interracial relationships are

challenging, but worth it. I have two beautiful children, and I know my husband loves me. I'm the most secure woman I know. I have some black girlfriends who are worried; they don't feel treasured. [My husband] puts me on a pedestal. He's learned how to do that. He's been interested in learning how to make me feel loved and secure. He's put out the effort and because he does, he gets more from me. We're well balanced. You have to be willing to give. People think they need to receive before they give, but it's the other way. I've had to learn not to criticize him about every little thing and to affirm him for what he does for me and our family. I remember reading an article once about a man who said his wife made him feel like he was on the bottom of her list. I really make sure my husband knows his place: as the man, as the top of my list. He's good to me and I make efforts not to take him for granted.

While I don't deny that my black male friend has heard the comments from white men about black women that he reports, I have problems accepting them, as the YouTube poster suggests, as a blanket indictment of every white man. There are two problems with the "all white men see all black women as sex objects" argument, and you'll recognize them; perhaps you're thinking them yourself. The first problem is the generalization: the "all" that lumps every white male person into the identical thought pattern. It's exactly like saying "All black people can dance" or "All black people love red" or some other ridiculous statement we all know to be positively untrue and racist. There's a double standard there that anyone concerned with fairness to both individuals and groups of people should not be willing to tolerate.

And if you can somehow overcome the first problem, there's a second: Do *black* men really see us any differently from white men? Isn't the only real difference that black men see us as "theirs" to objectify? Don't men of every ethnicity objectify women in some fashion? Doesn't this problem, like rape, really belong under the heading of "gender" and not under the heading of "race"?

Wouldn't it be better to judge a man's motives—and a woman's too—based on his or her actions?

Many of us as black women have been taught to believe that our beauty is not genuinely appreciated by men beyond our race and that nonblack men, white ones in particular, who express attraction to us are "deviant" or "predatory." Evia Moore points out that some black women "get angry or uncomfortable" when a white man looks at them with admiration or sexual interest.

> But black women should realize that many heterosexual white men are viewing them in that way because white men are men just like any other men. I recall how . . . when a white male commentator [Roger Rasheed] . . . drew complimentary attention to Venus Williams's shapely behind [at the Australian Open in 2008], it almost became a minor racial scandal. But I've heard *many* men, including black men, compliment the looks and body of Maria Sharapova [a white female tennis pro].

> White men make up the bulk of males in this society. When they are prevented from saying appropriately flattering things about a black woman's appearance, black girls and black women are deprived of the mirror that other women readily enjoy. . . . I notice this all of the time when I'm in major cities—those small gestures that men make when they like

the way a woman looks. Now, I'm not talking about catcalls and lewd remarks—because I think that any man should be arrested for harassment when he does that. I'm talking about respectful appreciation. Being deprived of that natural mirror is why so many black women wonder about their beauty and feel that they are invisible or that their beauty is unrecognized. This even causes some black women to go to great lengths—wear revealing clothing, for example—just to get noticed by men. This is because many non-black men are virtually gagged from commenting on black women's beauty in this country. It is still considered improper and somewhat "taboo."[9]

Nikki Doughty agrees, up to a point. "We're so used to being ignored that we have forgotten that we're beautiful. We're so used to being race-loyal black women that we forget that we're attractive to men beyond our own race. But if you're willing to think differently and widen your options, the possibilities are there. That doesn't mean you stop being careful," she cautions. "White is not always right. It's important to be aware and to use your better judgment. But the truth is, there are men who are predatory of all races, and there are men who are sincere of all races."

Real black women usually have pretty good judgment and have learned, sometimes by hard experience, to be wary when attention seems overtly sexual. But if you haven't really given it thought before, try widening the scope of your radar to receiving compliments from men of all races. You might just see yourself in a new "mirror"—and like what you find reflected there.

IN THE THICK AND THIN OF IT

Before we leave the subject of physical attractiveness, there's one other thing we must discuss—the painful subject of black women and obesity. Black women's rates of obesity are on the rise, just as our likelihood of remaining single for our lives rises too. Related phenomena? Maybe so.

We've spent some time talking about Jezebel—an image of black women as sexual animals, usually visualized as shapely, long-haired, and light-skinned. But there's another physical image of black women that pervades our culture: Mammy. "Mammy" is the dark-skinned, overweight caretaker who lives to serve. Often portrayed as old or at least middle-aged, Mammy is the opposite of Jezebel. The implicit assumption is that no reasonable white man would choose a fat, elderly black woman instead of the idealized white woman. The de-eroticism of Mammy made her an acceptable servant, safe to be in the household. Keeping Mammy fat and servile meant that the white wife and, by extension, the white family were safe, a fiction necessary to cover up the number of illicit relationships between white men and black female slaves—regardless of their appearance. For most of us, the Mammy image is immortalized forever in the person of Oscar-winning actress Hattie McDaniel for her role in the 1939 classic movie *Gone with the Wind*. McDaniel was a talented actress capable of many complex and difficult roles, but Hollywood of the 1940s and 1950s wasn't ready for her abilities and she was, for the most part, consigned to roles supporting white actresses.

To some degree, like Jezebel's, Mammy's descendants are alive and well in our media. She is the overweight black woman who populates commercials for necessaries like laxatives and cleaning supplies but never sells us makeup or beauty products. She's the heavier supportive friend to the white female lead but rarely has a story line of her own. She's the hardworking matron who balances a full-time job with rearing her children or the church lady who serves her pastor with zealous faithfulness. And very, very occasionally, she's a love interest, but usually, modern Mammy is manless and alone.

Just like Jezebel, she's an image of the African American woman that just won't die, but just like Jezebel, she's a fake. I don't know any black women who "mammy" white families—or black ones, for that matter— and I doubt you do either. We know black women who do their best to care for their children, their responsibilities, and their communities. We know—and sometimes are—black women who take better care of others than we do ourselves. But Mammy? Hardly.

"Mammy is just one of these stereotypes that people insist on projecting on us," says law professor Kimberly Jade Norwood of Washington School of Law in St. Louis. "But the fact is she's a sliver of personality, blown large. Somehow, the larger she gets, the further she is from any real black woman who ever lived. Even black women who worked in white homes as domestics weren't Mammy. They were women doing a tough job, who went home to their families and did another tough job. Mammy is a fiction and she always was."

In fact, perhaps the only aspect of Mammy that has any basis in reality for many black women today is the issue of her weight. While it's true that Americans are getting fatter across the board, the American Obesity Association reports that black women lead the way with 50 percent of us having a body mass index (BMI) of over 30 (considered obese), compared to 40 percent of Mexican American women and 30 percent of white women.[10]

Obesity has often been linked to poverty, but lately that link seems tenuous. In fact, it's *upper-income* people who have gained the most weight since the mid-1970s.[11] A University of Iowa study released in 2008 shows that since 1971 obesity rates have increased dramatically with the amount of cash flowing through the household:

- Less than $25,000: obesity rates increased 144 percent between 1971 and 2000
- $25,000–$40,000: obesity rates increased 194 percent
- $40,000–$60,000: obesity rates increased 209 percent
- More than $60,000: obesity rates increased 276 percent

Obesity rates are similar across all income groups now, with the poorest quarter just 5.7 percent more obese than the richest. In short, while it used to be true that being poor increased your likelihood of being overweight, these days that's not so.

Black folks have been comfortable with slightly heavier weights for black women for decades. Although many health practitioners consider a BMI of 25 as "overweight," that number has been challenged as an unfair measure for women in minority communities. In recent studies, epidemiology tables show that African Americans and Hispanics (particularly women) tend to be *healthier* at weights 10–15 pounds heavier than white women, so weight and BMI charts can definitely be culturally biased.[12] But while black women are both far less obsessed with weight than white women and able to carry a few extra pounds healthily and happily, there's a limit. Obesity (typically defined as being more than 20 percent over one's ideal weight) and morbid obesity (being more than 100 pounds over one's ideal body weight) involve far more than the 10–15 pounds doctors have found to be relatively healthy. And both have damaging short- and long-term consequences.

When black women carry too much extra weight, they hurt their long-term health by increasing their risk for heart disease, diabetes, hypertension, stroke, breathing problems, arthritis, gallbladder disease, sleep apnea (breathing problems while sleeping), osteoarthritis, and some cancers. Extra weight ultimately leads to poorer health and less happiness, which for some leads to more food, sought as comfort for our sorrows. If we're medicating our loneliness with food, we're caught in a vicious cycle with potentially deadly consequences. Feeling fat and unhappy often makes it harder for us to have the confidence needed to seek and accept real love. It can also keep us from the activities that bring us into contact with healthy, available men of any race. Finally, it tells the world something about how well we care for ourselves, and the message sent isn't usually a good one.

"I would say that overweight is another result of dealing with the stresses of being both black and female in a society," says Kellina Craig-Henderson. "There are so many pressures on black women that we can't control. Food is something we can easily enjoy."

In "Black Women's Weight Issues with Weight," Lisa Vazquez examines why so many black women choose not to put the effort into getting fit and healing their relationship with food.

> There are many sistas who pride themselves on having "a little junk in the trunk." There are some sistas who are indignant about not making changes in their appearance in order to expand their dating pool. "A man who values substance over superficiality will accept me as I am!" huffs the sista who orders a triple combo meal at Wendy's with a large Frosty. . . . I believe that accepting a dysfunctional relationship with food is always related to a fractured relationship with self.[13]

Rachel Sullivan agrees. "I think black women have it particularly hard. There is lots of pressure being put on them from all different corners. It's a heavy burden, and you look for release and comfort where you can find it."

Evia Moore thinks that the growing problems of obesity and loneliness among black women are inextricably related.

> We have beautiful bodies when our curves are not hidden by excess fat. Medical professionals have pointed out that, in fact, black women's skin and bodies age better than any other group's *if* we take care of ourselves . . . too many AA women are carrying an unattractive and unhealthy amount of weight around. Let's not mince words here. I've noticed that some people refer to themselves as "having a few extra pounds" or "thick." But is it just a *few*? As more and more black women die and/or are debilitated from weight-related illnesses, everyone—even those who say they love you—seems to be afraid to tell you that the weight is very excessive in some cases. Added to that, many of you have been bamboozled by the black community into thinking that it's okay or normal for black women to carry around excess weight, with ridiculous statements like: "Only a dog wants a bone." This is a lie. It keeps black women caged . . . with the belief that only black men will want them.[14]

DO BLACK MEN REALLY PREFER BIG WOMEN?

The black man's supposed preference for heavier women can be read as another way that some of us have been discouraged from dating interracially. No other men would be interested in us, is the message. This concept is flawed on several levels.

First, several studies have, in fact, shown that there isn't that much difference between what white men and black men hold as the ideal female body shape.[15] In an article published in *Obesity*, a litany of prior studies supported the finding that the ideal female form doesn't vary by ethnicity as much as our popular wisdom might suggest:

> In examining a community sample of black, Asian, Hispanic, and white male and female dieters, studies found no significant race differences in ratings of attractive female (or male) shape, and . . . no ethnic differences among men in the female shape they found most attractive. . . . Black men and women did not differ from white men and women in perceptions of the most attractive female body shape and, moreover, overweight female figures were not rated as desirable or attractive by either group.[16]

In another study, researchers at James Madison University discovered that both black and white women get it wrong when it comes to predicting what men like.

> While all the women in this study believed that men would find thin bodies most attractive, there was a significant disparity in the level of thinness Black women and White women would have expected the men to find attractive. The Black women estimated closest to what men chose as ideal, whereas the White women believed that men would find extremely thin women to be most attractive. . . . It was found that while White males chose a thinner body as more ideal, there was not a significant disparity from the ideal body chosen by Black males.[17]

While the studies do suggest that both white and black men prefer slenderness, not all white men prefer superskinny women. "I love thick women," writes one white man on interracialdatingcentral.com.

> For me a thick woman has a better shape to her body, which makes her more beautiful. There is more woman to her, more to look at and feel. She looks better and feels better. She feels right. Most thick women have big wide hips, which I love, as well as a big bottom and thick thighs and nothing turns me on more than that, especially in bed. And to see a woman like that in tight blue jeans is heavenly. Not fat and ugly, but heavenly. Heavenly because I like the way it looks. Heavenly because I know what it feels like. When I hold a woman I do not want to feel her bones. When I run my hands down her back I want something I can feel when I get to the bottom, something that sticks out from her body that I can put my hands on. And I want to press my body into hers. I cannot do that with a thin woman.[18]

His post garnered dozens of responses from other white men who agreed, including one man who wrote,

> I love thick women who have a shape and [who] have hips! Women (in my opinion) push themselves too hard to be "models": it's not attractive, it's not natural. Give me a woman who has a solid hour glass shape any day![19]

The idea that fat women are more desired by the black community may ultimately discourage black women from seeking love and affection from nonblack sources. The implicit message is, stay fat—and stay within the black race. Whether you give that idea serious credence or not, the research suggests that men of all races like curves but not fat. And to be fair, most women admit to a preference for men who are athletic and healthy, rather than men who are very fat or very thin. If we're honest with ourselves about what we find attractive in a man, we have to be willing to present ourselves in a similar light. Don't get me wrong: I know how much grief black women get in our society. We're always too much or too little to someone, and it's not my intention to add to that perception here. There are men of all races who love and appreciate women of all sizes, and it's important to us to be open to receiving that love from all the men in the global village offering it. But it's also important to take care of ourselves—not just for the sake of attracting a man of any race, but for our own health and happiness. Black women don't need to embrace extremes of body shape or beauty, but we *do* need to make every effort not to embrace the fiction of Mammy either. If we do, we rob ourselves of our femininity, our sexuality, and our futures.

"Be fit," says Nikki Doughty. "Have the body that lets you do the things you love to do—and draws the best men of all races to you. That's really the key."

Consider these moving words from feminist scholar bell hooks:

All women dream of meeting a partner who will like our bodies as they are. We long for partners who will offer affirmation and unconditional acceptance, particularly if we have never been affirmed or were affirmed only as children in our families of origin. We long for acceptance of our physical beings, to be admired as we are, even as we withhold affirmation from ourselves. This is the worst form of self-sabotage. We can "start where we are" by offering ourselves that gaze of approval we long to see in the eyes of someone else. The more we love our flesh, the more others will delight in its bounty. As we love the female body, we are able to let it be the ground on which we build a deeper relationship to ourselves—a loving relationship uniting mind, body, and spirit.[20]

BLACK WOMEN HAVE BAD ATTITUDES?

The subject of self-acceptance leads us to the third of the fake but popular images of black women that stand in our way of attracting men of all races: the Sapphire. Masculine, aggressive, loud-talking, and overbearing. Finger-wagging, neck-rolling, lip-smacking.

Do you know this woman?

Almost every black woman I interviewed shook her head with dismay. "I don't know anyone like that," they said. "If that's a typical black woman, I guess I'm not a typical black woman." In Teresa's view, "Men of all races are always chiming in about how loud we are, how masculine we are, how fat we are, but I don't know any women like that. They keep talking about her, so I guess there must be someone like that, but I don't know her."

Men seem to find Sapphire everywhere. In an email to me in March 2009, one man wrote,

> There are a *lot* of angry people out there. A few years ago there was the stereotypical "angry white man" who was pretty much angry at anyone who didn't vote Democrat and asked questions; back in the 60s there was the "angry black man" stereotype. Of course, every stereotype started with a grain of truth . . . so where is this leading? There are a *lot* of angry . . . and justifiably so . . . black women out there. A *lot* of good women who have been dogged by men and then turn the anger generated by the last one on the next one and so on. We *men*—the ones who have got past the "if it moves, hump it" stage—are not (unless masochistically inclined) looking to spend a lifetime of domestic conflict. A smart man avoids an angry woman as much as possible.

The Sapphire image is yet another character—a fictional type of black womanhood that, we're told, repels black and nonblack men alike. Born out of both racist and sexist notions, Sapphire was created to oppose the virtues of white womanhood: gentleness, soft-spokenness, and weakness. Viewing black women as loud and aggressive justified the subjugation they were placed under: subjugation and oppression were the only ways to control their tendencies toward emasculating anger.

The name Sapphire came from the popular but racist radio and television program *Amos 'n Andy* in the personification of a hostile, nagging black female character. As Carolyn West, associate professor of psychology at the University of Washington, Tacoma, writes, "We see traces of the angry sister with 'attitude' . . . in reality shows and recent movies. . . . Popularized in hip-hop music and urban fiction, Sapphire has now become the 'gangsta girl' who is equally as violent as her male peers. Sapphire also provides comic relief as Tyler Perry's character Madea (a southern term for 'mother dear'). She is a pistol-packing grandmother who is frequently depicted rolling her neck, with both hands on her hips, telling off the person who has just offended her."[21]

Madea is just one example. Add the rapper Eve's shouting and tongue-lashing as Terri in *Barbershop*, Gabrielle Union in *Deliver Us from Eva*. What about Wanda Sykes in a scolding role in HBO's *Curb Your Enthusiasm* or Vivica Fox in *Two Can Play That Game*? Or Lynn Whitfield in a *A Thin Line between Love and Hate*? And many people consider Omarosa Manigault-Stallworth of *The Apprentice* the poster child of the modern formulation of a black woman with a bad attitude. At the time of this writing, I would say that the reigning "sister with a bad attitude" is one of the *Real Housewives of Atlanta* (or all of them, depending on the episode!). But of course, by the time you read this, there will be another Sapphire image dominating the media, or more than likely, several of them.

But what do all these women have in common? They are *characters*. Even NeNe Leakes admits her reality TV appearances reveal just a fraction of her personality, a stereotype exaggerated for entertainment purposes. And we *are* entertained (I know I am!), because we all know that Sapphire isn't us. Sapphire is a character. Sapphire isn't real.

But even as fiction, her image can be detrimental. Hollywood clearly loves to cast black women as feisty man-eaters, and in order to remain gainfully employed, it seems many talented black actresses play along. Maybe you too enjoyed Madea's antics in Tyler Perry's popular movies or liked watching "New York" swish her finger in some poor girl's face as she plowed her way through a dozen contestants toward the dubious prize of Flavor Flav or seeing Sheree Whitfield of the *Real Housewives of Atlanta* demand "Who gonna check me, boo?" of a party planner who failed to meet expectations. As black women, we know she represents just a slice of ourselves, and it seems like everyone else should too. After all, is TV fair to anyone? Isn't most of it just a jumble of stereotypes?

Yes and no. The result of our media saturation with Sapphire images is that all of us get painted with the same brush. When we speak out about any injustice, whether legitimately or not, we're "going off." When we challenge sexism, we're emasculating. When we demand fairness, we're "difficult." As Nikki says, "Black girls are perceived as scary, when actually we're confident. The perception is that we're masculine . . . the reality is we've often been left to do the jobs of men, so we're capable. Men are left out of the equation for reasons beyond our control, leading folks to believe we didn't want them there in the first place. That misconception buries us!"

Journalist Jane Musoke-Nteyafas explained in an article in *Afro Toronto:* "Throughout history, women's endeavors to stand up for themselves have been dismissed as the ramblings of angry women, whether they were black or not. An example is the case of feminists, who are always brushed off as angry, opinionated, and unreasonable women. But in a world where racism, sexism, ageism, single motherhood, misogyny, and even warped body images prevail, it comes as no surprise that some black women are angry. The truth is some women are angry because they are exhausted or they have been ignored and dismissed or they're not taken seriously, or they are being abandoned or they are being rejected."[22]

Being angry about racism and sexism is absolutely appropriate. Continuing our fight to achieve fairness in an unequal system is appropriate. "And those things are not just our jobs as blacks or as black women," adds Kimberly Jade Norwood. "Fighting injustice and racism, sexism and unfairness are the jobs of every human being on this planet. That's not the burden of black women alone, but of everyone."

"I'm reaching the point that I don't even like to hear the words 'strong black woman,' " writes Evia Moore. "Say 'confident' or 'self-assured,' but not 'strong.' Men hear the words 'strong woman' and they tune out. The truth is they see it as their role to be strong. If a woman is strong, then the men are like, 'What does she need me for?' "

While "strong" may be a code word for a level of independence that frightens some men away, I'm not sure those are the men we want anyway. I think the problem here is the perception some men have that all black women fall into the category of finger-waving, chip-on-the-shoulder, never-satisfied bitches.

And it just ain't so.

Some black women do have bad attitudes. So do some black men.

And some white men.

And some white women.

And some men and some women of every other race and demographic. Some *people* have bad attitudes. Period, end of story. Anyone who lays the Sapphire moniker on all black women without distinction has been watching too much TV and doesn't know the difference between fact and fiction.

What black women need are men who appreciate the difficult corners black women are backed into by a society that seems to damn us if we do and damn us if we don't. Not all of those men are black; in fact, black men seem to be some of the black woman's harshest critics (along with other black women!). Don't believe it? Search "black women" on YouTube.com. You'll hear a rundown of what's wrong with us that will make your hair stand on end.

Because these stereotypes are so pervasive, it is all the more important for black women to keep an eye out for men of any race who have the sensitivity to appreciate the difference between a woman with strength of character and the passion to fight against injustice and an angry woman with some personal issue that needs to be addressed. It is as important for black women to be open to supportive mates able to separate strength from stereotype as it is for us to work toward a self-definition that is liberated from both the sexist and racist narratives that continue to work against us.

CREATING OUR OWN IMAGE

Depressing as the uphill battle against Jezebel, Mammy, and Sapphire may be, it is important to remember that it's not just *white* men who cling to those images. Black men have been drinking the cultural Kool-Aid too, and so have we. Like some white men, some black men are intoxicated with the image of the loose black female and often act against black women in ways that are predatory. Both black and nonblack men can pursue black women for sexual purposes alone; the only difference is that when black men seek sexual conquest, it isn't considered a "fetish." Neither white nor black men will typically seek out a Mammy or consider one as a future mate. Both white and black men will avoid a Sapphire with unresolved anger issues.

To whatever extent Jezebel, Mammy, and Sapphire exist in our minds, that is our starting place. Many have advocated radical changes in Hollywood and hip-hop culture—and those are worthwhile goals—but effectively killing these negative images may require a more deliberate and individual approach, one that begins with truly examining and, where appropriate, eliminating the ways these traits appear in our own personalities.

In an essay called "Cutting the Ball and Chain of the Strong Black Woman," blogger Lisa Vazquez tells this story as an example of the kinds of changes in thinking, speaking, and behaving that may help black women change first our self-perception and ultimately our realities:

> One of my friends grew up in a fatherless home and never encountered responsible black men. She's used to seeing a single mother running the household and giving direction to male adults who were her live-in boyfriends. Once, we were on our way to a restaurant with a guy. He was figuring out how we would get there. She spoke up and told him which way to take to get there. I glared at her but she didn't notice. Later, when this guy wasn't around, I told her, *"It will be great when my sistas stop thinking they need to tell a man what he needs to do when he isn't asking them!"* She was shocked to hear me say those words. In her mind, it was common for black women to tell brothas what to do and when to do it!
>
> I explained to her that it wasn't necessary for her to step in and start giving that brotha any directions when he wasn't asking either of us for our recommendations—especially when we weren't wandering around lost. She felt it was okay to tell a man what to do who had not asked for her direction! She has seen black women adopt this behavior all of her life. When this mentality is unchecked, it becomes emasculating.
>
> Another time, this same sista was dining in a restaurant with a white woman and a white guy from their church. The bill was incorrect so the

white guy called the waiter and mentioned the error. She immediately spoke up and started talking over him to explain the situation to the waiter. She told me that as soon as she heard herself, she remembered what I had said about the other situation. She said that the white woman didn't utter a word when the problem was handled by their dinner companion. A week later, she asked this white woman why she didn't say anything about the bill dispute. The woman said, "That was not *my* problem to solve."

How often do black women decide that other people's problems are our problems to fix? This is part of the mentality of the Black Superwoman—the belief that we *have to be* the fixers, the rescuers, the doers.

Far too many black women have internalized roles based on modern interpretations of Mammy, Jezebel, and Sapphire stereotypes. We take on the mantle of "black Superwoman"—trying to handle problems that aren't ours, attempting to save whole communities, stepping into the gaps left by the men in our lives. But in the end, these roles don't make us heroes; they make us tired, overburdened, and alone. As Vazquez's post suggests, the first step toward creating new images of ourselves in the world around us is to recognize and redefine how we act in our own lives. It means isolating and dismantling those behaviors that no longer serve us. Little by little, black women are moving into more and more visible roles throughout our society and taking hold of the power to reshape their own images.

Instead of broad, sweeping reforms like "Down with hip-hop," we need new images of confident, smart, and powerful black women to take Jezebel's place. This is just one of the reasons First Lady Michelle Obama has been received with such enthusiasm by black women: we know her as one of us—a successful, intelligent, attractive black woman who keeps her derriere covered and receives admiration for her character, not her body parts.

Michelle isn't the only one. Each of us as black women has a role to play in changing the negative stereotypes that surround us, and a part of that role involves refusing to be subjugated to outdated images and interpretations surrounding our beauty and sexuality. That means seeing all men for the qualities and motives they present to us as individuals—

not as whites or blacks or Asians or Latinos but as men. As Nikki Doughty says, "We have to realize that Black women have to change the equation for themselves. We can't wait for them—men—or the world to change. We have to create our own platforms to attract what we want." It also means dealing with our anger and healing our own hurts. It means taking care of our bodies and our spirits. It means being willing to be vulnerable, to allow men to see us not only as strong but as gentle, compassionate, and kind. And finally, it means celebrating ourselves as exactly the kind of sexy, beautiful women men of all races adore—and other women of all races envy. From Marvine:

> I was out with my husband and my brother at a local club one night. I was looking good and feeling good. We got out on the dance floor—all three of us—and I was dancing with them both and just having fun. My brother sat down and my husband and I kept dancing. Then I noticed this group of white women on the edge of the dance floor glaring at me and talking about me. They must have seen my wedding rings because I overheard one of them saying, "Oh my God. Look at her. And she's *married*." Clearly, they were jealous. They thought my husband was attractive, but they hadn't connected that he was my husband. I was thinking, "Yeah, I'm married. To *him*. Eat your hearts out!"

NOTION 6

What About the Children?

One of the first questions a black woman considering interracial marriage will be faced with is "What about the children?" She may also get some unsolicited advice, as I did when I shared the news of my pregnancy with my good friend Regina. I had known her for years and we'd been through some of everything together. We were sisters in arms, with a lot of the same goals and values in life. Regina was a strong proponent of the black family and had been in a solid marriage with a black man for fifteen years, but she accepted my new husband easily enough.

The announcement of our pregnancy, however, was met with a very different reaction. I was expecting an expression of joy, but instead she stared at me for a long time and then said, "Well, I guess you'd better start looking for a good therapist right now. Mixed kids always have a lot of problems. They don't understand who they are."

Regina is an educated, intelligent black woman, but as her comment illustrates, the popular perception of "racial confusion" has sunk deep into our collective consciousness. So has the long-standing white supremacist "one-drop rule," which posits that if a person has one drop of black blood, that person is wholly black.

More realistically, in our present culture, the one-drop rule may be restated as "If you look black, you are black." For children of multiple cultures, the one-drop idea can mean that others, particularly African American others, can place an expectation on their ethnic identity that requires them to suppress the other, nonblack influences. But as deeply ingrained as those images and ideas may be in black culture and consciousness, the new realities of our multicultural society make this the perfect moment to reconsider them. What impact does being the product of parents who share values but not the same racial background have on their children?

"My husband's aunt asked, 'What are you going to raise her as?' " Crystal tells me of their five-month-old daughter, who, right now at least, has pale skin and blue eyes. "I told her, 'A human being.' But I know why she asked. She's white, but she adopted a black child and has her own concerns about being responsible for helping a black child navigate race. I really think it's going to matter less and less. Race was almost a nonissue for us as a couple because the area we live in is so diverse and has so many mixtures."

Jarrod recalls that his parents were fine with his relationship with a black woman. "But my mom did say, 'Well, you've always said you didn't want children, so I guess it will be okay.' And she's right. I don't want children. I guess you could say I'm too selfish for the job of father."

"His mother did say something along the lines of 'What about your children?' " Joan says. "I told her, 'If [the reaction to biracial children] is that bad here, I'll take them back to St. Vincent where it doesn't matter so much.' And that was the end of that."

"How you raise a biracial child really depends on what color he or she is," said Lorraine, who has two biracial children. "You have to prepare them to respond to the way people see them."

"Good parents, good child," say Cynthia and Mike. "It's more important that the parents be good parents and really make every effort to encourage and support the child. The racial stuff is really not the kid's problem. It's what other people want to project onto the child."

For interracial couples, ideas of how biracial children should be raised are as different as the parents themselves. While most hope that as the twenty-first century unfolds race will become less of a factor, most are still very aware of the difficulties of being black *and* white in a culture that is to a large extent still black *or* white. They point to the election of President Barack Obama—a biracial person—as an example of the heights a child straddling two cultures can reach. But President Obama himself has written about his own struggles with his racial identity—and been attacked for being both "too black" and "not black enough." Practicality requires parents of biracial children to be prepared to guide their children through some unique experiences.

But as an argument against interracial relationships, the "What about the children?" notion doesn't wash. The fact is *all* children are barraged with hundreds of issues, concerns, and crises, and much depends on how those closest to them respond and support them. When same-race couples marry, they are rarely asked "What about the children?"— though they probably should be! There is something in particular about a mixed-race child that seems to require the question and a particular answer.

Why?

BACK TO SLAVERY, AGAIN

Like the notion "Don't bring home a white boy," our notions about mixed-race children begin with the days of slavery and the sexual abuse of black slaves by their owners and other whites. In the very early days of slavery, when the United States was still a British colony, children of mixed-race sexual relations were considered to follow the "condition of the mother." In other words, if the mother was a slave, the children would also be slaves. If the mother was free, the children were free— regardless of skin color. This was true in those very early days partly because of the relatively small number of African slaves in the colonies. The other factor was the number of indentured servants who formed a part of the labor force of early America. Because indentured servants were both male and female, and because they worked closely with slaves, the rule allowed the children of free white women and slave men to assume the status of their mothers.[1]

However, by the early 1700s these rules had begun to change. Indentured servitude as the primary source of cheap labor was waning, and in an effort to boost the number of slaves, any child with a slave parent was considered a slave—whether the slave parent was mother or father. This system, pretty much the law until after the Civil War, seemingly would equalize slaves of any background, whether born in Africa, born of American slaves, or born of a slave and a free person. But of course slave status alone doesn't take into account the more complicated issues of slave children owned by their white parents and the perception that favorable treatment was afforded to slaves with lighter skin during slavery. Concerns about differing treatment and easier cultural assimilation of lighter-skinned blacks persist to the present day and still create resentments and intraracial undercurrents. Although most white people are ignorant of it, black people all know about colorism, the stratification of black privilege according to skin shade. Colorism has its role in the discussion of multiracial children; more on that in a moment. For now, let's stick with defining who got second-class treatment as a former slave or descendant of slaves.

The "one-drop rule" arose in many southern states during the period of racial strife and intimidation that followed the Civil War. As the name suggests, one drop of African ancestry made a person black. As explained by Randall Kennedy in *Interracial Intimacies*,

> The one-drop rule at once precluded the formal recognition of intermediate racial castes [mixed people], assuaged anxieties about the perceived loss of [white] racial purity, facilitated racial-group solidarities, and stigmatized any form of white-black amalgamation.[2]

It's ironic then that a standard used by whites to assert their "racial supremacy" and "purity" over blacks in the age of Reconstruction is now used by black Americans to identify—sometimes harshly and with condemnation—their own. "One drop" helped black folks to create a large community that proved critical to the advancement of African American people in defeating Jim Crow and assuming social and legal parity.

> By definition, the one-drop rule unites all those with Black ancestry. It enables the Black community to draw on the leadership of its light-skinned members who often have more credibility with Whites. It creates

a sense of racial loyalty that discourages members from passing as White or marrying outside the race. The rule, then initially used to enslave Blacks, has now become a unifier for Black people.[3]

Washington Law School professor Kimberly Jade Norwood describes the one-drop rule as something "meant for evil that black folks, in their infinite resourcefulness, were able to use" to create something helpful. In a telephone interview, she explained,

The analogy I often use in my classes is to pig's feet, tongue, brains, and intestines. These are the parts of the animal that got thrown away in the slaveholder's kitchens. The whites didn't want to eat them; they were offal. But slave women, who knew that back in the slave quarters their children were hungry, took those parts and figured out a way to cook them so their children could survive. That's good . . . but up to a point. The fact is that those parts were usually thrown out for a reason and now that we know better, we should do better. And I'm not just talking about food here. There are so many ideas and values that are holdovers from slavery times that we have been able to use . . . but they only serve us up to a point. The one-drop rule is one of them. We know better; time to do better.[4]

As it has been applied to mixed-race people, the one-drop rule is one of the places where, as a culture in general—and as African American people in particular—we should do better. If you marry interracially and start a family, you will be among those leading the charge. Black women have never been ones to shrink from a fight.

For far too many black people, mixed-race people are "suspect." For some, the perception is that if you're mixed, you lack black "cred" and you need to be called out for it until you subscribe to an acceptably "black" level of behavior. Journalist Elliot Lewis, himself a biracial person, calls this the "black backlash."

In the days before multiracial issues had received much public attention, saying "I'm biracial," in my experience, tended to elicit two different types of reactions. With white people, it was generally, "Oh, well, whatever," they would say, willing to play along even if they didn't completely understand what I was talking about. The typical reaction from black folks, however, was more along the lines of "Biracial? Boy, you better check yourself!"[5]

For black people, Lewis explains,

the argument goes something like this: even if you're only part black, our race-conscious society will judge you to be all black and treat you accordingly. So you might as well just say you're black and get used to it, and move on with your life. I've been called the N word enough times to know that argument has some validity. I also know that being biracial . . . doesn't necessarily make someone "all-black, all the time" in society's eyes. If it did . . . [people] wouldn't spend so much time wondering out loud [to me], "Hey, what *are* you?"[6]

"What are you?" is the question that mixed-race children have to be prepared to hear and that we, as their black mothers, have to prepare them to respond to. They may also have to answer to what journalist John Black calls the "Soul Patrol," "the legions of black people who force their definitions of blackness on other black people."[7]

WHAT *ARE* YOU?

What are you?

I think the first time I was asked that question I was in elementary school. That would have been the early 1970s. The last time I heard it was just a few months ago, directed at my thirteen-year-old daughter. Like me, she is light-skinned, but also like me, both her parents are black.

The question usually comes from other African Americans, though *very* occasionally it is asked by people of other ethnic backgrounds. These nonblack askers usually approach the question with some level of apology in their voice; they are embarrassed by their own curiosity. Fellow blacks, however, ask without hesitation or concern. They want to know. They demand to know.

Unfortunately, knowing doesn't help. As I came of age in the 1970s and 1980s, I was accused of being a "white girl" for my light skin and scholarly disposition. When we lived in a predominantly black neighborhood in 2003, my daughter got the same nickname, for the same reasons.

My younger daughter poses a new problem. She has a black parent and a white parent. When she's with her father, I think people assume that she is white. When she is with me, occasionally people ask me, "Is that your daughter?" with a look on their face that indicates that they believe I could be either the mother or the babysitter.

Being able to clearly categorize a person's race is a national pastime in America. It seems to matter less now to whites, but there was a time in our not-so-distant history when it mattered *greatly* to them. Only fifty or so years ago, in the Jim Crow days when determining racial purity was critical to separating the first-class citizens from the second-class citizens, determining who was black and who wasn't could be the subject of an actual lawsuit—perhaps giving a spouse grounds for divorce, a suitor the right to break an engagement, or relatives the ammunition to challenge the bequests in a will.[8] These days, when wealth and class do more to determine first-class citizenship than skin color does, white interest is usually little more than curiosity.

Money, however, doesn't change or mitigate black interest in defining who is in the black community and who isn't, which makes the question "What are you?" a loaded one. Simply answering "I'm black" or "I'm biracial" isn't enough. At the root of the question is authenticity, which is why the question is at the heart of many black folks' concerns about interracial marriages.

Sociologist Rachel Sullivan has written extensively on interracial families and cultural expectations. Based on interviews with interracial families, she determined,

> Black relatives and White relatives generally had different ideas about the child's racial identity and socialization. For some African American families, raising a child as "biracial" rather than Black was not seen as a challenge to the rule of hypodescent [the idea that children take the status of the partner with the perceived lower financial or social privilege], but as a sign that the relative in the relationship or the child was (or could

be) disloyal to African Americans. Given the long history of privileges bestowed on lighter-skin blacks and those who could identify as "mulatto," it is not surprising that a mixed marriage raises concerns in African American families. While White families appear to be more concerned with the loss of privilege that interracial relationships and biracial children bring, Black families are concerned about the privileges biracial children enjoy over their Black (especially darker-skinned) relatives.[9]

The possibility that their children might be perceived as "disloyal" or "inauthentic" is worrisome for many black women when considering partnering outside the race.

"I don't want my kids to have to go through that," said one woman who asked to remain anonymous. "I know there are people out there who will go out of their way to make their lives more difficult. Why put that on a child?"

Another woman agreed. "Kids have enough to deal with. Why add to it?"

Without using the words, these women seem to be referring to the "tragic mulatto" stereotype, which portrays black/white biracial people as poor, lost souls caught between two worlds and accepted by no group. According to this ideology, their mere existence is tragic, and they are destined to lead a life of sorrow because of their social ambiguity.[10]

Sullivan elaborates, "The question at the heart of family's objections/concerns is how children from interracial unions and their parents will fit into the current (and future) racial order. Will they be more closely allied with African Americans? Will they develop into a unique racial group (i.e., coloreds in South Africa)? Will individual children of interracial unions have the power to create their own racial identities? Or will they be forever lost souls with no group to call home as the tragic mulatto image would predict?"[11]

Remember the whole fracas when Tiger Woods identified himself not as an African American—as many were eager for him to proclaim—but as "Cablinasian" in recognition of the Caucasian, Black, Native American, and Asian influences in his ethnic background? Many black folks completely lost their minds over that announcement: how could a young man who so obviously had some African American heritage fail to identify himself in accord with the one-drop rule? Was he abandoning his blackness? Would it be more appropriate for him to abandon his Asian mother's race?[12]

"We need to 'flip the script' and analyze why racial categories have been created in particular ways, and why certain people who identify themselves with only one race feel they have the right to pass judgment on multiracial people and their families," says clinical psychologist Maria P. P. Root.[13]

Children aren't born with any concept of race, theirs or anyone else's. Instead, children learn about race and racial categorization through their interaction with others. That means that in today's multicultural environment, children's environments and experiences will play a large role in determining their racial identification. As a parent, you (and your spouse) will have a huge impact on helping your child shape her view of herself. How parents approach multicultural identity helps biracial children to adapt in society and ultimately helps them to avoid the "confusion" that many black women fear. Or as straight-talking playwright Mona Washington puts it, "Great parents, great kids. Fucked-up parents, fucked-up kids."

Parents of biracial children agree.

"My father did say something about biracial children having problems," said Lorraine. "But I know that children can have problems regardless of their backgrounds, so for me it was more important to love my children and stay aware. My daughter is seven and she's noticing how some white girls treat her and how some black girls treat her. One day at a friend's party, I noticed how three or four of the other little girls there went off to play without her. I decided to discuss it with her that evening. I asked her how it made her feel to be excluded. 'I move on,' she said easily. I considered it to be a 'teachable moment' and we talked about how sometimes other black girls might be jealous or just uncomfortable [because she has long hair and light skin]. We talk about history—but on the level she can understand it. If you teach them age-appropriately as the questions come up, then they can handle it. It's vital for their survival to prepare them. It's our responsibility as parents to raise them to understand the truths of our culture, so they can deal with it with their self-esteem intact."

Cynthia agrees. "My daughter is light-skinned with kinky hair and full lips. People think she's white until they meet me. She's thirteen now, but we started having these talks when she was about four years old when she said to me, 'I'm sorry you don't look like me and Daddy.' I told her, 'Don't feel sorry for me for being brown. You're brown too. You have two cultures in you. What you are is much deeper than skin.' And I taught her a little history, right then. Now that she's older, she has a much better understanding and is more sensitive to her black heritage and to the perceptions some blacks might have of her based on her appearance."

Crystal, the new mother of a five-month-old, says that she and her husband will openly discuss the various issues of race when it becomes important. They are grateful for geographic factors that will help their young daughter find common ground with others like her. "Where we live is important. We live in an area where there are so many different kinds of people, so many biracial children of so many different mixtures [that] I know our daughter won't be the 'only one' like her by the time she goes to school. If it does come up, though, I'd tell her to just answer 'My mom's black and my dad's white' and move on."

Color also plays a role in how biracial children will be treated. "I think it's also important to appreciate the differences in how they look. Biracial kids get different messages, so they need to be taught according to how they are treated," adds Lorraine. "As a parent, you have to understand that how they look dictates how they will be treated and prepare them for that. My son appears to be a light-skinned black. His hair is more textured; he's a light-skinned black boy in looks. It doesn't concern him because he's autistic, but I understand that, for all intents and purposes, he will be treated as a black man."

"My son is six," says Marvine, "and just beginning to clue in to race as a concept. He's still just identifying by color—'Mom is black, Dad is white, and I'm brown.' Every time he brings it up, I always tell him, 'That's right. You got the best of both worlds!' It also helps tremendously that President Obama is a mixed-race person. I tell my son, 'He's just like you!' and my little boy is absolutely tickled to know that he has something in common with the president of the United States! It also gives him a response to people who ask him about his racial background."

Indeed, several of the parents I spoke with mentioned President Obama as a role model and source of inspiration for them and their children.

"I remind my daughter of that often," says Lorraine. "I disagree with some of his politics, but I appreciate him as a source of pride and inspiration. There are no limits to what children can do—no matter what their backgrounds might be."

Indeed, the proliferation of openly mixed people in the media has offered parents and children more role models than ever before. Halle Berry, Vin Diesel, Dwayne "The Rock" Johnson, Derek Jeter, Rashida Jones, and of course Tiger Woods have also raised the visibility of being mixed in America. Seeing how famous people respond to questions about their identity helps the average kid gain strength and it also gives them powerful examples for handling the questions that might arise in their own lives.

"I think people project their color concerns on kids and that it's important for parents to challenge the people who do that—particularly when those remarks come from the extended family or from friends. If anyone ever calls a child of mine 'confused,' I'd say, 'If he is, it's because of people like you!' and that would be the end of it!" says Joan.

Every parent said, in essence, "We answer any questions the children have and we try to help them understand whatever situations they face as a result of being biracial," an attitude experts say is critical to helping children find their identities in a world where people still seem to have a need for an answer to the question "What *are* you?"

Kimberly Jade Norwood, author of "The Virulence of Blackthink," believes that the times are changing rapidly and that our children may be among the last generations to struggle with these questions. In a telephone interview, she said, "Interracial marriages—across all ethnicities—are becoming more and more common. That means we'll be seeing more and more children of all different mixes. Another couple of generations and hopefully we can retire the question of 'what are you' and devote our energies toward the more important work of ensuring opportunities of all people regardless of their race."

MOM'S BLACK, DAD'S WHITE, WHAT AM I?

Teaching children how to respond to outsiders who feel compelled to ask "What are you?" is, of course, only part of the story. Children of interracial unions will be asking us, as their parents, questions about themselves too. If Mom's black and Dad's white, what am I? Those questions get different answers today than they might have gotten even a decade ago. One reason is the sheer increase in numbers of mixed-raced children across the country. Another reason is the movement to recognize "biracial" or "multiracial" as official answers on U.S. Census and other forms.

In 1970, the U.S. Census Bureau estimated that our nation consisted of 460,000 mixed-race children. In 1980, that number more than doubled to 996,000. In 1990, it doubled again to more than 1.9 million. In 2000, it had once again greatly increased, to more than 2.8 million children of more than one race. Of course, these numbers include children from all ethnic and racial mixes, but the point is there: the numbers are on the rise. If the pattern continues to hold, the 2010 census is likely to identify more than 4 million mixed-race people under the age of eighteen.[14]

And with such a dynamic increase in numbers, attitudes about racial identification have begun to change. In their 2004 book *Raising Biracial Children*, University of Chicago professor Kerry Ann Rocquemore and psychologist Tracey Laszloffy explain the impact of the shift:

> Over the years, social scientists have shifted their position on what is considered *the* "healthy" ideal for mixed raced people, all the while clinging to the assumption that there is *one* ideal racial identity for this population. The clearest example . . . is in the case of individuals with one black and one white parent, where researchers have shifted between two different ideal identities: black and biracial. Before the mid-1980s, researchers assumed that the only healthy way for members of this group to identify racially was as exclusively black . . . and mixed race people who resisted [that] categorization were "confused." [But] beginning in the late 1980s, the study of biracial identity among mixed race people shifted as the "one drop rule" was challenged and re-conceptualized. A new gen-

eration of researchers, many of whom were themselves multiracial . . . suggested that biracial was the only healthy choice . . . and that those who defined themselves as black suffer from "denial."[15]

Rocquemore and Laszloffy argue that both these viewpoints suggest a "one size fits all" model that doesn't reflect the truth of being multiracial. Instead, they and other psychologists and sociologists offer several very different ways in which the children of interracial marriages may choose to identify themselves:

- *Single-race identification:* A person with parents from different races can identify with one and not the other. Usually, for a child who has a black parent and a white one, this means identifying as black, though obviously that's not the only possible choice. Here, skin tone, environment, and the racial community in which the child receives the most acceptance will play a large role in the child's choice.

- *Blended-race identification:* In this case, a person with parents from different races can identify with both races and may identify herself as "biracial" or "multiracial" rather than choosing to identify one race over the other. Tiger Woods's famous "Cablinasian" designation is a blended-race kind of identification. Since the terms *biracial* and *multiracial* are gaining in acceptance in our country, more and more children will be free to make a blended identification their choice.

- *Transcendent identification:* In this scenario, the mixed-race child rejects racial categorizations altogether. While most experts agree that, on a purely biological level, there are no races, the social constructs of race do matter in the United States for most us. The transcendent person refuses them entirely, however, and chooses to identify as "human," leaving others to worry about categorization based on their own prejudices, biases, and beliefs.[16]

Experts like Root, Rocquemore, and Laszloffy stress that at various points in a child's development she may choose a single-race identity, a blended one, or a transcendent one. These aren't fixed: they can and do evolve depending on the age of the child, the circumstances, and the child's needs. For example, at different points in a child's development, she might identify herself as white like Dad, then as both black and white, then as just a person, then as African American, like Mom. But the most important thing these scholars and researchers want parents and potential parents to know is that being mixed doesn't hurt kids, even when their racial identity vacillates between their parents' races.

"Children need help from their parents to verbalize racial thoughts and feelings," sociologist James H. Jacobs writes in "Identity Development in Biracial Children." "Supportive interest rather than alarm at the child's ambivalence will facilitate identity development. If the child's racial ambivalence is suppressed, he or she will feel that there is something inherently wrong with or degrading about his or her racial status."[17]

When mixed-race children announce that they're black one day, biracial the next, and white on the third, they aren't damaged and they certainly aren't confused, and they won't be unless you see them that way or surround them with others who believe that they are. Your children will be just fine, if you and your spouse encourage them to learn and explore both aspects of their racial history fully and completely. As Elliot Lewis writes in *Fade*, "For multiracial people, there is an additional layer in the identity development process. It involves creating a sense of self by assembling pieces of their heritage that others view as incompatible or mutually exclusive. No two people will assemble the pieces in exactly the same way. Some will end up emphasizing one part of their background over another. Others will end balancing them all with equal weight. For some, the process unfolds quite naturally. For others, it is a struggle."[18]

As there are more and more biracial children, the world will continue to change to accommodate them. In fact, our society already has changed greatly on this issue, since "biracial" has become a recognized term of self-identification and government forms now allow people to "select all that apply" when it comes to race. Furthermore, it's normal for children to change their self-identification as they age and their circumstances change. All kids really need is parents who love them—and each other— and who take time to listen supportively to them.

A WORD FROM A MULTIRACIAL CHILD

There are several organizations for young people of mixed parentage that offer support as well as resources and, in some cases, activism. One of them is Teen Project Race, an organization affiliated with Project RACE. Project RACE lobbies for the options to classify oneself as "biracial" or "multiracial" on various school, medical, and government forms. As its mission is stated on its website, www.projectrace.com,

> Biracial and multiracial people do not have a box to check on forms. Being forced to choose only one race forces us to deny one of our parents. It also requires us to do something illegal, since we are defining ourselves as something we are not. Multiracial people should have the option of recognizing *all* of their heritage. "Multiracial" is important so that children have an identity, a correct terminology for who they are. "Other" means different, a label that no person should bear. Also, without proper racial and ethnic classifications, multiracial people are "invisible" in the health care system.

Project RACE director Susan Graham comments frequently on the issues of identity facing multiracial people. In a recent interview addressing the concerns of multiracial children, she told a reporter that having a multiracial child is not something to fear. "People think everybody excludes them. I have not found that to be true. I have found just the opposite: that they are able to go between races and be very fluid and have a lot of friends of different races because they are themselves of different races. I don't think they feel excluded or denied. I am sure there are some who, for whatever reason, do, but overall, I have found that they know who they are." [19]

Through Project RACE and its sister organization Teen Project RACE, I met Kayci Baldwin, who told me her story. At seventeen, she is already an activist for multiracial identification. Hers are not the words of a "tragic mulatto." Instead, her story illustrates that biracial kids are finding it easier and easier to navigate in society, especially since they have some pretty powerful role models, including the president of the United States.

My mother is White (Irish, English, German) and my father is Black (African American but we do not know from which country his ancestors came). Although my parents didn't emphasize race, my siblings and I grew up thinking Daddy's Black, Mommy's White, and I'm Brown. Just as a matter of fact. We used to sing "Jesus Loves the Little Children" and change the chorus from "Red and Yellow, Black and White" to "Red, Brown, Yellow, Black and White, they are precious in His sight." They told me how lucky I was to have beautiful curls and a natural tan, but that what made me most beautiful was my happy heart.

I was born in Los Angeles but moved to central New Jersey when I was four. I have always attended predominantly White schools, but our family is very involved in our church, which provides tremendous diversity and role models of nearly every race. We have families that we are close to from church that are African American, White, Puerto Rican, Mexican, Haitian, and Filipino, as well as other interracial families. This has made a huge difference, I'm sure.

I haven't noticed any negative reactions from anyone—older people, strangers, relatives, teachers, or acquaintances—white or black or of any race. But I'm not one to look for problems or read into things. Kids my age think it's cool [to be mixed]. I'm growing up in the age of Disney princesses that look like me and a whole bunch of popular multiracial celebrities, not to mention our president. It is interesting that for the most part, White kids are more likely to consider me Black and Black kids are more likely to consider me White. I guess they take note of the differences, but never in an exclusionary way.

I typically use the term "multiracial" to identify myself when people ask or on forms. I've come to realize that proper terminology is important in a society where classifications are used to identify people. I think being multiracial is a huge advantage. So many people are raised with a bias, either because their families have some prejudiced thoughts that they pass on or because they are not adequately exposed to those of other races. Being multiracial helps a kid realize that race is not that big a deal and definitely not something that should divide us. It is not what makes a person who she is. It is a part of you, but it does not define you. Being multiracial allows you to flow confidently into different societies, families, and settings knowing that, in the ways that matter, all people are essentially alike.

The drawbacks of being multiracial? That's harder. I guess the fact that some of the older members of our family had a hard time with my parents' decision to marry. I know it's because of the generation they were raised in, but it is still disappointing. I guess it's also a drawback that when I'm in an area where a lot of Dominicans live, people speak Spanish to me assuming that I too am Dominican. Ha!

I have close friends of many races. I have only had one official boyfriend, and he is Puerto Rican, but now I date guys of any race. I date in the church where race truly is a nonissue. I typically find Black or multiracial guys more attractive, but not always. Maybe that's because a girl looks for a guy like her dad. Who knows?

If two people love each other and are devoted to each other and feel proud of their choice to marry, race should not be a concern. I know messed-up, insecure kids with two White parents, and messed-up, insecure kids with two Black parents. If there are messed-up, insecure kids of interracial parents, maybe it's not because of race! Many studies show very positive findings on the self-esteem and achievement of multiracial children. Of course, other studies find the contrary. Again, I say that race is probably not the problem.

Being multiracial is really just a small part of who I am. I am a Christian, an activist, a scholar, a singer, a writer, and a public speaker. I love to serve those in need, I love to travel, I love to shop, I love yellow and purple, I love to go to the beach at night and walk in the rain, I love my family, I love my friends, I love boys, I love chai lattes. I hate mayonnaise, I hate the sight of raw chicken. I hate insincerity. I want to be a political analyst or work in community redevelopment or go into the ministry or become a judge. Or maybe all of these! I'm looking forward to prom and BASH and going on a college visit with my grandparents, and returning to South Africa. I would like people to know that *these* things describe me a lot better than the fact that my mother and my father happen to be of two different races.

America is making great progress with racial issues. I am hopeful. I believe every generation sees race less than the generation before. I also think that the growing number of multiracial people will continue to blur the distinction between races. I think many people are "over" the whole concept of race. I think many others will get over it in my lifetime. But in the back of my mind I have the nagging feeling that some will remain who refuse to let go of the superficial categories and divisions of race.

THE FINAL WORD: GOOD PARENTS, GOOD KIDS

The experts have said it, the parents of multiracial children have said it, and Kayci has said it too. Black women considering dating and perhaps marrying outside the race don't need to worry about the children. What they need to worry most about is finding a good man with whom they experience love and affection and with whom they share common ground. A secure family builds secure children, no matter what the races of its members.

NOTION 7

He Must Have Money: Black Women as Gold Diggers

If you see a black woman with an overweight white man, her credit is fucked up!

> —*Chris Rock,* Kill the Messenger, *HBO Home Video, 2009*

It's as easy to marry a rich man as a poor one.

> —*Old saying*

Sometimes it's whispered, sometimes it's shouted. Sometimes you just read it in someone's face and sometimes he tells you to your face. Most black women in interracial relationships have heard it in one form or another: you married him for the money.

The bit from Chris Rock may be funny, but the allegation that a black woman with a white man must be using him for the money has serious flaws. It argues from the point of view that black women are impoverished and dependent, when you and I both know that for most of us these are the wrong two adjectives. We can make really quick work of this notion, since *gold digger* is absolutely the wrong phrase. The right one? Try "successful person, seeking same."

WHAT IS A GOLD DIGGER?

People are quick to use the term *gold digger,* but it turns out to have more meanings than you might think. A product of the American gold rush, a gold digger was originally someone who mined or dug for gold. Subsequently, it was extended to mean a person who used charm to get money or gifts from other people. The *Random House Dictionary* specifies the gender of this "charming manipulator" in its definition: "a woman who associates with or marries a man chiefly for material gain."

At urbandictionary.com as of March 2009, there are no fewer than fourteen definitions, the most popular one "Any woman whose primary interest in a relationship is material benefits. A woman who cares more about a man's bank account than she does about the man."

Finally, in their meticulously researched 2003 paper "Freaks, Gold Diggers, Divas, and Dykes: The Sociohistorical Development of Adolescent African American Women's Sexual Scripts," sociologists Dionne P. Stephens and Layli Phillips describe hip-hop culture's "script" or definition as one based on the old Jezebel image we discussed (and dismissed) earlier:

> A woman who explicitly seeks material and economic rewards above all else, and is willing to trade sex for it. Sex is her commodity because it is the only valuable thing she has in society. Gold Diggers are not traditionally viewed as being successful in educational, employment or other economic spheres. Instead, the Gold Diggers' plan is to "toss them titties around, shake that ass, make that money." Also known as pigeons or hootchie mamas, Gold Diggers seem to have the most obvious awareness that sex is their most powerful commodity. Sex may be used to barter for basic needs such as a bag of groceries, getting rent paid, or making sure their lights do not get turned off. However, manicures and pedicures, new clothing, vacations, or having a car note paid are also possible wants that Gold Diggers may be willing to trade sex to get.

> [Gold diggers] purposefully select male partners based on the lifestyle or affluence that they can provide. A man and a dollar sign are seen as being one and the same as the gold digger views the man's worth according to the balance of his bank accounts or the cash in his pocket.

As long as the money is available, the gold digger will make herself available. . . . Gold digger scripts most obviously show women engaging in sex for personal gain and using men. That is why it is one of the most resented scripts in African American culture by both males and females. *Money and sex are hot commodities and women are not supposed to have both.*[1] [emphasis added]

While maybe somewhere in the black community (as well as in the communities of other racial and ethnic groups) a woman who displays some of the characteristics of a "gold digger" probably exists, very, very few black women fit this stereotype—whether they date white men, black men, or men of any other race. Most women examining potential mates rate financial security important, and justifiably so, since money is one of the elements necessary to ensure a family's success. But most black women bring so much to the table of their relationships—including money and education—that the generalization "gold digger" as it applies to black women dating interracially is virtually always ignorant and inappropriate.

EDUCATION MEETS OPPORTUNITY EQUALS ADVANTAGE

Any woman of any race can be a "gold digger," but black women who date interracially seem to be prime targets for this appellation. It's a convenient moniker if you like living your life according to stereotypes—and according to notions that are rapidly becoming ancient history. But if you're interested in some facts, here are several.

First of all, the majority of black women have far more than sex to offer to their partners in any relationship. According to 2000 census figures, black women with at least some college education earn more than their Asian, European, and Hispanic American counterparts with the same level of college education.[2] Which means, in addition to their undisputed sexiness, black women with even a little college under their belts have money of their own to contribute to their partners—*more* money than women of any other ethnic group! Since more and more young black women are going to and graduating from college, the 2010 census should show even greater gains in educational and economic advantage as they join the ranks of graduates and become members of the workforce.

Second, studies show that black women in interracial relationships tend to be in economic parity with their white partners: that means that you won't see a black woman with no money with a white man with cash to burn. Instead, you'll see couples in which the black woman and white man make similar money—something you're less likely to see in any other interracial pairing. In their 2008 book *Interracial Families: Current Concepts and Controversies*, George Yancy and Richard Lewis find that:

> socioeconomic status plays a unique role in spouse selection. Some early socioeconomic research studies suggest socioeconomic homogamy [sameness] is an important factor in the development of romantic relationships [citations omitted]. However . . . interracial couples tend to be comprised of individuals who, as a group, exhibit slightly higher socioeconomic status (educational attainment and personal income), for instance, in comparison to the adult population overall. . . . There is some work that suggests that African Americans and Hispanic Americans who are in interracial marriages tend to have higher socioeconomic status than others from those two groups [citations omitted]. This higher socioeconomic level may help equalize their economic status with majority group partners since Whites on average have higher incomes than people of color.[3]

Yancy and Lewis found that the research suggests black women in interracial relationships are the exact opposite of "gold diggers." They earn as much as their white spouses, and those who assert otherwise don't have the facts on their sides. Are these accusers just "haters"? Evia Moore thinks so.

> I find it beyond interesting that some black men tend to think that the sole reason I married a white man was because of his money. My husband is comfortable financially, but he's certainly not rich. All white people are not rich, just like all black people are not poor. People sure do live

and breathe these stereotypes! The thing is that many black men can't believe or don't want to believe that a white man can offer a black woman anything aside from money. That is just limited and wishful thinking.[4]

The person who calls a black woman dating interracially a gold digger is basically advertising his or her ignorance—and a determination to see the world as it was in the 1960s and 1970s, rather than as it exists today. In other words, this is really yet another old-fashioned notion that casts white men as a group as "rich and powerful" and black women as a group as "poor and powerless." Of course, disparities still exist in gender and racial equality, but the socioeconomic status of black women has risen dramatically over the past several decades. Knowing just a few facts reveals the "gold digger" argument for the garbage it truly is.

As the song says, "sisters" are really doing it for themselves, and that's part of what makes us attractive companions for men of all races. Most black women don't have to date any man for financial reasons. Indeed many black women who date and marry out aren't looking to their partners to provide for them: they are looking for a partner who will fit with the lifestyle they have achieved for themselves. And that means a man with similar education, interests, and yes, income.

JEALOUS?

Many times black women who ask whether a black man has a job are considered to be interested in him for his money—or labeled a gold digger. I also must point out what many black men overlook—that black women do know that many black men don't really have substantial monetary resources or gold to "dig," so if [money] were a black woman's main reason for being interested in a black man, she'd often be out of luck and would instead only look at white men. [This isn't the case since] in 2008, most black women still gravitate toward black men.

Compare these comments by Evia Moore to what Phil Cohen, a blogger at www.dvrbs.com, had to say in an email to me:

In a "fair world," one that doesn't exist and never will, no effort would
be required of men and women for anything. Well, it's not a fair world.
A man has to make himself "eligible" . . . that is, worthwhile of consider-
ation . . . in appearance, behavior, and economics *to be real about it.*
So does a woman, but she has different hoops to jump through, different
standards to meet, and that's just the way the species is built.

Money is a part of what men can offer women in a country where the
average woman makes 70 cents for every dollar a man makes. Economics is a real part of every relationship. Fact: deal with it. Some black men
love the phrase *gold digger* and apply it to just about every woman who
asks questions about a man's education, ambitions, and income. But I
love what one black comedian, Steve Harvey, has to say about men and
women and words like *gold digger* in his book *Act Like a Lady, Think Like
a Man*. He speaks the truth, as a man to us women, revealing that men
use words like *gold digger* to get what they want—and to keep us from
getting what we want.[5] Men who don't want to share and invest their
money in women drop the phrase *gold digger* to keep women second-
guessing themselves and struggling to prove themselves "not like
that."

> If he takes you out on a date and lets you pay, or only kicks in his portion
> of the bill, he's [not serious about you]; if he pays the bill, he's showing
> that's he's willing to provide for you, which means he's likely looking for a
> keeper. . . . If he does not have himself together financially, emotionally
> and spiritually, he may [not be serious about you]; if he is capable of
> providing and protecting his potential family the way a real man should,
> then he might be searching for a keeper.[6]

In other words, a man's willingness to pony up his cash—to
provide—is a signal not of his wealth but of his level of commitment.
A man doesn't have to be wealthy, he has to be willing. When his interest is sincere, words like *gold digger* don't even cross his mind.

Add race to money, however, and you have another round of
complications—but with a similar bottom line. The man accusing a black
woman of "gold digging" when she becomes involved with a white man

uses the phrase in his own interest: in this case keeping a supply of black women available for black men. It also keeps our assets—that money that black women earn with the education they get at twice the rate of black men and work hard for—available for some black men to use and abuse.

You know what I'm talking about. Too many of us, in our search for love, have ended up supporting a man, believing that we are being "good black women" by doing so. Unfortunately, some of those guys just weren't interested in reciprocating. Funny, but it seems like those are often the same guys who are quick to accuse women of gold digging—or worse, selling out—when we date outside the race! Men who accuse women of gold digging may not only be using the term to get what they want, as Steve Harvey suggests. They may also be projecting their financial insecurities about what they can attract and what they lack.

Teresa, a successful black woman with a college degree and her own business, says, "Sometimes it seems like black men expect us to get excited because they have a job and a house. I'm like, sure, I've got those too. A person *should* have those by the time they get to a certain age. What do you want—a medal?" Teresa is currently dating a physician of Indian descent. "If it makes me a gold digger to expect that any man I'm involved with will have at least what I have, then fine, call me what you want!"

Tori recalls an incident that happened once when she was leaving a movie theater with a white male friend.

We were both in college then; neither of us had any real money. And we weren't dating, we were just a couple of friends who had gone to the movies together. As we were walking home, this black guy approached us, offering to sell us a lady's watch. My friend declined and so did I. I didn't need a watch, and I didn't expect my friend to buy me one. But this guy got really angry and started yelling, "See, he don't care nothing for you! He won't even buy you a watch, sister! He won't even buy you a watch!" It was clear that this guy thought we were dating and that my friend had money and I didn't. [He thought] that I was only with him for the cash I might be able to get from him. That guy was wrong on just about every level, and it says something about his thought process: he had to make it about more than we just didn't want the watch.

A guy hustling watches on the street might very well have issues with his own economic significance. But any man who insinuates that a woman's romantic choices make her a gold digger is showing his colors: he's either using the phrase as an attempt to control, insecure about his own financial viability, or just plain ignorant.

"In my interviews, I also heard the gold digger accusation from some black women who asserted that they would never date interracially. In fact, the more vehemently against interracial dating the woman was, the more likely it was that she might accuse fellow black women of being 'sellouts' or 'gold diggers' for their choice," Kellina Craig-Henderson observes.

I came across this sentiment too in the voices of women who said they would feel like they were "abandoning the brothers" if they dated outside the race. These are women who value the idea of loyalty—to their vision of the black community, to black men, and to the concept of "black love." Fine. Every woman is entitled to her convictions, but both common sense and experts suggest that a black woman shouldn't settle for less than she deserves from a man of any race. In fact, if you apply an economic analysis to black women's dating lives, same-race-only dating puts black women at a disadvantage. Check out this economic analysis by Kurt Davis published in the *Virginia Law Weekly*:

Analysis has been provided over the years as to why black women are one of the demographic groups in America most likely not to be married. Considering past arguments ranging from the high incarceration rate of black men to a lack of highly educated black men, I choose to inject my economic analysis into this argument. The marriage rate of black women has encountered a huge market failure. . . .

How does this apply to marital rates among black women? Sadly, but truly, a black woman pays a higher cost for a successful black man, as he is a limited commodity in the marital partner market. Furthermore, a black woman pays a high cost for a black man who does not meet the standards she expects in a marital partner, further undermining efficiency in the market. In other words, a black woman pays a high price for a black man who may not put in much effort. For example, a black woman who earns a Ph.D. should not think that she is wrong in expecting a similar educational status in her partner. However, many black women do feel that way, and may lower their standards to find a black partner. Thus, the black man puts in less effort or assumes less marginal cost but still comes at a high price to a black woman.

In the financial realm, government intervention is easily justified in the face of market failure. In this case, social programs that range from minority recruitment to jail-to-work serve this purpose despite their flaws. With that said, personal behavioral changes unrelated to governmental intervention can affect the market dynamic. A black woman's rightful choice to limit her market solely to black men reinforces the market failure, just as her choice to date interracially would alleviate it. Increased interracial dating by black men only underlines the last point, as the market of black men will decrease. For example, interracial dating by Asian women has often been equated to that of black men. Studies have shown that, as a result, Asian men marry at similarly low rates as black women.[7]

And here's a real-life story from an email I received that illustrates the same point:

I'm a white man, married to a black woman. We've been married for 20 years come August, and while the questioning comes from all directions, I think it has been particularly rough on my wife in dealing with disapproval from other black people. She heard it for years—from her family, friends, colleagues, strangers. I recall one of her friends saying disapprovingly how she would never date a white man—"I believe in the black family," she said. This is a woman who at the time was single and having an affair with a married man, and who has had multiple abortions. My wife has about 8 close friends from her college days. None of them has had a successful relationship with a black man and none are married. Several have had children out of wedlock. All remain single. But none to my knowledge have ever considered dating outside their race . . . the reason why: this pressure to put ethnocentrism above all else, including the right to be happy and the freedom to choose whom to love.

No doubt, at least some of this attitude is rooted in the financial and racial inequalities that still exist today. Labor department statistics reveal that white men do still have earnings advantages over black men. The criminal justice system still deals overwhelmingly in black defendants, and black men with criminal records are stripped of many of their opportunities to improve their lives. Educational inadequacies still put black children at risk.

"Black women tend to think that we must bear the burden of these injustices, that these are 'black' problems that we must work to solve," Professor Norwood reiterates. "But once again, the truth is these are not 'black problems.' They are American problems. They are human problems. All of us have a stake in solving them, regardless of race, because they impact our nation as a whole."

Loyalty is a good and valued thing in any person, but blind loyalty is dangerous. Blind loyalty leads the women who practice it to believe in a stereotype that paints us as poor and powerless, with sex as our only asset, which we "sell" to the white man for a shot at some temporary privilege. It's as ridiculous as it is wrong, once we really look at the motives behind it—and the facts.

It's human nature to notice couples that appear not to go together in some striking way—and human nature to explain the discrepancies in ways that balance the power between the couples. For Craig-Henderson, seeing the "white man" as "the power" and the black woman as exchanging sex for proximity to power is a phenomenon she calls "mismatching." "It's basically studying what brings certain people together," she explains. "And when you see certain pairs of people—people who are mismatched in some way—we take a second look. When you see an attractive black woman with a less attractive white man, you'll often hear a whispered 'gold digger.' But you'd also hear it if the attractive woman and less attractive man were of the same race. Couples that are visually mismatched are likely to attract those kinds of responses, even though, once you look more closely at the details of their relationships, there's often far more common ground between them than their appearance might suggest."

Mismatching does at least partially explain why the phrase "gold digger" continues to circulate for black women/white man interracial couples. But, as the women I interviewed will tell you, mismatched or not, gold digging is not a part of the reality of their relationships.

"I was the primary breadwinner in my first marriage," says Cynthia.

"And my second husband just got his second degree and is starting out in a new career path. So for now I'm still the primary breadwinner while he gets his footing in his new career. I enjoy working, so I probably would always choose to do it, but if I chose not to, I know Michael could provide for us. That's what couples do: support each other."

"Jacquetta and I met on craigslist.com and I remember reading through her height and income 'requirements,' " said Greg, a white attorney married to a black woman who teaches special education in the New York City public schools. "I just ignored them; I always have. Who knows what women mean by that stuff? They check off these boxes like a wish list, but in the end, I think it's more about, do you like each other? Are you compatible? Besides, I'm confident about my income. I think women just want to know a man can take care of himself."

"My black girlfriends actually asked me, does he have money?" Marvine laughed. "The answer? No. My husband and I work *together* to keep our family financially secure. We both contribute. But we're doing well because he's smart, and he's a go-getter and so am I."

At least in part, this whole discussion about who is digging for what is about perception. Is the glass half full or is it half empty? Do we see ourselves as black people in need of power, or do we feel powerful? Clearly, some people—both black and white—are moving past the idea that white people have the power (and aligning oneself with them is betrayal in some form) and into a stronger and more realistic truth: like attracts like. Education attracts education. Money attracts money. Ambition attracts ambition. People with these qualities often attract others with those same qualities, and race shouldn't limit us from exploring the possibilities that result from socioeconomic similarities.

Clearly, men and women of any race attract and seek people who have similar interests, assets, and backgrounds. There is nothing wrong with expectations, and having them doesn't make a black woman a gold digger. How many women have you known who have lowered their financial or educational standards while looking for companionship— with disastrous results? Buying into a dated notion and letting the fear of being perceived as a "gold digger" guide your romantic choices is giving away power, power that you have earned and that you deserve.

NOTION 8

You're a Sellout:
Perception of Black Women Who Date White Men

My name is Tiffany. I'm a 27-year-old African American female who is married to a Caucasian/Hispanic man. We've been married for 4 years and have a 2-year-old son. My parents tried to give my brother, sister, and me a better life, and for them, that meant buying a home in the suburbs. While I was growing up, I was around mainly all white people. Of course I had my extended family, but they were in St. Louis, so I wasn't always around them. Growing up, when you're around mainly one race, you start to . . . identify with them, you're attracted to what's around you, and that's how it always was with me. I dated a lot of white guys. My family was always accepting of it, but the black friends I did have would always ask "Why?" I never had an answer.

When I married my husband, we didn't really get a lot of looks from other people. I figured that since we are from a younger generation, people would be more understanding. Most people don't seem to care, but black men my age seem to have the biggest issue. I've gotten the remarks about how I'm a "sellout" and my husband has gotten remarks that I find incredibly insulting such as, "You don't know what to do with that." We just laugh it off, but sometimes, it does hurt because you can't help who you fall in love with.

A couple of years ago, after a piece I'd written about interracial marriage was published in the *Washington Post*, I got a short and succinct email from a person—gender unknown—that went like this:

"I read it. After seeing your photos [on your website], he can have you. No loss to us."

The message was unmistakable: as far as this person was concerned, my choice to marry interracially had exiled me from the black race. Many African American women who have had experiences like mine—or like Tiffany's in the email excerpted above—have been accused of being sell-outs for their choice of partner. Washington College of Law professor Kimberly Jade Norwood calls it getting "de-blacked," and it illustrates just how much work we still have to do to define—or redefine—black identity.

Ultimately, "de-blacking," as Norwood explains, "is about whether you're going to let other people decide your identity or not. And it manifests in all kinds of ways. You can be de-blacked for being good at school, or for moving to the suburbs or marrying interracially. It's really sad, what we black people do to each other. In my view, we have too many real problems to be clawing at each other like this, accusing each other of selling out and not being black enough. It's the power of slavery and Jim Crow and the psychological traumas black people as a collective still haven't healed from."

Although certainly no one would argue that all black people think or believe the same things, the black community as a whole has, however, struggled to maintain common allegiances as a part of the effort to achieve group benefits in a society in which racial discrimination and prejudice still hinder our advancement. Remaining faithful to those allegiances has been a part of what has traditionally been defined as "blackness." Marrying interracially is just one of the ways that a black person can become vulnerable to the epithet "sellout," but the real question is whether that derogatory term is accurate or appropriate.

The black women in interracial relationships whom I spoke with were well aware of the perceptions some black people had of them. But each of them asserted pride in their African American heritage and rejected a narrow definition of "blackness" that excluded them.

"You can call me [a sellout] if it makes you feel better," said Cynthia. "But I know I'm proud of my African American heritage."

"Black women get blamed for everything," added Teresa. "We get educated and other black people get jealous. We interact with white men who have similar education and economic status, then we're sellouts. They've stacked the game so we can't win. And if we can't win, we might as well do what makes us happy, because those people aren't ever going to be satisfied."

Mona agreed. "I think these people are full of hate—and projecting it on other people. People who are comfortable with their own black identity have no need to fixate on what other black people are doing. Black identity is not a monolith."

Norwood calls this the "myth of one voice":

> Just as Black people's skin color spans a spectrum of shades, there is a spectrum in every other facet of our being. We range from the very poor to the very wealthy, from the well educated to the academically disadvantaged. Some identify with conservatives, others with liberals. Some support affirmative action, some do not. A single Black voice is an oxymoron. One voice is a myth.[1]

Black people are not a monolith and one voice is a myth, and yet, some black folks still seem certain that they know who has "stayed black" and who has "sold out."

WHAT'S A SELLOUT, AND WHO GETS TO DECIDE?

In his book *Sellout: The Politics of Racial Betrayal*, Harvard Law School professor Randall Kennedy defines a "sellout" as a person who betrays something to which she is said to owe an allegiance.

> When used in a racial context among African Americans, "sellout" is a disparaging term that refers to blacks who knowingly or with gross negligence act against the interest of blacks as a whole. Defining it that cleanly, however, offers a misleading sense of clarity. Sellout is a messy, volatile, contested term about which disagreement is rife, especially when it comes to applying the label to specific persons or conduct.[2]

Norwood adds that, along with "oreos" and "Uncle Toms," "sell-outs" is "used to describe Blacks whom the labelers believe do not act Black, do not support 'Black' issues, and more importantly really want to be White."[3]

Social psychologist Kellina Craig-Henderson offers a slightly different perspective. "I'm not sure that the term is particularly helpful in the discussion of what it means to be black in our current society. But what 'sellout' *does* indicate is a kind of cultural identity and affiliation that you can assume when you meet a person who appears to be African American. When black folks call a person a 'sellout' it connotes a person that we can't assume certain things about, even though their color might have originally suggested we could. Sellout is really the only term that captures that feeling. It's something felt and reacted to on an almost visceral level. When regular folk say someone is a sellout, they mean they can't categorize the person. They can't put them in the box. If you look at it that way, the term still has potent currency in the African American community."

There's also an economic edge to the word, as in one has literally "sold" her African American heritage for money, status, or power—which for black women in interracial relationships harks back to the "gold digger" label.

At various times, certain conduct (being too bookish, speaking too "proper"), occupations (in the 1970s being a police officer, for example), and political affiliations (being a conservative or a Republican in the 1980s through the present—think Condoleezza Rice or Supreme Court Justice Clarence Thomas) have opened one up to the accusation of "selling out." "Sleeping white" is a perennially popular basis for applying the term. Kennedy dates concerns about "sleeping white" back to 1884, when former slave and abolitionist activist Frederick Douglass married a white woman and ignited a sense of racial abandonment and outrage, in spite of the fact that Douglass had previously been married to a black woman for more than forty years and only remarried after her death.[4]

"I confess I still do a bit of a double take when I see black men with white women," says Janine. "It used to make me mad—not because I thought the guy was a sellout, but because it meant that there was just another brother who wasn't available for us black women. But now that

I'm dating a white guy, I'm over it. My boyfriend and I notice, but it's different now. It's more like 'Hey, there's an IRC—interracial couple. They're like us.' "

But not exactly. "In my research for my latest book, *Black Women in Interracial Relationships*, I did find black men—and black women who had very strong feelings against interracial dating—seemed to be the most likely to use words like 'sellout,' " says Craig-Henderson. "There was definitely this sense of disloyalty that was expressed in very strong terms."

Some "brothas" do react, but once again, there appears to be a double standard for black men versus black women. While sitting with my husband in a restaurant in Boston, I had the feeling of being stared at. I looked around and found myself under the scrutiny of a black man in a nearby booth. If looks could kill, I wouldn't be writing these words right now; I'd have perished in that restaurant that night. He wasn't alone, but because of the angle of our table, I couldn't see his companion. I tried to enjoy the rest of our meal but it was tough: every time I looked in that direction the guy was staring daggers at me. Finally we got up to leave, and as we passed his booth I could see his dinner companion: a white woman. My emotions at this revelation were mixed: I wanted to laugh at the irony of the situation, but I also wanted to scream my fury at this man at the top of my lungs. What was so different between what he was doing and what I had done?

It's obvious a double standard is still at play. For black women, "sleeping white" and "marrying white" still touch on some uncomfortable history. In her groundbreaking book *Black Feminist Thought*, Patricia Hill Collins writes about the kind of double standard black women face. "The history of sexual abuse contributes to a contemporary double standard where Black women who date and marry White men are often accused of losing their Black identity. Within this context Black women who do engage in relationships with White men encounter Black community norms that question their commitment to Blackness." [5]

Losing "blackness" is at the heart of the allegation that a black woman involved with a white man is a "sellout." But what exactly is blackness and can one actually lose it? Who gets to decide what's black enough and what is not? On the surface, these seem like silly questions—questions barely worth any serious discussion. But in actuality they are questions that get a great deal of thought, both from scholars and from average black Americans trying to determine just what it is about inter-racial dating that bothers us so much.

WHAT IS BLACKNESS?

Blackness is one of those things: we all think we know what it is, but it's very hard to define.

Academics and average people alike struggle to get the right com-bination of phrases. Here's an attempt by John McWhorter, author of *Authentically Black: Essays for the Black Silent Majority,* as it appeared on the popular blog TheRoot.com a few years back:

> What is black culture? Definitions will differ. But we can't treat the defini-tion as so "fluid" that it isn't a definition at all. I will toss out a few param-eters of what "black" is:
>
> - The dialect: which is *not identical to Southern white English, and not just slang*, but a sound and a series of grammatical patterns.
>
> - Music: yes, most of hip-hop's listeners are white. But there are *pro-portionally* more black people who listen mostly to black music than there are whites who listen mostly to black music.
>
> - Bodily carriage. Culinary tastes. Dress style. Christian commitment. Juneteenth. And yes, skill on the dance floor.
>
> There are whites who have some of these traits. What I have pre-sented is not a bag of "stereotypes." These would be stereotypes if I claimed that all black people exhibited all of those traits to a maximal degree. But I have not claimed that. I have listed a few aspects of black culture: what an anthropologist might identify as traits unique to the black community—i.e., what it is to be black.[6]

He elaborated in another entry, stating, "There are definable cultural characteristics and behaviors that link black people to one another culturally, and this complex of characteristics and behaviors can be des-ignated 'black culture.' This particular complex of characteristics and behaviors does not describe Jewish people or Armenians. It describes black Americans."[7]

Another definition is offered by Kimberly Jade Norwood:

Some might argue that Black blood alone makes a person Black, but sole reliance on the one-drop rule is troubling given the reason for the rule's creation. And while others believe that being Black is a way of life, a culture and an attitude, it is clearly more than that. Indeed, no matter how much of a Black culture style or way of life or thinking one adopts, if the genealogy/ancestry and/or phenotype/visual perception indicia are lacking, the target will be not be recognized as Black, will not be treated as Black . . . mere support or desire, no matter how vociferous, is never enough to turn that White person into a Black person without the requisite biological bloodline.[8]

Yet in a recent Wikipedia.com entry, *blackness* was defined as "the degree to which one associates [oneself] with mainstream African American culture and values."[9] In this view, being black is not so much about skin color or tone as it is about culture and behavior. Blackness can be contrasted with "acting white," where black Americans are said to behave with assumed characteristics of stereotypical white Americans, with regard to fashion, dialect, and taste in music.

Confused yet?

"It's impossible to define," says Craig-Henderson. "But it matters. Unfortunately, black people who have education or different political ideas, or who have light skin or date interracially have to expend additional energy defeating the perception that they aren't black enough. They have to live in two worlds, which takes up a lot of energy. That energy takes a toll on the body that some physicians now believe may play a role in health problems in the black community. Little things that, over time, cause more hypertension, more heart attacks. Researchers are studying that now at Howard University, the physiological effects of dealing with 'being black' and 'being black enough.' You have to wonder what it would be like for black Americans if we didn't have to do that. If we could just live our lives as ourselves, without those burdens."

Norwood is more blunt. "We're just messed up," she told me in a telephone interview. "Black people are incredibly hard on other black people. It's not traitorous to date outside your race. A woman can marry interracially and still be as committed to fighting racial injustice as a woman in a same-race relationship. But there's still the perception that she's somehow opted out in a way a black woman in a same-race relationship has not."

At least one way to attempt to live a life without the burden of proving black authenticity is to leave the United States and live abroad for an extended period of time. Angela Shaw lives in France, where

> it is easier . . . for me to exercise my own imagination in defining my own identity than it would be in the U.S. . . . There are a thousand overt and covert ways in which the habits and manners of living in the United States inhibit one's own imagination. . . . This is to say, living abroad, outside the circle of formalized American identity, I have been required to define and hence to imagine my own life for over 20 years, without the comfort zone that you probably take for granted in being within American geographic and cultural borders.

Angela's life has taken her and her husband (who is Belgian) to China and all over Europe, changing her perspective on herself as a black American woman and allowing her a different view of the ongoing American discussion of race. More and more, black women are traveling abroad to experience a fresh perspective for themselves. But for now, for most of us, the black American experience is our grounding, our home. And that means that both being black and being black enough are very real considerations for black women living in the United States—especially for black women dating interracially.

When we examine these issues critically, it seems simplistic to say that a black American woman has sacrificed her blackness because she likes rock music or preppy fashions or speaks "proper" English, just as it seems ridiculous to assert that, by virtue of one's choice of partner, one loses one's cultural identity. Does her white spouse erase her work teaching inner-city children? Does her white spouse negate her volunteer work with other black women who have been battered and abused? Can one really "sell out" if one still embraces black history and literature but also appreciates the history and literature of cultures other than ours?

"Not a day goes by that I don't know that I'm black in America. I live in Chicago, which, even though it's one of America's largest cities, really isn't integrated," says Janine. "It's neighborhoods—chunks of blacks here, chunks of whites there. I live on the Southside, which is predominantly black. There are folks who've lived their entire lives on the Southside and never been Downtown, don't know any white people at all. And my parents still live in Lynchburg, Virginia, a smaller southern city where segregation and prejudice carved deep footholds that are still there today. What I'm saying is, I'm very connected to my black heritage, and while my boyfriend is white, I know where I came from, because I'm still living there."

Like Janine, the other women I talked to were very proud of and connected to their black heritage. They really *do* work with inner-city children, help battered women, do mission work in Africa, perform legal advocacy services for less fortunate blacks in this country, write novels and plays and other books for African American audiences. They are an educated, thoughtful, interested, and activist group of women, and their white partners appreciate them for these qualities.

"It's not like being with Mike made me white," says Cynthia. "I'm perfectly happy and proud of the skin I'm in. I don't want to be white. I want to be myself and do the things that matter to me. And my husband wants me to do the same."

I remember once having a heated discussion with my cousins (both ministers) about integration, education, and the future of the black race. When my husband came into the room, my cousins fell silent, while I continued my rant about blacks and whites and racism and prejudice. Finally I noticed their uncomfortable glances in Kevin's direction. "Oh," I said, "don't worry about him: he knows I'm black. He's heard all this before." In fact, when a particularly disturbing news story comes on, or I've just about had it with someone of the Caucasian persuasion, I've occasionally said "Crazy white people"—in my husband's presence—in just about the same tone that I might have said the words to any black person in my life. It's become something of a joke in our household. In order for us to be spouses—to be best friends and partners—we both have to be free to express ourselves and our frustrations, even when those frustrations involve race.

The point here is that no "blackness" has been sacrificed in the relationships of these women—or in my own—and that defining who is black and who is not is a slippery slope.

In an article in *Diverse Issues in Higher Education*, Elwood Watson reflects on the divisive and derogatory language used by blacks to describe other blacks. Words like *ghetto, bougie, Uncle Tom, Negro, oreo, incog-negro, Aunt Jemima,* and of course the granddaddy of them all, *nigger,* are pejoratives used with frequency by blacks to describe other blacks—always with the aim of questioning a person's blackness.

> The larger question that emerges from this is how and what do we define as Blackness? economic situation? educational attainment? skin tone? religious affiliation? clothing attire? racial genetic makeup? geographic region? . . . Are lower income Black people in the Huff section of Cleveland more Black than those who live in the wealthy Los Angeles suburb of Baldwin Hills? Do Black people who have doctorates, law degrees and MBAs embody less Blackness than those who only have a high school diploma or even more minimal level of education? Are darker skin Black people like Wesley Snipes more racially legitimate than lighter skinned Blacks like Beyoncé Knowles?
>
> Do Black Pentecostals and Southern Baptists have more *soul* than their Presbyterian and Methodist parishioners? Do Black men and women who wear clothes by Damat and Tween and Tracey Lee [represent more] of a fashion racial consciousness that is absent among those who wear J. Crew and Timberland threads? Are biracial Black people like Halle Berry and Barack Obama less authentic than those of us who have two Black parents? Are Blacks who reside in the heat sweltering, largely agrarian Black-belt states of Mississippi, Alabama, Louisiana and Georgia more racially aware than their fellow Blacks who live in the picturesque, snow-capped mountain states of Maine, Vermont and New Hampshire?[10]

Dr. Watson's answer is a resounding no. But some black people feel not only that there are some experiences that are more black than others, but that they hold ownership over what (and who) is authentically black and what (and who) is not. And they are usually the first to let you know when you've stepped across the black line.

BLACKTHINK

Pat is a black woman in her midforties who has been married to a white man in his midfifties, Tom, for nearly ten years. When they met, Pat was round-faced, favored comfortable ethnic clothes, and wore her hair in dreadlocks (imagine the author Alice Walker and you've got her), while Tom was rocking a big "Santa" belly and a long beard (think something out of a Hollywood biker bar and you've got him).

"I'll never forget it. We were in this buffet-style restaurant having dinner. It was before we got married but we'd been dating a while," she told me in a phone interview. "And this black woman at a nearby table kept glaring at us. Then I realized she was saying something, over and over again, just loud enough for us to hear. She was saying 'perp'—like 'perpetrator.' She was insinuating, I guess, that in spite of my dreads and my attire and my skin tone I wasn't really black because I was dating someone who looked like Tom."

Clearly, this woman was a member of journalist John Blake's "Soul Patrol" and as such felt qualified to judge Pat's "blackness" based on her dinner companion. Pat had been "de-blacked" by a process Kimberly Jade Norwood calls "Blackthink™," a prejudice exercised by both non-blacks and blacks based on "the assumption and demand that all Black people think a certain way. . . . Autonomy and difference are stifled; acquiescence is embraced and rewarded." Blackthink™, she argues, uses various methods to challenge one's blackness and to ultimately "de-black" those who have been found wanting.

> De-blacking also occurs if a Black person decides to date or marry out-side the race. Although this standard has not been consistently applied, it remains true today that dating or marrying a non-Black person . . . speaks volumes to the Soul Patrol about the person's acceptance of a Black racial identity, or rather a person's denial of such.[11]

That's what many black women fear—the perception that dating outside the race may lead to questions about authenticity and identity. But as these scholars with their multitude of definitions and arguments illustrate, and as we all already know, "blackness" isn't a monolith of skin tones, dance steps, and seasoned chicken. Those may be cultural traits that many of us enjoy, but they are only parts of a much larger fabric.

> The problem comes when we begin placing value on one's level of identification with blackness—when being more black makes you "down" and being less black makes you a sellout. That's also the point at which we cross the line from talking about blackness to talking about black authenticity. Black authenticity contains the value judgment of blackness; it concerns whether you are a *real* brother or sister or whether you're some Uncle Tom cornball. It's also about assigning or rejecting membership to the black community based on adherence to acceptable behaviors. And that's a problem—especially when based on trivial behaviors like how someone dresses, dances or speaks. No doubt that there's plenty of that going around.
>
> So where does that leave us? Is it even worth attempting to define blackness? Is it too diverse to place any parameters on it? If we can define it, do we only create more division by doing so? Or is the issue of authenticity the real problem?[12]

If authenticity is the real problem, we're stuck. We can't define blackness, so we can't define who is authentic. In fact, the whole discussion is like a dog chasing its tail: we go round and round, but we never really get anywhere. And without a definition of authentic blackness, it's very difficult to define the behavior or circumstances that qualify as a betrayal of that blackness. In other words, if we can't define "blackness," it's really tough to label *anyone* a sellout. In the end, those who insist on using labels like "sellout" and "betrayal" reveal themselves to be believers in Norwood's "myth of one voice." Ultimately, "one voice" robs all of us of the opportunity to imagine our identities for ourselves. It steals our choices.

Tori says she always knew that she would be with someone of another race.

> I always knew there was a bigger world than the one that I was in. My mom said I always did my own thing. I did what made me happy. And I'm still that way. I love hair metal, and I want someone [as a partner] who

understands that. I love literature theory and I want [my spouse] to have something that he's just as passionate about. Some of the black men that I've come across are just so closed-minded about all the possibilities in the world. They accuse me of not being black enough when I ask if they've read W. E. B. DuBois. They're quoting all the lyrics to rap songs and they don't know DuBois first wrote about a lot of what they're rapping about. When I go home [to the housing project in Woonsocket, Rhode Island], some of the guys I went to school with are still there. They accuse me of being a sellout [because I got an education, a good job, and date interracially]. They say I always acted like I was better than them. I tell them no, I acted like I wanted something better than [the housing project]. I wanted to learn. I remind them that we went to the same schools in the same neighborhood. They had the same access that I had, but they chose differently. They chose to believe it wasn't "black" to be good in school. That it wasn't "black" to like to read. That "black" was only certain music and certain relationships. And look what that got them.

Tori illustrates the kind of thinking that many black women must embrace in order to reach beyond narrow and confining definitions of black identity that not only limit their romantic opportunities but also cripple their ability to reach for their highest good in all areas of their lives.

NOT SELLING OUT BUT DIVESTING

The concept of "selling out" is rooted in questionable notions of black solidarity. Divesting from those notions altogether makes "selling out" irrelevant. "Divesting," as defined by Lisa Vazquez, who writes about the issue frequently on her blog, blackwomenblowthetrumpet.blogspot.com, is the way for black women to achieve a new empowerment in our multiracial culture. It involves four steps:

1.   Dismantling the notions we have been conditioned to believe in without question in all-black constructs;

2. Removing financial, intellectual, and emotional energy from those concepts and situations that do not serve to further our individual goals and needs;

3. Diversifying to other cultures and ways of thought to expand our knowledge base and seek common ground; and

4. Dominating in a multicultural sphere by learning the ways in which power is used in a variety of settings.

These steps don't come with a manual or qualify as a "movement," Vazquez says. Instead, they require each individual woman to make her own journey into her heart and mind to heal the fractured racial and personal issues that lie there.

"Divestment is an imperative of our self-preservation as black women," she argues in an essay titled "Divestment and the Spiritual Quandary." "There are some women who believe that racial loyalty should have precedence over self-preservation. Where did *that* teaching come from? Racial loyalty is based on external identification and *not* on spiritual identification. Therein lies the problem. Too many of us claim that we are God's women but our mentality reveals that we place racial validation *above* any and everything. Many black women quickly bond with those who share their external characteristics rather than forging alliances with those who share spiritual characteristics that are aligned with our spiritual principles."

In other words, instead of circling the wagons around "black," we should seek to form loyalties with those of like mind and with those who show loyalty to us, whatever their racial backgrounds. Race loyalty may blind some black women to a more careful analysis of the realities of their situation—and of possible solutions, Vazquez suggests.

> At this think tank, we have examined many aspects of the conditioning that occurs in [all-black] constructs. The emotional baggage that most [black women in all-black environments] have unknowingly accepted seems to have fostered several fallacies:
>
> **Fallacy #1:** Black women have to take responsibility for black children.

Fallacy #2: Black women have to *prefer* black men above other men.

Fallacy #3: Living among all blacks proves blackness and affirms racial loyalty.

Fallacy #4: Black women should uplift/rescue black men in order to solidify their own destinies.

Fallacy #5: Black women are not highly desired by men of other races, so they should do everything they can to be validated and chosen by black men.

Fallacy #6: Leaving all-black constructs will result in social isolation among non-blacks and rejection by blacks who are in black constructs.

Fallacy #7: Divestment requires the rejection of black men.

When black women become divestors, several patterns will emerge:

After mastering effective vetting processes, more black women will forge economic and political alliances *outside of* the black community that will reap long-term tangible returns.

After dismantling racial baggage involving non-black men, more black women will choose non-black men as marital partners and will be in biracial and bicultural relationships.

After seeing masses of black women who have removed themselves from all-black constructs, black men will realize that they no longer have an automatic admission pass to the black "community."

After embracing the need to establish and enforce *their own* criteria of solidarity with black men, black women will no longer internalize the *"black pact"* mindset that reinforces nonreciprocal emotional contracts.[13]

In this essay and many others, Vazquez offers ideas for reexamining many of the notions that keep black women not only from exploring interracial dating, but also from breaking the bonds of other potentially dysfunctional relationships and situations. Her blog provides many useful insights for women ready to rethink what they've always thought and open themselves up to some new results.

The concept of "selling out" is really only relevant when "blackness" is at its narrowest scope, and a narrow definition of blackness robs not just single black women but all of us African Americans of a world of choices.

NOTION 9

We'd Be Too Different

> *I feel disconnected from white men, like I have to explain things that
> I wouldn't have to [explain] to a black man.*

> *I think some black women stay loyal to black men because they feel they
> have more in common with them. They don't have to worry about
> explaining certain things—culture, habits, beliefs, traditions, etc.*

As these email messages illustrate, many women assume that sharing a racial or ethnic background with a man gives the couple a "leg up" on compatibility, and for some, that assumption may be true. However, in 2008, the Centers for Disease Control's Annual Survey of Vital Statistics found that the divorce rate for African American couples was 12 percent compared to 10 percent for white and 7 percent for Hispanic couples in the period between July 2006 and July 2007. Clearly, a shared culture isn't enough to keep couples together.

Instead of race, most relationship experts say that compatibility, a sense of "shared mission," and acceptance of your partner's differences are the keys to a solid relationship. For the interracial couples I talked with, their racial differences led them to take more time in getting to know each other, which enabled them to determine their ultimate compatibility. Spending more time talking—before engaging in any kind of physical intimacy—enabled them to determine if they had the qualities that would enable their relationship to survive.

Evia Moore of blackfemaleinterracialmarriage.com relates this story from her own life in her book *First and Foremost:*

> I've also heard some black women say that they can't have a white mate because he won't be able to relate to the ins and outs of the "black experience," which means racism, the way a black man can or will. . . . A few years back, I went through a bout of unfair racial treatment with a white supervisor at work. I talked with my husband about it throughout the whole stressful time I was going through it. Though he had never experienced *racially* unfair treatment, he has experienced unfair treatment. Therefore, he could and did empathize and support me emotionally and otherwise during this ordeal because he saw the situation as being an example of the massive power difference between whites and blacks. The white male supervisor was simply taking advantage of the historic power embedded in the role of the white male who functions in the typical U.S. racist structure. Therefore, my husband helped me as I essentially reduced the power of the supervisor in this situation, and things turned out fine for me.
>
> The bottom line is that a good husband is a loving mate and he will somehow find a way to understand and support a woman he loves; it doesn't matter whether they share the same racial, cultural, or religious background.[1]

In my own experience, my husband has had a new sensitivity to racial issues that he admits he would not have had were it not for being married to me and having a daughter who is biracial. He often says that he sees the world completely differently now that he has a personal stake in another culture and is more conscious of racism and the role we all must play to eliminate it. As Kimberly Jade Norwood says, fighting racism isn't just for black people, it's for all people. In a way, black women in interracial marriages take the struggle against racism to, as they say, a "whole other level."

The best way to dispel the notion that people from different racial backgrounds are just "too different" for a relationship to work is to listen to actual interracial couples. Their stories reveal the ways in which people who look different on the outside can find a shared sense of mission, mutual acceptance, and a love that has the staying power to last a lifetime.

Jamie and Jarrod

Jamie: I'm really interested in fitness. I'm a longtime runner, and in 2003 I decided to train for the Chicago Marathon. The training regime is pretty strict and I knew I would do better if I joined a group. There are a lot of people training, so when you join, you end up in a pace group—a group of runners who run at about the same speed you do. Jarrod was in my pace group and we ended up running side by side for mile after mile, day after day and week after week.

Jarrod: When we met, I hadn't dated anyone seriously for years. I felt like I really needed something different—something life-changing. One of my clients had suggested that I run a marathon. "It's truly life-changing," she said. I thought about it and I decided to give it a try. I joined a running group that met on the Southside, which is a mostly black neighborhood in Chicago.

Jamie: Before meeting Jarrod I had dated only black men. It hadn't been going well. I was a professional woman with a college degree and a good job, but it seemed like I met nothing but losers, including one brother who stole money out of my purse while I was in the restroom. A couple of my friends in professional circles were saying, "You should date white guys." I wasn't opposed to it, but no white guys were approaching me, so I just figured there wasn't any interest there. Meanwhile, my girlfriends and I were trying everything looking for a good black man: church, online dating, sports bars. *Essence* did an article once called "Date a Blue-Collar Man" or something like that. I remember all of us dutifully followed their advice. I was dating a city bus driver for a while. And that was fine; he was a nice guy. But we had nothing to talk about. I couldn't imagine taking him to one of my work events. He would have been out of place and uncomfortable. In the end, it just sort of fizzled out.

Jarrod: Jamie is the first black woman I ever dated. When we met, I hadn't dated in a long time—several years. I'd been in school, finishing my PhD, and that had been the focus of most of my energies. But with school behind me, I was ready to meet someone and be in a relationship. I had started looking online and the profiles I was looking at were only white women. Nothing was really clicking with anyone from online. Meanwhile, I was doing the running group on the Southside and most of the participants were African Americans, just because the Southside is more of a black neighborhood. I was probably one of just a handful of white people in this fairly large group. Janine and I were just running buddies at first. We ran and we talked and we ran. Sometimes after a run we'd go out with a group of fellow runners and hang out. I started to realize that there was a connection there, that I really enjoyed talking to her. But then she got hurt and couldn't train anymore. We kept the connection alive with emails and occasional phone calls for a few months. Then in January 2004, I called her and said, "I want to take you out. On a date."

Jamie: He called and asked me to dinner and the movies. I really thought at first he was asking me to just hang out with him as a friend, but he made it very clear that wasn't his intention. He said, "I like you, and I'm asking you out on a date." There was this split second when I strongly considered telling him no. I thought, "Where could this possibly lead?" But it had been a long time since I'd had a date with anyone, and I was intrigued by his directness. I already knew him from all that time in the running club, and so I knew we'd have things to talk about and a good time. So I said yes and now I'm really glad I did. I would have missed out on a good thing if I'd said no that first night.

Jarrod: We went to dinner and a movie, and then we went to one of my friends' birthday party. I introduced her to almost everyone in my life that first night!

Jamie: He was a total gentleman. He picked me up at my house, paid for everything, was very charming and respectful. We had fun together. By our second or third date, he told me, "I consider you my girlfriend." That sort of surprised me. Usually when you go out with someone, there's this awkward period where you know things are going well, but you don't know whether it's serious or not. There's all this back and forth: "Does he like me? Does he like me as much as I like him? Are we a couple?" Jarrod made it clear that he wanted me, but I was still nervous about it. For the first year we dated, I kept waiting for the other shoe to drop. I kept waiting for him to say, "So, I've been thinking maybe we should see other people." It never happened.

Jarrod: In the first six months that we dated, I was aware of people staring at us, but we've been together now for five years, and I really don't care anymore. Race does come up in our relationship from time to time. Jamie tends to see things I don't see, especially on issues like gentrification and crime. I sometimes think she sees race when it isn't there. But I also know I have it easier than she does. I know being white brings privilege in this country.

Jamie: We don't fight, but we do have disagreements. We don't scream and we don't yell, but we definitely see the world differently from time to time. He was shocked, for example, when I told him that I had been a member of [controversial minister] Reverend Jeremiah Wright's church. He started telling white people that I was an "internal terrorist," which is hardly true. Things like [Wright] get taken out of their context by people who don't understand the culture that creates them. So we disagree from time to time—strongly. But in terms of our personal relationship, there's very little drama on a day-to-day basis.

Jacquetta and Greg

Jacquetta: I grew up in farm country in a little town on Maryland's Eastern Shore. I was raised by my mother, who had a master's degree and worked for a nearby college. We didn't integrate well with the other blacks in the area. First of all, I was interested in school, which separated me from most of the kids in the black community. They teased me because of the way I talked and because I liked school. Second, my mother was very liberal, very forward-thinking. My mother dated men outside her race: white, Indian, and others. Some of her extended family members had real trouble with it. Even as a kid, I really hated the small-town life. I couldn't wait to get out of there.

Fortunately, I was admitted into a gifted and talented program. It saved me. I had been miserable in the regular school setting, but the GT program put me in classes with a mixed group of students from all different ethnic and racial backgrounds that were philosophically liberal and focused on achievement.

At fourteen, I went to a boarding school for high school, which was yet another academic environment. I spent summers as a camp counselor and I met a lot of men from other countries doing that. After high school, I went to Sarah Lawrence College in New York. In high school and college, I dated a lot of British guys; for some reason I seemed to attract them. I have never been approached by black men at all. I guess I was too nerdy, or too preppy and academic. Also, because of the way I was raised and the places where I went to school, I wasn't as clued in to the sexuality that was part of the culture.

After college, I found myself in London, dating British guys, of course. In Europe, there's a clear difference between Africans and African Americans. You are really more of an American than anything else. It was freeing. Liberating. I remember thinking, "Wow, I can actually date whoever I want and no one cares." I had no problem meeting men. Easy to meet a guy and date and move on. Eventually, I met my first husband, who wasn't British at all. He was Hungarian. We were married for a couple of years, but it just didn't work out. We divorced and I decided to make some life changes. I went back to school and got a degree in education. I teach elementary school by day, but by night I'm a comedian. I play frequently in several New York City comedy clubs.

When I was ready to date again, I put an ad on craigslist.com searching specifically for a white guy. Over the years I've just realized that that's my preference. They give me the least hassle, they're less macho, and I'm used to them. I like what a lot of black people consider to be "weird stuff." I like music that's not black. I'm not at all religious. I like to travel. I like gay people. I'm interested in medieval studies. None of these things is considered "typical" in the black community.

My ad got a ton of responses—mostly from older Jewish guys and Italian guys, but also some from angry black guys who didn't like that I was a black woman seeking a white man. I was like "Why are you on here? Why are you trying to harass me?" That was really frustrating. My feeling is that black men expect black women to cater to them. They seem to think they are endangered and that because there's so few of them, women should be turning cartwheels to be in their company. To be honest, that's not me. And then there's something about the approach. If you're not going to approach me respectfully, then just don't bother. And there's the issue of parity. Once you get education and property, you want someone with the same level of education. If you don't have those things, I don't want to talk to you. And finally, there are more white guys, period.

Greg was one of the people who answered my craigslist.com ad. I liked his response and we started emailing. I was emailing lots of people and I really thought I'd be meeting and dating a lot of people for a while. But when we met, I knew it was all over. We dated for two years and married in 2007.

Sometimes when we're walking together in New York City, my husband will get some angry glares from black men. Occasionally someone will yell something or mutter something just loud enough for us to hear. But I really don't care. As far as I'm concerned, those people have issues, not us. Unfortunately, his parents have had a hard time with our relationship. They are Greek immigrants and I think they've been insufferable. I hope they'll get over it in time, but so far, no good.

We don't have kids yet, but we hope to. We live in a mixed neighborhood with lots of different cultures. That's what's great about New York City; it's a pretty good insulator because it's so diverse. But I expect we will have to raise our children to appreciate how color can shape identity in this country. I wish that weren't so, but it is.

Greg: My parents disowned me when I decided to marry Jacquetta two years ago, and while I sometimes talk to my mother, I haven't spoken to my father since then.

Both my parents are Cypriot Greeks. There is a difference between the culture of the island of Cyprus and that on the Greek mainland. There's a lot of history there—not all of it friendly. Up until 2003, there were still demarcation lines between Greeks and Turks on Cyprus and there was still a wall between sections that are Cypriot and sections that are Turkish with border patrols to maintain those separations. Cyprus is part of Greece, but even Greeks recognize that, in many ways, Cypriots are a people unto themselves.

My father came here when he was seventeen. My mother was born here, but her parents immigrated to this country from Cyprus. She grew up in New York City, but after my parents married they moved to Webster, Massachusetts, where I was born and raised. Webster is a small community, a very Polish Catholic town. Not at all diverse. There's a small Greek community of which we were a part. For my elementary education I went to a small private school that was mostly Polish Catholic, then I did one year in a Catholic high school. I didn't like that at all and transferred to a public high school, but it was still a very small school. My graduating class had one hundred students: all Catholic, a few Greeks, very few blacks or Latinos.

After high school, I went to the University of Massachusetts, then Brooklyn Law School. I wanted to do criminal law, and after law school I started working with the Brooklyn District Attorney's office, which I did for seven years before opening my own practice three years ago. I didn't start dating until I went to college. My parents were very strict, all about school, determined that I graduate from high school with good grades. As a result, I was number two in my high school class and got a scholarship to UMass, but I didn't really have much time for girls. In college, I did date. I dated white American women, spent a summer at Oxford and dated British women. I also met a Cypriot girl in London. I also dated a black woman in either my freshman or sophomore year, I don't recall which.

I did well at University of Massachusetts, graduating with two BAs, English and poli-sci. Minor in journalism. I was also in a serious relationship with a white woman, but it didn't work out. After law school I just dated who I met on the occasions when I went out to clubs or bars or wherever.

When I turned thirty, I decided to give the Greek thing a try. My parents were involved in the Cypriot community and arranged some dates. They were terrible experiences . . . just really bad dates! I tried some Greek dating sites, then looked for Greek matches on craigslist .com. I remember I went back to Webster for a really bad first and last date on my birthday and that was enough of that.

I knew I wanted a woman who was educated, liberal-thinking, and athletic: those are the three most important factors for me. When I read Jacquetta's ad on craigslist, she had mentioned these same criteria and she sounded smart and independent and fun. I remember her advertisement mentioning all the usual stuff too: height requirements, income, etc. I ignored those. Who knows what a woman means by those? I knew that, as an attorney, I was financially secure, so I just focused on her qualities. We started emailing back and forth and our first date was six days later, March 27, 2004.

We really hit it off. We were both sort of dating other people, but those others got dropped pretty quickly. We were so compatible that things between us got pretty serious pretty quickly.

My parents were *not* happy.

My dad—being non-American-born—has been very upset about it. He wanted a Greek Cypriot girl. He might have been upset about any non-Greek girl. To his way of thinking, the only thing worse than [choosing Jacquetta] would have been a Turkish girl [because of the history between Turks and Greeks]. My mom is in a tough spot. She's American-born and taught school in New York City for a while. She's used to more diversity. I kept telling my mom, "Once you meet her, you'll love her. She's a teacher, you're a teacher. You have a lot in common!"

But neither of my parents has ever met my wife. When I told them we were getting married, my parents drove from Webster down to

New York. I thought they were finally going to meet Jacquetta. But when they got there, they called and asked me to come outside, where they begged me to break it off with Jacquetta. When I refused and begged them to come in and meet her, they said no. My dad shook my hand, then he and my mother got back in the car and drove back to Webster.

Jacquetta and I were married in 2007.

None of my family came to the wedding. My brother lives in Japan; he says he can't get in the middle of it. My aunt met Jacquetta but didn't want to get in the middle of it either. I don't think my extended family really cares about my interracial relationship one way or the other, but they don't want to anger my father.

One of my friends actually went to my parents and told them, "This is crazy," but my dad got up and left. When Mom calls, she says he loves me and he misses me, but he still can't accept the choice I've made.

I look at it as Greek stubbornness. They will come around. Time flies, I have a life. Running a practice is a full-time job, being married and spending time together, we barely make time for friends. I'm sure they miss me more than I miss them, aging in their big house alone. Eventually, I believe my mom will start to reengage and pressure my dad into getting together with us. In the meantime, I'm not overly concerned. If they lived closer, that might be a different story, or if I were sitting around doing nothing. But as it is, I have a very full, busy life.

We're talking about starting a family, and I think when we do my parents will come around. But will we want them to then, after all this? I don't know. God help anyone who says anything to me about my kids—including my parents. I just won't stand for that. I won't.

At this point, I'm not pushing Jacquetta to meet them, not when they've behaved in such a bigoted, disappointing way. It would be nice if they apologized, but they think I need to give *them* an apology because I "just threw this at them." I think that's ridiculous. They're wrong, plain and simple.

As for Jacquetta and me, I have no regrets. None whatsoever. I'm a pretty lucky guy. I've found a wonderful woman whom I love and who loves me. We're happy, enjoying our life together.

Cynthia and Mike

Cynthia: We met online in March 2007 on Yahoo Personals. His profile said, "God, family, country," in that order. I liked that. I had some very specific things I was looking for in a man, and I had listed them. Also on most dating websites you'll check off things like height and weight and income. I'd done all of that. He wrote me a very nice email, saying he liked my profile but he didn't meet my income standard. He told me he hoped I found what I was looking for. I thought he was very nice, very honest. I liked his approach, so I answered him.

Mike: I had been married before. Twice. I had done some real soul-searching before looking for another relationship and I knew I was looking for some very specific things. I wanted someone who saw the world as I did religiously and spiritually. Someone who shared my work ethic and my values. I was looking for someone who I knew that, as we grew older, we would be friends. I was hoping that she would be attractive, but the package didn't matter as much as the qualities. I really liked her profile, but I didn't really expect for anything to come from my reply. She was in Kentucky and I was still in school in Florida [pursuing a second bachelor's degree as a part of a career change] and I was pleasantly surprised when she answered me. [The two exchanged emails and eventually started talking on the phone.]

Cynthia: I liked him. Almost from those first emails, we just hit it off. He's very humble and able to laugh at himself. Talking with him felt very natural, like meeting a friend you didn't know you had. Once we started talking on the phone, we kept talking. His roots were in Kentucky—along with his children from his prior marriage—and I was in Kentucky. But because he was in school in Florida when we met, it was May before we actually sat down across from each other, face-to-face.

Mike: Cynthia was the first black woman I'd ever dated. I had some slight concerns in the back of my mind when we both started to realize that there was potential there. Not just because of race, but for all kinds of reasons. As I said, I had been married before. I have two kids; she has one. There are a lot of things to think about when you realize you're falling in love. But I remember we had a conversation and she asked me how I was going to handle the potential racial complications. The people I was most concerned with were my family, mostly my mom. I have a stepfather, but we aren't that close. But my mom's reaction was important to me. I called my mom and I said, "What would you think if I dated a black woman?" She was real cool about it. She said there might be issues with other people, but not as far as she was concerned. My grandfather—her father— he wasn't happy. But he comes from a different generation. He was a career military officer and I think he was always very concerned with appearances, what other people are going to think. He didn't come to the wedding, but later, when he met Cynthia, they got along well. He got over it once he met her and understood what kind of person she is.

Cynthia: Mike is my second husband—my second white husband. My family was sort of over the whole interracial thing when I told them Mike and I were going to get married. We'd already been down that road. My mother was more concerned that we hadn't known each other very long. She thought the whole thing was happening too fast, but other than that, she was fine with it. She met Mike just a couple of weeks before the wedding, but they got along well. It helps that he's such an honest, Christian, humble man. My daughter likes him too. That was very important to me. Other than family, I really don't care what other people think. I'm proud to be a black American, but the truth is most of us are mixed somehow. My grandmother was a white woman and most black Americans are mixed with something. This country is a melting pot and culture/heritage can be a double-edged sword. It's something that gives you pride and roots, but it's also something you can hold too tightly to. Defining yourself in a limited way can ultimately be a problem.

Mike: I think Cynthia is beautiful—inside and out. I'm a lucky guy.

Brian and Crystal

Crystal: I'm twenty-three and we've been married for four years. When we got married, I was nineteen and a sophomore at University of Maryland. I married Brian six months after I met him—I know, no one does that anymore. But we did. Our daughter, Madison, was born five months ago.

I grew up in northwest Washington, D.C., in a very large house near Rock Creek Park. In addition to my parents and me, there was my grandmother and my aunt in the household. Both of my parents work for the federal government: my mother has been with the National Institutes of Health for most of her career, and my father has worked for several federal agencies. He's currently with Homeland Security.

I went to an all-black, Catholic preschool as a very little kid. But when I was six, my family moved to Montgomery Village, Maryland. Then I went to an almost all-white public elementary school in Bethesda, Maryland. There were a few other black kids in the school, but I was the only one in my grade. It wasn't until high school that I really had classes with students of all different backgrounds, but I adjusted well. I've never had a problem with finding friends and I've always had friends of very stripe.

All of my boyfriends before my husband were men of color— usually African Americans, but I also dated guys from Puerto Rico and Panama. I don't really have a type, though I do like athletic guys. I dated the quarterback of the football team in my senior year. But I'm athletic too. I play soccer, I dance, and I was a cheerleader. I'm attracted to bad boys—the angry ones who like to fight—but I've mostly dated nice guys who were kind of quiet and reserved. I think I attract those guys because I'm very social and outgoing.

After high school, I went to Hampton University in Virginia. It's a historically black college and I went there because, after all my experiences with diversity, I wanted to see what it was like to go to an all-black school. I transferred to University of Maryland College Park after only one year there. It just wasn't what I thought it would be. I wanted to go to school far from home to have freedom, but Hampton was actually very restrictive. We had dress codes and curfews and I was like, no. That wasn't what I had hoped college would be like. I had more freedom at home, so I transferred to a school less than ten miles from where my parents live.

On the night I met Brian, some girlfriends had asked me to go with them to a club downtown, and I almost didn't go. I hadn't been dating much, and I didn't have a boyfriend. Even though I was young, I knew that I wanted marriage and a family. It seemed like I wasn't meeting guys who were interested in anything serious or long-term. And it seemed like I was having bad luck attracting "good brothers." I had joked to my mom that I was fed up with black guys. "I'm going to find myself a white guy!" I told her. I was being dramatic and she just laughed. But then I went out that night and did exactly that.

He was with a whole group of guys; you could tell they played football or something, they were all huge. All of the guys I saw were black; I didn't see Brian at all. My girls and I started dancing near them, thinking maybe when they saw a group of girls dancing, a few of them might ask us to dance. So I'm there dancing and this guy says to me, "Are you just going to dance in front of me and not *with* me?"

That guy turned out to be this cute white guy. He was a terrible dancer but he asked for my number and I gave it to him and he called me the next day and asked me out on a date. I'd never been formally "asked out" before. It's always been you just start hanging with someone until you're girlfriend and boyfriend. There was no way I was going to turn him down, after being asked like that.

Things got serious fast.

Brian: She was dancing right in my space—in the bubble, you know? I figured if she was going to get that close, we'd better dance. She says she didn't see me, but I think she did.

We danced, but it was hard for me. I'd hurt my knee running the bleachers at the stadium earlier that week. I knew I was on the verge of quitting football too. I'd been hurt before, but that was the moment that something deep inside me said no. I knew I wouldn't be a football player much longer and I didn't have high expectations of what my dating life would be like without that.

The best way I can describe my dating experiences before Crystal is to say that I was not the predator but the prey. Girls were always hovering around me: girls of all races, girls of all backgrounds. I was an All-American and I guess they thought I was some kind of "golden ticket." So I had "hookups" but I never really had a serious relationship. I just didn't trust these women. In the beginning, I wasn't sure of Crystal either. When I finally did quit the team and walked away from football, I fully expected her to disappear. She didn't. For a while I sort of wanted her to disappear . . . but she didn't.

"You love me," she told me when I told her I thought I wanted to see other people. "I know you do."

She was right, but it took me a while to understand and accept what that meant.

I'm the kind of guy who does his own thing. I like to do what no one else does. I've always been like that. I grew up in Rockville, Maryland, which is a suburb of Washington, D.C. My neighborhood is mixed and I'm still friends with the kids I grew up with. One of my best friends is Pakistani; another is white; another is black. Playing sports, you build bonds with your teammates and race isn't a factor.

When it was time to go to school, I was tested to be significantly above grade level, so I skipped from the first grade to the fourth at the age of six. The stress of being a six-year-old fourth grader was too much and I just stopped going. I guess you could say I was an elementary school dropout. Finally I was enrolled in the Episcopal Center for Children, which is a kind of alternative school, and by sixth grade I was back in public schools. Middle school was a nightmare: I went to four of them in three years, basically because I would finish my work, get bored, and just leave. I'd walk around the building until dismissal. This would go on until, eventually, I'd get expelled. Then my parents would enroll me in another school and we'd start all over.

It wasn't until high school that things started to change. I decided I wanted to play football and made the junior varsity team, even though I was sort of small and scrawny. Over the next year I had this huge growth spurt and shot up a foot and gained about sixty pounds. And I learned football and got very good at it. Good enough to get a football scholarship to University of Tennessee. I played there for a year, got hurt, and got sidelined for a year. I decided to transfer: I really hated Tennessee. It was a real culture shock for me. My family isn't religious, but they had a bus come to take the entire team to church every Sunday. For me, that was a turnoff. But there wasn't anything else to do! I was bored, bored, bored, and while I was recuperating, University of Maryland called and asked me if I'd like to come play there.

I transferred. Again I had a scholarship, but after I got there, I just didn't feel like football. I quit. They were pretty mad at me. Of course they yanked the scholarship. I wasn't sure what I wanted to do, so I took just one class—enough to stay enrolled—while I sorted myself out. After I'd had time to think, I decided I did want to play, so I had to go try out. Hundreds of guys tried out, but only about two made it. I made it. They let me back on the team—without a scholarship this time—and I was playing when I met Crystal.

She was the only girl I met that night at the club who was memorable. I thought she was pretty and seemed smart and fun. I was with a bunch of my teammates. We almost didn't go out that night and we'd made it to the club very late.

The more we hung out, the more I liked her. When she didn't quit on me when I decided not to pursue football as a career, I liked her even more for that. I had been around so many girls who were only interested in me for being a football star that I was a little jaded. But Crystal didn't seem to care whether I played or not, she just wanted me to be happy with my choice. It's weird when you meet someone who cares about you that much. I guess that's why I wanted to break up with her after quitting football—I was a little scared of being in a relationship with a woman who really just wanted me, as I am. But when I realized she was right, that I really did love her, that was that. Like I said, I tend to see things a little differently than most guys my age, and from my analysis, it seemed stupid to wait. I asked her to marry me and we went to the courthouse and just did it.

Crystal: Then we did it again for our families.

Brian: I pretty much dropped out of college, then started our [home inspection services] business. Crystal finished her degree but now we work together, building the business and raising our daughter. It works because she really understands me and how my mind works. A lot of women try to change their guys; she's never done that. She accepts me for who I am, not what I do. Don't get me wrong, Crystal's not shy about telling me how she feels about something—or when she disagrees with me. But she's not trying to change me and I'm not trying to change her. We accept each other for who we are as people.

Crystal: Our parents really haven't had any trouble with our relationship. My parents really wanted me to finish college, and I did. But that was their most serious concern. We live near both our families and see them often. It's really been no problem. But once again, living in an area like ours [suburbs of Washington, D.C.] where there are so many different cultures and nationalities makes a big difference. I think people here are more used to seeing mixed-race couples and their children.

Joan and David

Joan: David and I have been married for seventeen years and I'm sure we'll be married for the rest of our lives. But it really is sort of amazing that we got together. We are so very different in just about every way. First of all, I was born in St. Vincent in the Caribbean, the fifth of nine children. I grew up very poor in a two-room house that had no electricity or running water until the late 1970s. My father was a farmer, and so all of us kids had chores: tending animals, fetching the water for washing and cooking. But my mother was absolutely militaristic about education, and all of us attended the British schools—St. Vincent was a British colony until 1979—and the schools provided a very proper British education, even though it was basically a one-room schoolhouse.

At fifteen, all students took an examination that pretty much determined your future career path: teacher, nurse, or police officer. I took the teachers' examination and passed it, but that was just the first step to actually becoming a teacher. You have to work as an aide, you go to school, and you take more tests. While I was still a teachers' aide, there was a union dispute with the government and I and some of my fellow students joined the strike. We were arrested, dismissed from the teaching program, and that was that. They finally let me finish my degree but I couldn't get a job. So when I got out of school, I immigrated to the United States.

My experiences with law enforcement made me realize just how important having a good attorney was, so I decided that I would go to law school. It was a long road, because I basically had to go to college again first, then apply to law school. I ended up at State University of New York Syracuse School of Law, and that's where I met David. He went to a different school, but he was there doing a summer mini-course. He used to hang out in the library where my friends and I congregated.

I didn't like him. He was this quiet type who just insisted on hanging around me and my friends. He was always talking to me. We couldn't have been more different: I was this social, Caribbean woman with a big natural and a criminal record, and he was this very pale, very easygoing white boy. But he was very persistent and very patient.

At the time I was dating another guy—a man from St. Vincent who was tall and dark and good-looking, but who was also unfaithful. David was the opposite: he did what he said he would. He went out of his way to take me places and to do what I liked. He put me on a pedestal. I knew I wasn't competing with other women. And more and more, I started to trust him.

I was raised to believe that you could tell a lot about a man by the way he treats his mother and his sisters. In the islands, they say that a man who loves his mother and gets along well with his sisters will make a good husband. David took good care of his mother. Even though he was in law school in Connecticut, he frequently drove back to Syracuse to check on her. And when he did, he also checked on me. I had no doubts about his sincerity or his fidelity. When he asked me to marry him in our third year, I said yes.

We really didn't experience any problems as an interracial couple until I came to Washington, D.C., in 1990, after I graduated from law school. David's job kept him in New York, but I got a two-bedroom apartment, thinking that it would be good to have the extra space when David moved down for good. In the meantime, I advertised for a roommate to help cover expenses. This Nigerian medical student took the place, but I guess he thought I came with it. He kept making passes at me, and finally, when David came down and this guy saw him, he got nasty. "What a waste!" he said contemptuously. I kicked him out immediately. It was ironic to me because this man clearly had only sexual interest in me, while David had offered that and so much more. I don't know why so many black men find it so difficult to be faithful to just one black woman, but it's an experience I've had and seen many, many times.

After that, we decided that David should just move down to Washington and look for a job here. We had other experiences like that, walking around Washington together. Black guys made us miserable in those first few months. "Sister, you're with the wrong man!" and things like that. A lot of stares. A lot of whispers. I don't notice it much now, but I did then. David didn't react to it much at all. I know he was preoccupied by his job search then. He had money on his mind and he just didn't let any of those comments distract him.

We were married in 1992, and within a few months of being husband and wife, I admit I was a little rattled by it all. There was a moment where I thought, "What have I done?" I was actually a little surprised at myself to have married this soft-spoken white guy who was so different from me. I wondered if it could really work "till death do us part." I had said the vows, but I still hadn't really sorted it all out in my head. So I decided to go back to St. Vincent for a few months. I was studying for the bar examination [to practice law there], but I was also trying to figure out how I really felt about the marriage. It wasn't really the interracial part—though that was part of it. I just wasn't sure. I loved David, but I worried that our personalities would clash. I was afraid that love wouldn't be enough when he was so quiet and laid-back and I was so outgoing.

My trip to St. Vincent saved our marriage. I had the chance to really think about what I was doing, about why I married David, about what mattered most to me in a relationship. I missed him. When I came back, I knew we would be okay.

We have two children, a girl who is now thirteen and a boy who is ten. In our neighborhood, there are kids of all different races and mixes and so being biracial usually isn't a problem for them. In fact, my son likes to say that he is "gray." We usually don't identify them as one race or the other, though some of the forms in the schools are changing. They want to require us to check the boxes, which I would prefer not to do. My daughter has had a few struggles because of her light skin and long wavy hair, but to me, that is far less important than her education. It's most important to me that both of my children do well in school.

Pat and Tom

Pat: I was born in Alabama, but when I was almost two, my parents moved to Indianapolis. That was 1966. I was the middle child of seven and I started public school in 1971. I spent the first few years of my education in a neighborhood school that was all black. But by the time I was in fourth grade, I was bused from our home in the projects to an integrated school.

I wasn't apprehensive about going to a new school at all: I was excited. And the experience was on the whole a positive one for me. I was constantly being teased by the black kids in my neighborhood because my skin was dark. At the integrated school I hung out with mostly white kids who really didn't make much distinction between one black kid's skin tone and the next one. I remember this one girl yelling "HL! HL!" at me one day. I had no idea what that meant, and finally I had to ask her what she was saying. "Honky Lover!" she said. "HL!"

I don't remember being particularly hurt by that: the kids who were my friends were my friends. I was invited to their homes to play badminton and for other games but they never came to mine. That was mostly because my parents divorced in 1976 and my mother had to work very hard to support the seven of us. My father was supposed to pay just forty dollars a week in child support—just forty dollars a week! He never paid any of it. He was an alcoholic and he had issues, but it still makes me angry. He was my earliest role model for how a man was supposed to treat a woman, and I don't think he did a very good job.

Even though I had so many white friends, my boyfriends were all black. At thirteen, I had my first serious crush on a guy named Michael, but we never really dated. I didn't go to my proms because I got involved with my older sister's boyfriend's brother, a guy named Raymond. He was very streetwise and verbally and emotionally abusive to me. Being with him left me very depressed, very insecure. He would say he was coming over and he wouldn't show up. Or he'd show up drunk at two or three in the morning. I finally got so depressed I went to see a psychiatrist and started to realize that it was my father all over again. I was re-creating my childhood. So I decided to break up with him and start seeing someone else.

Raymond didn't want to break up. He came over with a gun and started slapping me around. Fortunately my mother came out of her bedroom and stopped anything worse from happening. After high school, I joined the Army and was in the military for eight years. I started a new pattern: dating married men. Not intentionally. A couple of times they told me they were separated or in the process of divorce, and I later learned that wasn't true. Other times I didn't find out until there was a relationship going. I dated five men who turned out to be married in a row while I was in the Army! It was like my energy was bad. I just kept attracting men who would treat me badly . . . and unfortunately, they were all black men, because I never thought of dating outside the race at all. I just felt like I couldn't do it.

When I left the military at the age of twenty-six, I had had it. I didn't date anyone for a long time. I just worked and came home, and worked and came home. Sometimes I went out with my girlfriends and we'd talk about getting a man. But I just felt like I'd been through so much with men, I wasn't that interested.

I had one white male friend who was really into the sisters. He used to say that he was a black man trapped in a white man's body. He was a good guy and he thoroughly enjoyed and appreciated black women—including me—but I just wasn't attracted to him. Boy, did he try to convince me to give him a chance. But I couldn't. I just wasn't physically attracted to him at all. He was sort of big, with a big gut. That's never really turned me on.

Meanwhile, I met this guy at my church that I kind of liked, but it just didn't seem to be going anywhere. I learned later he was just flirting with me to try to make someone else jealous, so that was that. When I turned thirty-five, I decided I'd really give the whole "manhunt" one more shot. I was talking to one of my coworkers, and she said, "If you want to find a man, you have to go where the men go," and she suggested working in a hardware store. After all, that's man heaven! I already had a pretty heavy work schedule, but I decided to get a part-time job at the local hardware store. Tom was one of my coworkers. I saw him around, but I really didn't pay him much attention. Not only is he white, but he's got this big long beard and a belly on him. He just wasn't my type at all. My vision for my husband was a slender, dark-skinned black guy, well-spoken and clean-shaven. I did meet a guy like that at the hardware store, but he was ten years younger than me. The age difference meant I was always explaining things to him, and worse, I discovered he had a bad temper and tended to drink too much. I'd already been there, done that, too many times before. I cut him loose pretty quickly.

Then one day, Tom started talking to me in the break room. We were just standing there, near the vending machine, and he struck up a conversation. He showed me a picture of his son. Then he asked me if I was married. As soon as he asked me that, I thought, "Oh no." I suspected he was interested in me and I just didn't want to go there.

He was waiting for me after work. He told me he was going to ask me out soon and I was like, "Okay, sure, right." A couple of weeks later, I could tell he was ready, so I tried to avoid him. Finally he caught me long enough to ask for my number. I didn't give it to him but took his instead. But I didn't call him. Weeks went by and I didn't call him. Finally he called me at work and we talked. It was a nice talk. He called again and we talked. And he called again and we talked again. I still wasn't into him, but he was easy to talk to. I had never dated a white guy, but this was comfortable. I told my mother about him and she seemed excited for me. She kept saying, "This could be the guy. The one you've been waiting for." So finally I agreed to go out with him.

I have to paint this picture for you. I'm about 5'3" and at the time I was a little heavier, maybe 180 pounds. I had dreadlocks and dark brown skin. Tom is this heavyset guy who looks like some kind of biker or like one of the members of the band ZZ Top—big long beard, big belly. I'm sure we made an odd-looking couple, but after my initial hesitation, I found myself very comfortable with him. So much so that I forgot about how we looked. We were at the mall a couple of weeks after we started dating, walking along, holding hands, and this young black woman stopped in the middle of the concourse and glared at us. "I don't believe this!" she said, shaking her head at us. "I just don't believe this!"

I didn't know this woman at all. She was a total stranger, but she felt like she could just start in on us like that. It was very upsetting. I was sweating, I was so upset. I really wanted to run out of the mall. Another time, a black woman kept hissing "perp" at me from a nearby table while we were having dinner in a restaurant. "Perp" like "perpetrator." Like she felt I was betraying blackness with my dreadlocks and this white man. It's been my experience that the black men just glare at us, but the black women? They're right up in your face.

But my family loved him and that was all that really mattered to me. He's a great guy, a real sweetheart of a man. We've been married nine years and are still going strong. All of those things I thought were problems in the beginning are so unimportant now. He's the last thing I expected and the greatest thing I could have ever imagined. I know how lucky I am to have found him.

Tom: When I first met her, the first thing that I noticed was her great cleavage! But the second thing I noticed was how pretty she was: she has the prettiest smile and the most beautiful lips. Once we got over the initial b.s., we found we really enjoy each other. We can really make each other laugh and that's a good thing in a relationship.

The girlfriend I had before Pat was also black. Before that, I was married, and my ex-wife is white. We have a son together; he's twenty-two now. My family is small—just my mother and a sister and brother. They all love Pat and so does my son. That was all that mattered to me: that she get along with my family and my son, and Kurt, my best friend. Kurt and I have been friends since the first grade, back in 1956; he's like a brother to me. If I have some distant cousin who has a problem with my wife being black, I couldn't care less.

I was born and raised in Indianapolis. I started school in the 1950s—before integration—so there were no black kids in my schools until high school. There were no blacks in my neighborhood either. I saw black people when we visited my grandparents, who lived in a more mixed community. But I didn't really have black friends until I moved to Oklahoma and the only job I could get was working with an all-black bricklaying crew. Those guys were my friends, I got along with everyone. But that's really how I approach everyone: I like people, all kinds of people.

I work for the city of Indianapolis and a lot of my coworkers are black. Recently, this young black guy joined the job, and when he saw Pat's picture on my cell phone, he was surprised to learn she was my wife. It was funny, because after that he started trying to talk to me about rap music and stuff like that! My wife is black, but I really don't know anything about rap music! I think that's a generational thing, but it was kind of funny.

If people react to us as a couple or because of how we look, it doesn't really matter to me. I think that's *their* problem, not mine. Pat's a beautiful and sweet lady and I love her. To me, that's the most important thing.

Marvine and Chris

Marvine: I was born in 1971 in Brooklyn, New York. Both of my parents are Haitian immigrants. My father emigrated in the late 1960s, but he lived in Canada for few years before moving to the United States. My mother came to Brooklyn from Haiti in 1969. They dated long-distance, then married and lived in different neighborhoods of New York City for sixteen years. Then we moved to Springfield, Virginia, which is one of the suburbs of Washington, D.C.

I went to elementary school in Brooklyn and I had a lot of black friends, but my best friend was a little white boy named Phillip who lived across the street from me. I remember playing with him after school a lot because we were the same age and lived so close together. Our neighborhood was racially mixed, but our building wasn't. By then we had moved from Brooklyn to Queens and we lived in a co-op that was probably 90 percent Jewish.

I think my very first crush was on a Puerto Rican kid. I was probably eleven or twelve. I don't recall race having anything to do with it. I just thought he was cool!

We moved to Springfield, Virginia, when I was in high school. I dated white guys because there weren't that many black guys at my school. The guy I went to prom with was white. My parents didn't have much of a reaction to that; they are from Haiti and the whole "black/white" thing is different in the Caribbean. But I do remember my black high school girlfriends being critical of my dating choices. They accused me of being "not black enough." They said things like "You're different." I took that very personally because I felt they might be right. They talked about things I had no idea about. At first I thought it was because my parents grew up in a foreign country, but my younger sister was completely different than me. She was very connected to black culture while I wasn't. By comparison she seemed really "Black Power" and I seemed really out of it. Black people tend to assume that I'm from a southern background, but I relate more to the Caribbean. Maybe it's the difference between being the oldest child and the youngest; I don't know.

But in high school, I really wanted to connect to a black American heritage, so I decided to go to college at a historically black university, Virginia State University, in Petersburg, Virginia, which is about two hours from where my parents lived. I was enrolled there for three years and dated a black guy for two and a half of them. My friends back in Springfield were surprised that I was with him; they always assumed that I would marry a white man. That relationship might have led to marriage, but he ended it. He felt we were getting too serious and he wasn't ready for a long-term relationship. I knew there were a lot of issues going on in his family, so I didn't try to hang on. He went on to date someone else. I've heard through a friend that he regretted breaking up with me, but it doesn't matter now. Life goes on.

What I did notice at Virginia State was that there seemed to be a "type" that most of the guys were into: light skin, straight hair, light eyes. That was the standard of beauty that the black men preferred. So the women all put a lot of effort into straightening hair and trying to attract the most desirable black men.

I loved Virginia State and wouldn't have transferred to George Mason University if my grades had been better. The fact was I loved it so much, I had a little too much fun. And my parents weren't having the "five-year plan," so they encouraged me to come home, go to a school close enough that I could commute, and live with them so that I could focus on getting my degree. Education is extremely important to Caribbean families. My parents were telling me things like "You have to finish or you'll disgrace the family."

At George Mason, it was back to what I knew, which was white guys. I dated a lot. Some of my old friends from high school had ended up at Mason, and I made a lot of new ones. For whatever reason, the people I got along with were white guys. After college, I didn't date any more black guys. Not because I was against dating black guys; it just seemed like white guys were what I was comfortable with. There was no other reason. When I was being myself, hanging out with my friends, that's who would approach me—white guys. My brother used to joke that I seemed to attract the kind of white guy who you'd think would never look at a black girl seriously. But those are the guys I dated, and it wasn't just one of them. I always had a date. There was always a guy.

I met Chris at the 1999 Virginia Wine Festival. A girlfriend of mine ran a dating service and she had a booth at the wine festival. She was trying to get clients by giving away a Bahamas trip and encouraging people to sign up for a bachelor auction she had planned that was a few weeks away. She'd invited me to join her at the festival and help out with her booth. Chris was a friend of the people who ran the festival and he was there helping out too. I saw Chris and I thought he was good-looking and had a nice build—just right for a bachelor auction. So I asked him if he'd be interested. We started talking and he agreed to do it. I took his information. I gave him mine too, in case I lost his.

Though I found Chris attractive, I didn't think he was my type. I actually intended to fix him up with my roommate. But my friend kept saying, "He's not going to date your roommate. He likes you!" I just laughed it off; I really didn't think anything of it until he called me two days after the festival. We talked for almost three hours. I told him that a group of my friends and I were going to Ocean City [Maryland] to the beach. I invited him, but it was really just politeness. I didn't think he'd come, but he did and we had a great time. He told me he was interested in me and that he'd like to take me out on a date. I had gotten to know him a bit by then and thought he was cool.

Chris had dated other black girls, briefly, but nothing serious. He doesn't like skinny women—and fortunately, I'm not! He told me later that what attracted him to me was my personality: I'm a people person. He's more shy and reserved. He said I made him feel comfortable and relaxed and that made him want to know me better.

We started dating and that was pretty much that. We dated for the next three years and got married in 2002.

Chris's father and mother are divorced. His father had his doubts about us; he told Chris he didn't think it would work because of the differences in race and culture. But he was never unpleasant to me in any way. My mother-in-law was on board with us from the beginning, as was my own family. My parents might have preferred I marry a Haitian doctor or lawyer, but as I said, there's a whole different history with people who were born and raised in the Caribbean, so they were not as bothered as parents who were descendants of American slaves might have been. My mother loves him. She tells me all the time how smart, handsome, and obedient he is. Obedient to *her*, that is! She loves how handy and creative and willing to help her he is! I've got to say, Chris is smart—smart enough to make sure my mom is always in his corner!

My friends, of course, were not surprised. Several of my black girlfriends have dated white guys because where we live, there are just so many more of them. But some of the others, who have never dated out, have asked me those questions about sex and penis size. I had to set them straight. It's funny, though, that so many black women ask that. The other question some of my black girlfriends asked was "Does he have money?" The answer? I wish! No, we have to make money together and we're doing fine because I'm smart and ambitious and he's smart and ambitious.

I have also met several black women who are afraid of white men—just because they're white. One of my acquaintances said that she was afraid to be alone in an elevator with a white man and that she certainly wouldn't date one. I confess I was a little surprised by that. It just seems to me to be as bad as when white people cross the street when they see a black guy. It's just offensive to judge people as a group like that. Any people.

Chris and I have two kids: a daughter who is four and a son who is six. Once when my husband was out with our son, a complete stranger walked up and asked, "Is that your little boy?" and when Chris said yes, asked, "How?" My son often gets asked at school, "What *are* you?" At home he says, "I'm brown, Mommy's dark brown, and Daddy's white." He used to call me "black" but he's gotten more sophisticated in his appreciation of colors! So now he says "dark brown." When we talk about race, Chris and I tell him, "You got the best of both worlds!" As he and our daughter grow older, we'll answer any questions that they have. I remind them how beautiful they are every day. I remind our son, "Our president is half and half and he's just like you!" They are so comfortable. They understand that when we go to Grandma's house it's different than when we go to Mindy's [Chris's mother].

It helps too that my husband is well traveled: he's been to Zambia and Ghana on mission trips with our church. We belong to a nondenominational church with a wonderful pastor and several other interracial families. The fact that there are lots of mixed and multiracial people there helps us all to feel comfortable.

Being married to me has made him respond more aggressively when he hears or observes things that are racist. He's a commercial diver and most of his work involves bridge inspections. He sometimes has long-term contracts that can take him away from home frequently. Right now, he's in Slidell, Louisiana, and he's told me that sometimes the guys he works with say things that he considers racist. He tells them up front, "My wife is African American, and my children are mixed. I don't want to hear that stuff ever again."

Sometimes, when we're out together, I've heard people say things under their breath about me and my husband. Things like "What's she doing with him?" Just a few weeks ago, we were at the mall together and there was this group of young black guys, just staring me down. It's uncomfortable.

Don't get me wrong: things aren't perfect. We have been through a lot. We have had to work hard—maybe twice as hard because of our racial differences. There have been some tensions and there are things we disagree on violently, like affirmative action and politics. We argue about these things. But I would tell other black women: never say never. Try it, you may like it, you never know. Interracial relationships are challenging but worth it. I have two beautiful children and I know my husband loves me. I'm the most secure woman I know. I have some black girlfriends who are worried: they don't feel treasured by their husbands. Chris puts me on a pedestal. He's learned how to do that. He's been interested in learning how to make me feel loved and secure. He's read and learned and put out the effort. He's been putting it out there, and he gets more from me. We're well balanced. You have to be willing to give. People think they need to receive before they give, but it's the other way. I've had to learn not to criticize him for every little thing and to affirm him. I've learned not to nag about every dirty sock. I remember reading an article about a man who said his wife made him feel like the bottom of her list. I really make sure he knows his place, as the man, at the top of my list.

Lorraine and Joe

Lorraine: Joe and I met through a friend at church. He was on a "mission" to find a wife and he specifically wanted to marry a black woman. He says he loves brown skin, that it's what he finds attractive. Before Joe, I met three white guys who were all dogs. One of them was a fetishist; I could tell he was really into the idea of having a sexual relationship with a black woman. That revealed itself on our second date and completely creeped me out. Acutally that may have been the issue with all three of them. They didn't come out and say it, but I felt it even if it wasn't something that I had words for. Thankfully, I realized there was something wrong and nothing happened with any of those men.

I met Joe in 1994 in Washington, D.C. He had gone to Howard University for his master's in social work and had been engaged to a black woman before me. He had even lost a job opportunity with a church because he was in an interracial relationship. That relationship ultimately fell apart for other reasons. We shared religious beliefs, we were from the same state (Indiana), we had both lived in Denver, Colorado (though at different times), and we knew a lot of the same people, but I was turned off at first. In fact, I really didn't like him at all. It wasn't his physical appearance—though he had long hair then, and I really didn't like that look. I was put off by his forwardness. He would say things like "I love dark skin" that just seemed inappropriate. He made it very clear that he was interested in me, with the end goal of marriage. I not only avoided him, I think I went out of my way to be mean to him.

I went home to Indianapolis for Christmas that year, and he did too. That annoyed me: I didn't think he was just going to see his family, I thought he was following me! Reluctantly, I agreed to go to Christmas services, knowing he'd be there. But I told him the wrong time (by accident) and he missed church. He was so persistent! Missing us at church didn't stop him at all, he just came by my family's home to see me. I'm embarrassed now to say that I hid in the closet because I didn't want to see him.

But when we returned to D.C., all my rejections had finally gotten the message across. He stopped calling but he did send me a card. I remember being annoyed when the card arrived, until my brother reminded me that Joe "was human too." That he had feelings and that I hadn't treated him with much kindness, even if I wasn't interested in him romantically. Another family member said to me with a knowing smile, "You're always saying bad things about him, but you're always talking about him."

I prayed about it and I realized how many women—myself included—complained about not being able to find a good Christian man. And here I was, pushing one away.

So I called him. He had just graduated and didn't have a job yet.

He was just a poor student, so I asked, "Can you afford to take me to a movie?" He laughed and said yes. After that date, we were inseparable because I finally saw him for the man he is. He is a good guy, very different from the guys I had met up to then. Once I allowed myself to know him, I loved him.

We weren't taught to hate in my household, so there really wasn't any problem with the racial difference. I have six siblings and of the four of us girls, three are married to white men. My father was more concerned that each of us girls marry a Christian than about race. If Joe hadn't been a Christian, that might have posed a problem. I didn't realize marrying interracially was a big deal until I met other women who were told things like "Don't bring home a white boy" or who felt that they shouldn't date outside the race.

Joe and I have two children. Our son is autistic and that places him outside most of the issues that biracial children face. He's just not conscious of it in any way. Our daughter, however, will more than likely have some questions and perhaps meet some bumps in the road. She is really beautiful, with long hair, and sometimes for African American people there's this tendency to get all excited about hair. I hate the whole "good hair"/"bad hair" classification. I make a point of telling her "It's just hair." I also think the child's skin tone is important when you're raising a biracial child. A kid can think of herself as biracial, but as a parent, you have to prepare them for the way the world is likely to see them, whether that is as a black person or as a white one. Our daughter is still very young right now, but as she grows older, Joe and I plan to make her fully aware of her two heritages. I have traced my own descendants back seven generations and there is a tremendous legacy there. Joe hasn't done as much of his, but I'm working on it. We want her to know all about her family, black and white, and to be able to claim her history proudly.

Valerie and Andy

Valerie: I was born in 1967 in Camden, New Jersey, but I grew up in Acto, which back then was a really rural area about fifteen miles south of Camden. It was farm country: the nearest house to ours was a mile down the road and we were the only black people who lived anywhere nearby. All of our neighbors were white. I would call my family lower-middle-class: my dad worked as a New Jersey health inspector and my mother was a homemaker.

My father was mixed-race himself, with light skin and blue eyes. He was older than my mother by thirteen years and very aware of the racism he'd faced growing up in North Carolina. He'd also gotten a lot of abuse from black people who felt he wasn't "black enough" because of his looks. But he directed his anger at white people. I remember him saying "White people are the enemy" more than once. At the same time, he was eager for my brother and me to go to integrated schools and live in integrated environments. He'd say, "Go to their schools. Know the enemy."

My mom grew up very differently in southern New Jersey in a very Italian area where hers was one of only two black families. She likes to remind me that Italians weren't considered "white" until the 1950s, and in a way, when she was growing up, Italians and blacks had some common ground. Her upbringing made her far more liberal and accepting of people from different backgrounds.

Their marriage was stressful and difficult on a number of levels and they ultimately divorced when I was twelve. We moved to Berlin, New Jersey, and that's where I lived from the age of seven until I went to college. My father moved to Trenton, which was about half an hour's drive. My younger brother and I visited him every other weekend.

My first school was a Quaker Friends school in Morristown, New Jersey. It was predominantly white. I went to public school in fourth grade and experienced some culture shock. I was used to classes no larger than fifteen students. In the public school, the classes were much larger. And there were many more black people than white people. I would say the school was 50 percent black, 40 percent white, and that ratio stayed constant from the fourth grade through high school.

Because of my parents' emphasis on education and because I'd gone to the Friends School, I was more studious than most of the other black students. I wore glasses. I had white friends. So of course, I heard, "Oh, you think you're white." But I wasn't the only one:

there were a whole group of us that got that accusation and we did tend to hang out together. I remember in my room I had a poster of Stevie Wonder—and Duran Duran. I was sort of straddling a couple of different cultures. Shaun Cassidy was my first TV crush. Remember *The Hardy Boys* TV series? I thought he was *so* cute!

I'll never forget, when I was about thirteen or fourteen my father asked me, "V, are you going to marry a white man?" I remember answering, "I'm going to marry who I fall in love with." That was the end of that. He didn't ask me that again. When I look back on it now, I'm a little surprised by my answer, because my father could be intimidating and he really, really distrusted white people. But the answer was the truth, so I guess that's why I said it.

I was a late bloomer on the dating scene and really didn't get into that until college. I was asked to prom by a black guy I knew, but I didn't go. I'm attracted to black guys, but not all black guys! This guy just didn't do it for me and I didn't want to go with someone I didn't really like.

At Temple University, though, I met a whole new range of people. I had more black friends than I had ever had before, and I dated mostly black guys—but usually the ones who got accused of "acting white"! And I had a huge crush on a white South African—during the height of the struggle against apartheid. He was older, he had been in the SA army, was an economics major. He knew I liked him, but I only spoke to him once. I actually was so smitten with him that I wrote him a love letter just before he left school. He called me after he read it but I missed the call, and we ended up never finding out if there was anything more there.

I left Temple after about a year and a half and started working and taking classes at a nearby community college. I love music and play several instruments and I love to sing, so I joined the school's choir and met a white guy named Mark there. There was this white girl in the class who liked him and she hated that he was interested in me. He asked me to dinner after choir concert and this girl overheard it and tried to make something of it. Mark didn't pay her any attention and neither did I, at least not on the outside. On the inside, I was thinking, "Ha ha!"

I liked Mark, but nothing much came of that relationship. I used to go out a lot then, clubs and things with girlfriends, and I met lots of men of all races and dated a few of them. I met white guys who were jerks and black guys who were jerks. I met a white guy who thought he was a black guy; I met another one who was interested in dating me but didn't want his parents to find out even though he was in his thirties. None of those encounters lasted very long. But my dating came to a screeching halt when I started working at a church and started spending evenings at services and rehearsals. I did that for three years until I realized that I really needed to finish my college degree.

I transferred to DePaul University in Illinois in 2000 to work on my BA in music education and performance. It was tough because I was trying to pay my way through school, so I was working, practicing my music, and really struggling to do it all. It got to be way too hard, so I stopped school again and ended up just working full-time. I stayed in Chicago for four years, doing a little internet dating, but mostly working. Then I started to feel like I wanted to move east again, but not back to New Jersey. I felt like I had already dated *everyone* in New Jersey! My cousins lived in the Washington, D.C., area, and in the summer of 2004 two things happened that paved the way: I got laid off my job and my lease was up at my apartment. I moved to D.C., started working in a law firm, playing for a church, and teaching piano.

When I turned thirty-nine, I gave up on men. I told myself it was time to give up on the entire idea of getting married. I really just sat myself down over a weekend and grieved for the whole idea of marriage and family. I told myself, "If I'm single for the rest of my life, it's fine. I'll be fine." I cried some tears, but at the end of that weekend, I was really over it. I decided to keep looking, but I made peace with the idea that I might not ever find "my man." And of course, I met a guy—the guy who is now my fiancé.

Andy is a writer and I met him on match.com. He's Italian, from Philadelphia, and seventeen years older than me. He has three grown children, all of whom have accepted me without incident. His mother has also been very accepting. His father is deceased.

My father only met Andy once before he died. He was nearly eighty, suffering from Alzheimer's and a very different man from the one who'd asked me point-blank "Are you going to marry some white guy?" when I was a girl. He didn't seem to register Andy as white at all. He made some joke about his last name sounding Italian, then disappeared again, the way Alzheimer's patients sometimes do. He died in 2007.

We got engaged in 2006 and live together. We haven't set a date for the wedding and that's fine too. We're both happy and this is definitely the healthiest relationship I have ever had. When we go out and people stare at us, he is even *more* affectionate toward me— just to see if it bugs them. I guess that's the in-your-face Italian in him. Once, when we were shopping, there was an older black man (maybe in his fifties) behind me and Andy in a line. All of a sudden he started kissing and hugging me and I was actually sort of surprised. Later, he told me he'd done it because the black guy behind us was looking at him cross-eyed. What's funny about that is the double standard: two lines over, there was a black man with a white woman, but the old guy wasn't staring at *them*.

Keith and Jackie

Keith: I am an upstate New York–born white Anglo-Saxon–Celtic–Germanic–Polish–Pennsylvania Dutch–French blended mutt, whose lineage in America began in the 1600s. I am married to the most beautiful, accomplished, amazing woman, who is black, and also likely a mix of many ethnicities. She refers to herself as a poor girl from the South, since her parents and older siblings are Mississippi-born.

We met through one of my best hometown friends, who, like me, migrated to the Albany, New York, area from our Binghamton, New York, area hometown. Our introduction and first date were twenty-seven years ago, this month. We have been a couple that long, and married for almost twenty-two years. What is most surprising is how irrelevant our color difference has been. It has impacted me almost not at all, at least not in any significant way, other than that it took a couple of meetings for it to smooth out with my parents. If I have lost anything due to the color difference, it escapes my notice.

I have observed that my wife is somewhat more impacted by the mixed relationship. She is a masterful and independent person, and to the extent it has created notice or concerns, she has finessed them with some degree of delight. I am very close to her family, even to her once reluctant oldest sister. Her family is truly my family, and since we have lived close to them, they have greatly supplemented my original family.

I just had the best Father's Day with our twenty-nine-year-old daughter, who is my wife's child from a prior relationship with a black man, but I consider her to be my daughter and I will until the end of time. While we were not blessed with children from our union, we have had surrogate kids in our nephews, nieces, and godchildren, with whom we have often filled our lives.

I had never even thought about addressing my wife, child, or extended family with any racial epithet. My wife and I have had some very heated arguments, where fur came close to flying and maybe a few objects were airborne. No blood, no bruises, never hatred, no racial insults, and no long-term damage. I had never even thought of it. This woman is my wife, my all-consuming love, my best friend, my partner, at times my mentor (although I am a decade older), and we trust one another, completely, to never hurt the other. Never would I cast aspersions upon her, in regard to her race. She is the best thing to ever happen to me.

Diversity nourishes relationships. It brings more promise and strengths than challenges. While we were the first lasting interracial relationship in her family, there are now a number, approaching a dozen, including her youngest sister and only brother, numerous nieces and nephews, and now even our daughter is in her first relationship with a white man, which just celebrated its first anniversary.

This barrier of race to relationships is forever broken. Thanks to the Lovings and many other unnamed pioneers in the generations before us, we have no legal impediments in any U.S. state. I have come across quite a few of these black-white relationships in the two generations before mine. For us it has been easy; I applaud those for whom it was not. Love does have a way of making things right, if given the time and generosity it needs to do so.

NOTION 10

It's the Same Story Around the World

> *When I told my family that my college offered a semester in the Nether-*
> *lands and that I wanted to go, some of the biggest criticism of my plans*
> *came from my grandfather. My mom was horrified that I wanted to do this*
> *semester there too, but I think she was more worried about my safety and*
> *my being so far from home. But my grandfather said, "There are no black*
> *people in Europe. What you wanna go there for?" I was determined to go,*
> *and when I got scholarship funds to finance it, off I went. And everywhere*
> *I went, there were black people, people of color. I took pictures of all the*
> *black people in Europe and I sent them home to my grandfather. I wanted*
> *him to know we're everywhere and that there's this whole world beyond*
> *what we're used to in this country. And it was liberating for me. People*
> *didn't know what country I was from until I spoke: I could have been from*
> *Germany or France or Sweden and still been a person of color. You see the*
> *image of us from a new worldview . . . and it makes it that much more*
> *clear that these black/white distinctions just don't matter. What matters*
> *is the kind of person you are and the choices you make.*

We tend to think that the issues we face in the United States are the same
issues that will follow us wherever we travel on the planet, but black

women who have roamed the globe like Tori, quoted above, report something very different. Traveling the world—and meeting men from other countries and cultures—can offer American black women a new view of themselves as desirable.

"I tell black women all the time: for what you spend on shoes in a year, you could go to Europe, and you should. It will change the way you see yourself," says Nikki Doughty of Black Women Who Date Interracially (bwwdi.org). "I've been to Europe seven times, and every time I go, I come back thinking, 'I really need to emigrate,' because I don't like to date American guys. The bulk of my personal relationships with them have been disastrous and disappointing, but I love men from Europe. They have a natural understanding and appreciation for black women. It is extremely common to see many white men with women of color. Interracial dating is not as big a deal as it is for us here in America."

"It has been my experience, as a black American woman living first in Belgium, then in Sweden," says Adrianne George, founder of Black Women in Europe, a support and activist group for black women living abroad, "that I'm seen first as an American, then as a woman, then as black. It was an experience that was new to me, to be perceived first as an American. I don't think that ever happens to me in the United States. I'm perceived as black first, then as a woman. It's refreshing, even while it can be challenging," she adds. "Because depending on the prevailing sentiment toward Americans in Europe, I'm either the flavor of the month or a complete pariah."

Adrianne's sentiments were echoed resoundingly at a January 2009 gathering of members of her organization in Washington, D.C. The women, who ranged in age from their early twenties to late fifties, discussed their experiences as African Americans living in Europe—particularly with Caucasian men. Most have married or date interracially, and they find abroad a far different attitude toward their freedom to do so than exists in this country.

While it would be a lie to say that there is no racism in Europe, the women and men I spoke to indicated that black American women experience treatment different from that accorded black women from other nations. As Adrianne put it, "African American women are seen as high achievers. For example, Condi Rice was admired, and of course so is

Michelle Obama. The only incident I've had that I perceived as racist was when I was stopped [by immigration agents] in the airport in Amsterdam and asked questions in Dutch. When I told them 'I speak English,' I was told to go on. This was after going through customs and immigration. Being an American prevented any further questioning. For good or ill, being an American dictates your treatment. It's usually good, though, because America is perceived as a leader through most of the world."

Being a black American woman can also attract fascination and a protective impulse. "In the Highlands of Scotland they weren't used to seeing black people. I got bought drinks and asked questions about myself and my background. They were absolutely fascinated with me. It's really interesting to be the focus of that kind of attention," says Mona Washington. "And, weird as it might seem, in Somalia, which is a Muslim country, I felt safe, as a single woman, traveling without father or brother. The people were solicitous, very concerned for me, and took me under their wing, so to speak. It was my experience that they protect women in a way that we don't here, though of course that protection can pose other problems and limitations for the women who are born into those cultures. For me, however, as a foreigner, I experienced those limitations as a form of kindness."

A TOE IN THE WATER: LONDON

For many black American women, the United Kingdom, because of the shared language and the historical link of colonialism, is the easiest nation to visit and explore. As a result of its colonial reach, Great Britain has a large population of black West Indian immigrants (from Caribbean nations like St. Vincent, Jamaica, and the Bahamas) and East Indian immigrants from India and Pakistan, as well as East Africans, Vietnamese, Russians, Poles, Bulgarians, and others from Eastern European nations.

"On my most recent trip," Nikki told me in a phone conversation in March 2009, "everyone was warning me about the Bulgarians. Don't go out with a Bulgarian, be careful of the Bulgarians. It was weird. It was some of the same stuff you might hear about black men in this country . . .

applied to men of another nationality. And I didn't like hearing it. Being a black American woman makes you very sensitive to those things."

Nikki also commented on the response she received from nonblack men: "European men first and foremost have backbone and confidence when it comes to courting black women. They are eons ahead of their white American counterparts. They are able to ask black women out directly in social settings and are very comfortable in our presence. I always felt that there's more acceptance of a black woman's look and features in Europe. European men appreciate what black women look like in all forms. What's so strange is that I guess I have been so Americanized about what I think a black woman is that I hardly know what black beauty is. I typecast as well. I would gawk at black-female interracial couples and think to myself, 'Damn, that woman is *not* pretty.' As I reflected and witnessed more, I became aware it isn't just the lovely black women who get love; the not-so-pretty (or the not-so-Americanized or the not-so-young or the not-so-stylish) ones get love over there too. Now, I don't want to say that there isn't racism over in Europe too. Lots of European men only date their own kind. However, it still remains a haven for interracial couples. I keep telling my 'brown girl' sisters, if you've never been to Europe, you really *must* go."

A white male Briton wrote me in June 2008 to offer his perspective on the difference in interracial dynamics between the United Kingdom and the United States:

> *There was, of course, no experience of slavery within the UK, notwithstanding the part played by the UK in profiting from slavery. Black migration into the UK commenced in the late 1950s. Regrettably, the government made no attempt to assimilate these migrants, settling on a policy of multiculturalism. The problem with multiculturalism is that when you have more than one culture, one will always be dominant. This is not a problem for minuscule cultures such as punks with interesting hairstyles and body piercing. It is a problem where there are more substantial alternative cultures.*
>
> *I appreciate this will contain generalizations, and it will always be possible to identify individual cases that do not fit the mold. Interracial relationships existed from an early stage, but in the beginning they were*

almost always black men with white women, frequently with a concept
of subjugation.

West Indian society, from where these migrants came, had always
appeared to be more matriarchal. Men saw it as their responsibility to
provide financially for their children but not necessarily to live with them.
Many West Indian mothers strove manfully to ensure their children had
a good education. Overall this worked much better with their daughters
than their sons. A large number, but fortunately by no means all, of black
boys (it is no longer correct to call them West Indian) saw conforming in
school and learning as "white" and so rejected it, sinking into an unedu-
cated gang culture.

On the other hand, black girls, doubtless encouraged by their mothers,
have performed much better at school and have assimilated into the domi-
nant culture. It is by no means unusual to see black women with white
partners. Black men who have assimilated are also frequently found with
white partners. The change is that, from casual observation, black women
with white partners now substantially outnumber black men with white
partners. Those black boys who have established their own counterculture
would not be seen dead with a white partner.

"It's true," said Nikki. "London is very diverse. I always see lots
of mixed couples—lots of black men and white women, lots of black-
woman, white-man couples. They are virtually ignored because there
are so many of them. They're just regular people on the street, nothing
special. And the couples seem to cut across income, class, and socioeconomic levels. Over there, I feel more viable romantically, because I know
I am perceived differently. On a 'romance level' I get identified as a pretty
woman first, race second. The two are never far from each other, but it's
refreshing to be romantically pursued and courted. It's like a job that
men (black and white) have forgotten or don't think they have to do for
black women in the United States. I get offers of help on the street in
London in ways I never do in New York. When I went out to nightclubs
or bars, I was never without a drink and an offer to dance. It tells you
that you're sending out the signal and it's really being received. I felt a
little like Josephine Baker or James Baldwin, happy to be appreciated for

the black and all the other parts of me. The European difference for black folks has been going on for some time. My grandfather, who is usually silent on the topic of black women dating out, always spoke highly of his time in Paris during World War II. According to him, the French were very happy to see the American servicemen, black and white. He was treated well in Paris. My grandfather was born and bred in the Deep South, so he has experienced the ugliness of American racial history firsthand. I've only introduced one nonblack boyfriend to my grandfather. He was the French one."

Mona spent five years living in London and traveling in Europe, the Middle East, and Africa. "You have different shit projected on you [when you travel abroad]," she said of her experiences. "But it's not the usual shit and it's refreshing. For example, when I was stopped at Israeli checkpoints, the guards asked if I was Ethiopian. I loved it. I loved that there were new assumptions about who and what I was and where I was from. I found on the whole when I'm traveling the world, there's less pigeonholing, less judgment about what I 'should be,' with the exception of in London, where there are some similar issues about race, second-class-citizen status, and a history of white privilege. But even with that said, I feel much freer abroad. If they're stereotyping me, it's in a way I don't know."

How a black-female/white-male couple are perceived might depend on where they settle in the wide world.

"My husband is Belgian," writes Angela, who has lived with her husband and their three children all over Europe and Asia.

We first met during the 1972 New Year's Eve celebration at Maxim's in Lisbon, Portugal. They were playing Stevie Wonder's song "Superstition." Georges came over to my table and asked me to dance. I responded by saying, "Why are you speaking to me in English? Don't I look Portuguese?" He laughed. Of course, I danced with him and he asked me out to dinner for the next three nights until my return flight back to the United States. We dated for several years, but we rarely lived on the same continent with each other! When we married four years later in March of 1976, and we moved in together in our D.C. apartment, we both had kept those torn pieces of paper that we had written our addresses on from one of the Portuguese restaurants that we had dinner at on one of those first few dates. We still have those torn pieces of paper, thirty-seven years later here in our apartment in Toulouse! I guess that Stevie Wonder's song was prophetic. We believed in things that we didn't understand, like the loyalty and devotion of our love.

Angela's life as a globe-trotting black American woman in an interracial relationship has given her a unique perspective on race, culture, and marriage. In a series of emails, she discussed how black/white interracial unions are perceived in America versus how "dating out" is seen in other cultures:

Georges's job took us first to China, where we were interesting only because we were not Chinese. In China there are rather rigid interracial taboos against Chinese males [marrying out] as opposed to females. Females are considered "spilled milk" because they can neither sweep the graves of the ancestors nor register the births of their offspring in Chinese society. Thus, Chinese women often marry interracially, but you will find less than 5 percent of Chinese men doing so.

Now, you can contrast this phenomenon with matriarchal societies like the Jewish community. There you will find more than 50 percent of Jewish males marrying cross-culturally, but not so with Jewish women. Much like in the black American community, females are charged with carrying the culture. In migrant, pilgrim cultures like the Jews and, as quiet as it's kept, for black Americans as well, educational nurturing is for the most part left to females. Rabbis are held in high regard religiously, just as many of our black American ministers are similarly held in higher regard than our female black ministers. So not surprisingly there are cultural similarities there.

Of course, Australia gives the best example of how tolerant Asian and Aboriginal people are of interracial marriage and how intolerant the white Australians are. Not only did white Australians ban their own interracial marriage with Aboriginals, but they tried to ban it between Asians and Aboriginals. Thus, many Asian men gave up their lives in Australia and returned to China or Japan with their Aboriginal wives and their offspring. White male Australians watched as their Aboriginal offspring became the stolen generation, just as white males did in New Zealand, Zimbabwe, and South Africa and Canada.

In the Middle East, I saw considerably more white European women married to Muslim men than I saw Muslim women married to European men. Usually white men have an unfettered choice of women that they will marry the world over, except in the Middle East (among Jewish and Muslim women) and, it appears, in the United States in regard to black American women.

Angela sees the status of black American women in comparison with their sisters of color around the world and reminds us, "It's a privilege to be a black American woman. In spite of the legacy of slavery, compared to how many women of color live in other nations and cultures, we have accomplished so much and are still rising. World travel is certainly one way to realize just how much has changed for us. I'm very proud to be a black American woman, even if I haven't lived in the United States for many years!"

Adrianne, who is from the District of Columbia, after stints in London and Belgium has settled in Sweden. In October 2006 she started the blog Black Women in Europe (www.blackwomenineurope.ning.com) in an effort to connect black American women living all over that continent. "I started the Black Women in Europe (BWIE) blog after moving to Sweden because I wanted to connect with other black women in Europe. I also wanted to raise our profile with the positive things we were doing. As an offshoot I started the BWIE social network because I found that we weren't doing a lot of networking on the pan-European level. The sisters in the UK seem organized but somewhat insular and not connected to the rest of the continent. I found organizations in Germany and France too, but there wasn't anything that crossed borders for the sake of building social networks and connections." The group currently has nearly 600 members, who live in countries all over the world. The group also provides support to black American women considering European travel.

Adrianne's story is an interesting one that speaks to the wide range of opportunities available to black American women as multinational corporations expand their reach around the globe. She made her first trip abroad—to London—almost fifteen years ago while in college. After several years working with PolyGram Records (now a part of Universal Studios), she returned to Europe in 2002, spending several years in Belgium. She met her fiancé while studying for her graduate degree.

> He was on a business trip [in Brussels] and I was studying a lot and rarely went out, but that Friday I was compelled to go out with friends and have a drink. We met at a bar and really just hit it off. White men have always been attracted to me; I had been approached by them in the United States as well as in London and throughout Europe. Italian men are probably the most aggressive. They tell you how beautiful you are and bluntly ask if they can spend time with you. Others are generally more subtle. There is more of a dance, approach and retreat, while they try to figure out if you're interested too. Still, you can be pretty sure a man is interested when he gets very talkative and asks a lot of questions about you. The Brits have a great expression for it: "chatting you up."

> Jonas was definitely chatting me up, but I knew there was a possibility for something more serious when he told me that he liked Americans. He understood Americans. His aunt married an American and raised her family in Maine. This was in 2005—at the height of anti-American sentiment in Europe because of the war in Iraq. After that evening, we corresponded by email and Skype and visited each other monthly. Jonas is Swedish. When I finished my degree in October 2006, I moved to Sweden; we became engaged in February 2007.

> I am a marketing consultant and do a lot of work in social networking (Facebook, MySpace, and the like). While in Brussels, I worked for an internet marketing agency. A former colleague, a German guy, moved to Copenhagen the same time I moved to Sweden (his wife is Danish and I am godmother to their youngest daughter). He was working on creating the website JobsinCopenhagen.com and recruited me to start JobsinStockholm.com. From that experience I learned a great deal about using social media to drive traffic to a website. It also got me on the path of building communities for expats. I run BlackExpat.com and Stockholm Expat.com as well as the blog for Black Women in Europe and Women of the African Diaspora and their social networks.

My family has met Jonas and like him, because he's a very engaging, likeable person. There have been no issues with family acceptance for us on either side. At this point in my life, my family just want to see me happy, and I am. Jonas and I are committed to each other, and I feel wherever he is, I'm home. Though I still love Washington, D.C., and cherish my time there when I visit, for the time being, I belong in Europe. Sweden is home. Fortunately, English is the lingua franca, but of course speaking the local language helps. I get by in French and am learning Swedish.

My second husband was a white American man and there were issues from time to time. I recall when we lived in D.C. there were a couple of instances when black men called me out for being with a white guy. "Sellout" and "gold digger" and those kinds of implications, although I don't think those exact words were used. And once in Amsterdam we passed some black guys on the street and they had something to say about us.

I do feel free to be myself living abroad, but I'm not sure how much of that has to do with geography. I think more of it has to do with getting more confidence and giving up trying to please other people. I got over that a long time ago. Still, as a black American woman, I do my best to "represent" for my black American sisters wherever I am. I felt that responsibility first in the U.S. and still do here.

In general, I think a black American woman is more likely to be approached by a European man than an American white man, but that's really changing with every passing year. For example, I spent some time in Southern California. I found white men there are very straightforward when they are interested in a black woman.

I want black American women to know that, in the wider world, we are perceived as smart, hardworking, and talented. In short, the world thinks you're awesome. Think Condi Rice and Michelle Obama. Think Josephine Baker, and even Beyoncé. While I understand that not everyone wants to make Europe or Africa or Asia her home, I think black American women should definitely make international travel a part of their vacation planning. Go everywhere you can! I've had great experiences in Africa, Asia, and Europe. Travel is the best education one can get.

AMERICAN APHRODITE

Yvette Jarvis is a woman who has used the freedom to create herself, free from the stereotypes typically imposed on black women in the United States, to maximum advantage, though I doubt anything in any country could hold her back! Nicknamed "American Aphrodite" in Greece, her adopted country, she's led a life that reveals how black American women living abroad are able to create their own identities in ways that can be very different from life in the United States. Profiled in 2004 by the *Washington Post*,[1] Yvette had been living in Greece for twenty-two years. She was born in Brooklyn, New York, and went to schools there until attending Boston University on an academic scholarship. In college she played forward on the basketball team. After graduating, she was a substitute teacher who occasionally moonlighted as a basketball referee. Then one night at a club, she met Stelios, a Greek student at Hellenic College, a Greek Orthodox seminary in Boston.

"It was New Year's Eve," she told a group of us at the gathering of Black Women in Europe. "He swept me off my feet. I came to Greece for love. I had no idea I'd end up living here for the next twenty-seven years!"

In Greece, she and Stelios married, she played professional women's basketball, became a model, and ultimately starred in a TV commercial that made her a household name. While she and her Greek husband ultimately divorced, the failure wasn't based on race. "The machismo of Greek men!" she said, rolling her eyes heavenward dramatically. "Hey, I'm a sister from New York. I wasn't having that!"

Then in 2003, she ran for a seat on the Athens city council—and won, making her the first African American to ever hold elected office in Athens. She served from 2002 to 2006 and currently works as a special assistant to the city's mayor on immigration issues. "Immigration is something that is very important to me. It's very difficult to get Greek citizenship unless you are born here or married to a Greek. And it's getting even harder, which puts immigrants from various countries, many of them African, who come here and work for years and years in a very precarious position. They have very few rights, very little access. I want to help change that."

"My self-image as a black woman has always been powerful and I'm not one for believing in limitations. In the U.S., I know some people might find me 'uppity' or 'aggressive' because of my confidence, but that's their problem. I keep on being me. Here in Europe, whether you are perceived as confident or aggressive depends on what you are doing. For me it was easier to take career risks here and to develop talents and skills that I may not have readily pursued in the States."

Yvette's second husband, John, is a white American who, like Yvette, has made his home in Athens. "In the beginning, my brother reacted to Stelios, my Greek first husband. He was a little uncomfortable with my having brought home a white boy, even though I had dated white men before. But after he got to know him, my brother really liked Stelios. He found him so cool he even used to tell him, 'You're not white,' making a distinction between him as a Greek and American-born whites. He felt that Stelios as a Greek had nothing in common with the whites in America. I did have some trouble with John's parents when we first got together, though."

I met his nieces and nephews first. When they reported home about Uncle John's girlfriend, I guess I had impressed them so much that they never mentioned my color! When his parents found out that I was black, they had a very different reaction. His dad wrote him a scorching letter letting him know that he was welcome at home but that I was not. At that point in his life, John had lived away from home for more than twenty years. Still, they let him know that he wasn't allowed to upset their peace of mind with their neighbors by bringing me to their home. After lots of talking and the welcomed support from their grandkids (John's nieces and nephews), who let John's parents know how great I was, the situation thawed a bit and I was invited to their fiftieth anniversary. When we got there, John's nephews pulled me aside and told me that if things got ugly, they "had my back" and would defend me! But everything was fine. Once John's mom and dad sat down and talked with me, they fell in love with me almost instantly! His mom even came over later in the evening and whispered in my ear how sorry she was for the letter. She was happy just knowing her only son was happy! Since then, we've become great friends, and she was ecstatic after the birth of our son.

Our son was born in Greece and holds dual citizenship. John and I believe the most important thing is to raise him to be a good human being, with respect for others. He is well aware of his roots and well schooled on stories of his dad's Italian/Austrian family in Philadelphia. He knows his dad had problems in school because of his German-sounding last name, so he knows racism can affect many people for different reasons. I have taught him well in black history and he is proud to be black. I think he enjoys being different and having such a rich cultural background. However, there have been a few problems. His first year in Greek school there was an incident with some boys making fun of his color. The teacher nipped it in the bud immediately by addressing the issue and confronting the children in class. She stood my son and the boy who was teasing him up in front of the class and asked the children to comment on their appearance. The children shouted out, "They look like brothers, miss!" When she questioned the boy why he had called my son the derogatory name and what it meant, the boy had no clue. It was a rocky start, but the incident made my son very popular with the kids in elementary school!

While Yvette still considers New York to be at least one of her "homes," she loves her adopted country. "I get emotional when I sing both national anthems," she writes. "After almost three decades, I truly feel at home in Greece. My sense of belonging is very strong here."

Like the other women living abroad, she encourages black American women to at least visit Europe and widen their horizons to the entire world. "I think European men are very forward in letting you know they are interested. They call out, they'll walk up to you and introduce themselves, they'll kiss your hand, and they'll send drinks to your table. The Europeans seem to have fewer taboos when it comes to dating across racial lines, or at least that has been my experience. I also think it's important to step out with the attitude of Maya Angelou's poem 'Phenomenal Woman.' " She added, "Be proud of who you are no matter where you go, and go everywhere! Travel! See the world, go wherever your heart desires, and don't be afraid to meet someone different from yourself. You may be pleasantly surprised!"

MEN ARE MEN . . . ARE MEN

At the end of the day, though, regardless of race or nationality, all men are men.

"None of them put down the toilet seat, and in my experience, they're all bad at details," says Mona. "They're still men, when it comes down to it. Hell is other people, but so is heaven. There is something essentialist about men. Heterosexual men are simply men. They seem to deal with ideological pressures in the same way. They're visual, they're testosterone-driven. They're men." She continued, "I've dated Austrians, Ghanaians, Sierra Leoneans, white and black South Africans, Italians, British, French, Dutch, and Mexican guys—which sounds like a lot of men, doesn't it?" She laughed. "The conflicts usually come over issues of gender and machismo rather than race. What I found was that sometimes, when you meet a man from another culture in a neutral setting—like at school or when you're both visiting or living in another country—and then you go with him to his home, you'll see him differently. A man is a product of his culture, and when you as an American woman go and live in his culture, he changes. His culture won't let him reject its values. It's a kind of oppression too: the men react to whatever his culture's social construct of manhood is."

AFRAID TO GO ALONE?
TRY BLACKGIRLTRAVEL.COM

Of course, there are all kinds of tours and opportunities to help get you started if you're interested in seeing the world. You can even start at your local university, where there are special courses that may allow you to brush up on old skills—or pursue new ones—while visiting a foreign land. But if you're looking for something that's geared especially for and to black American women, you may want to look up www.blackgirltravel.com.

Fleacé Weaver is an African American woman who is no stranger to worldwide travel: as a model, she did her time in Europe strutting the runways of the fashion capitals of the world. Then she married and divorced and ended up in the Los Angeles area as the creator of the popular website blackweekly.com.

"I have 28,000 subscribers," she told me in a phone interview in March 2009. "Over 67 percent of them are black women and most of them are single. Time and time again, the message boards would light up with the topic of being single, of looking for a man and not being able to find one. The women would also talk about wanting to travel but not wanting to travel alone. And in 2006, I put those two together and first the Bella Italia tour was born. Then Bella Italia turned into blackgirltravel.com."

Blackgirltravel.com offers single black women the chance to tour with other black women, usually about fifty women at a time. Some women sign up with a group of friends, but most are on their own. "I think many of the women find themselves wanting to do something that their friends don't want to do. That's why they like blackgirltravel.com so much. They can go somewhere exciting but still have the security of a group. And usually the women become fast friends on our ten-day whirlwinds. It's really a drama-free zone."

"Most of the women are between thirty and forty-five, though we've had women as young as twenty-six and as old as sixty-two on our tours," Fleacé said. "Every September we offer the Bella Italia tour of Italy— which is our signature tour—but for 2010 we're also planning trips to the French Riviera and Dubai."

The Bella Italia tour capitalizes on the attraction between black American women and Italian men. In fact, some have called Italy the black woman's Brazil (in reference to the popularity of the South American nation for single black men on holiday). "The tour hits all the cultural high points—the Sistine Chapel, the Colosseum, Trevi Fountain—and of course there's plenty of shopping! But we make a concerted effort to gear our stops to single women. That means going to clubs and bars to enjoy the nightlife and give the women opportunities to meet local men," says Fleacé. While most of the travel participants enjoy the attention, for some it's a little difficult to take in. "Italian men are very affectionate, very aggressive. They love women of all nationalities and for black American women, it can be overwhelming. Black women aren't used to the level of attention they get from the men in

Italy. In a way that's kind of sad. But it's also why the ladies have such a great time. It's fun when fifty or so black American women descend on a popular club in Rome and find themselves to be quite literally the 'bellas' of the evening. And then there's the Vespa tour through Rome: we hire a Vespa scooter and driver for each woman, and she gets to motor around Rome with the hottie of her choice!" The Vespa tour is a signature event for Bella Italia. "The women love it," Fleacé reported. "Of course, we don't just have fun. On every tour, we do spend a few hours doing some volunteer work. Blackgirltravel.com is affiliated with an orphanage in Rome and with the international Girls Club organization. The women have a good time, but they also give back."

Fleacé considers travel to be one of the most important things black American women can do—for themselves and for the world. "We're rare and different in places like Germany, Italy, and Israel, so there's a lot of interest in us. It's exciting and empowering and does wonders for the women's self-esteem! Since blackgirltravel.com started in 2006, I've had several women repeat the tours: that's how much fun they had."

And there have been a couple of genuine love connections made through the group, though Fleacé does urge the women to be cautious. "It's a foreign country and we do not encourage anyone to 'just hook up,' and that's usually not the style of the women who participate anyway. But a couple of women have met men on the tour with whom they are still involved."

Surprisingly (or not, depending on your expectations), some have had negative reactions to blackgirltravel.com in general and the Bella Italia tour in particular. "We did a press release to some of the more popular black blogs and websites a couple of years ago. I was surprised at just how negative the reaction was—from some black men, in particular. Really hateful stuff, suggesting that no one in the world wants the black American woman or that the women should just go to Italy and stay there because they aren't wanted here. Not for the faint of heart, reading those posts. But we didn't let it deter us in any way. First of all, I know that's not true, and secondly, I really think that some black American men really hate the idea of black women expanding their horizons. And that's how they express it." She explains, "It's not that I'm against black American men—or black men from any country. It's just that I'm *for* black women. I think we should have every option when it comes to dating, just like men do."

The criticism has done nothing to stop either blackgirltravel.com or the Bella Italia tour, which seems to be gaining in popularity. "We're thinking of doing a world tour in a few years—something like 'Black Girls Around the World'! My goal is to make it as easy, comfortable, and fun for black women to travel the world as possible," says Fleacé. "One of our slogans is that we're introducing black American women to the world, and the world to black American women. We're having fun, but we're also ambassadors. We're making sure that the world sees us in a positive light—one different from popular images of us in music videos and movies that get exported around the world but have nothing to do with the reality of who we are."

GO, WOMAN, GO!

I confess: I haven't yet seen as much of the world as I would like, but after interviewing these women, I'm eager to go and I hope you are too. I'd also like to visit some of the nations of Africa and to experience what it's like to be a black woman among a sea of a billion Chinese. I'd like to go to South America and Australia. I want to see the world—and not for the men, but for *me*.

After reading these women's stories and experiences, I think Nikki Doughty said it best: for what we spend in shoes, we could have an experience that completely changes the way we see ourselves and what we know about the wide world. So start putting your shoe money aside, ladies, and go, woman, go!

CONCLUSION

Monumental changes are taking place right now in this country. Black women are on the move.

A mixed-race man is president of the United States, and no fewer than seven of the twenty top advisers to Mr. Obama are black women. Michelle Obama has captured the attention of the world, representing us in an image that breaks apart the old stereotypes from movies, TV shows, and music videos and sets a new standard for beauty that is decidedly and wonderfully African American.

Black women authors are some of the most successful and revered in the world. Think of Maya Angelou and Toni Morrison. Think of poet Nikki Giovanni. Think of Terry McMillan or Tananarive Due or Mary Monroe—each writing from her unique point of view and telling stories her way.

Look at Hollywood, where some black female actors are among the highest paid and most sought-after in the industry. And look a level deeper, at who's producing and creating shows, and you'll see black women moving into realms once occupied almost exclusively by white men. We are in the process of completely renovating the image that the world has of us. We're showing ourselves to be confident but not strident, honest but not emasculating, feminine but not hypersexual. We are everywoman—and everything a smart man should want in a woman.

White men are beginning to realize this in greater and greater numbers.

Just the other day, I caught a TV commercial for a dating service that featured a mixed-race couple: a black woman and a white man. A few weeks before, my literary agent, Audra Barrett, brought me an issue of *Vanity Fair* that included a fashion layout featuring a black woman and a white man. As you're reading this, there probably will have been dozens more images of interracial relationships featuring a black woman and a white man.

Soon we'll also have the data from the 2010 census, and no one will be surprised to learn that the number of interracial marriages has vastly increased and that there are more mixed-race children in our country than ever. As social psychologist Kellina Craig-Henderson wrote in *Black Men in Interracial Relationships,*

> When African Americans as a group have achieved sufficient parity with Whites in society, interracial relationships between African Americans and others will occur with as much frequency as interracial relationships now occur between members of other races, and as frequently as same-race relationships occur within groups. Furthermore, with a sufficient passage of time, we would expect that Black men and women would be involved in interracial relationships at comparable rates.

More and more of us are taking leading roles in workplaces once dominated by white men, in schools and universities that were once the exclusive province of white men. As we do so, we come to realize that, as Mona says, "Men are men." There are good ones and bad ones, playboys and altar boys, tough guys and gentle souls, and they all come in all colors. Just as generalizations made about us as black women damage us, so do the generalizations we make about white men and any other group. If nothing else, generalizing reduces a man to a stereotype— and never gives him the chance to defeat it. As black women, we more than any other group know about how unfair it is to be on the receiving end of a generalization.

At the beginning of this book, I shared with you my experiences with interracial dating and the reactions that I have received from various people over the years and how those comments expressed the notions we've explored in this book. But from the beginning, I have also seen this book as an argument—not with you, but for you to use when people offer notions to keep you single if you don't want to be. Knowing for yourself that most of these notions are just plain wrong—or worse, sprang from a history in white racism that black Americans have twisted into a source of pride—helps you to take a fresh look at your romantic options. And options, as we all know, mean everything. The more options you have, the better your ultimate choices.

There's one more thing I'd like you to consider. In several places in this book, the concept of "racial healing" has been touched upon. We've noted that these notions about interracial dating have been controversial for so long because of the difficulties that black folks, as a people, have had in coming to a place of healing on so many issues that result from racism. For some people, seeing a black woman with a white man provokes thoughts of those issues and they react. That's when you'll hear comments about oppression and slavery, about gold digging and selling out, about what it means to be "authentically black" and how mixed-race children are disadvantaged.

If you decide to expand your options and consider men of all races in your dating and marriage pool, you will more than likely experience some level of reaction. You should consider this a good thing.

Yes, a *good* thing.

Why? Because it's important now, more than ever, that black people begin a new racial dialogue—not just with white people but among ourselves. Those who are uncomfortable or angry when they see a black woman with a white man will have to confront their issues. They'll have to ask themselves why they're *really* bothered by interracial dating. We have to address the controversy. And we have to get over it. Yes, get over it. Instead of worrying about who's being "black enough," respecting their heritage enough, and so on, we have to move on to the real work of defeating racism and sexism in all their forms. And, as Kimberly Jade Norwood has said so elegantly, that work is the responsibility not just of black men and women but of all people of all races.

The more black women date and marry white men, the more reaction there will be, in the short term. But in the end, for every one of us who moves into this territory and provokes conversation and commentary, there is a greater potential for ultimate healing—for black and white people alike.

As Angela Shaw states so eloquently,

I want to see black women no less than equal to white men, in their abilities and willingness to help as well as their power to hinder each other. The truth is that black women can help white men as often and as thoroughly as white men can help black women. Similarly, black women can impose as much pain on white men as white men can impose on black women. It was over forty years ago that Dr. King said that the only choice is between "nonviolence" and "nonexistence." At this point in time in first world countries, we can all agree that the biblical reference of lion and lamb can best be personified by white males and black females. There really is no choice but for the lion to lie down with the lamb. It's a step on the way to peace—and to progress.

Amen.

NOTES

Introduction

1. Details about Paula, her work, and her services can be found at www.artofabundance.com.

Notion 1: After Slavery, I Would *Never, Ever* Date a White Man

1. See Randall Kennedy, *Interracial Intimacies: Sex, Marriage, Identity, and Adoption* (Vintage Books, 2007), 163–207.
2. Danielle L. McGuire, "It Was Like All of Us Had Been Raped: Sexual Violence, Community Mobilization and the African American Freedom Struggle," *Other Souths* (University of Georgia Press, 2008), 300.
3. Ibid.
4. Ibid., 298–327.
5. Patricia Hill Collins, *Black Feminist Thought* (Routledge Classics, 2009), 176.
6. Maya Angelou, *And Still I Rise* (Random House, 1978).
7. Angela Shaw, from an email to the author, received February 26, 2009.
8. Jerry Harkavy, "Alabama Teen's Bus Defiance before Rosa Parks Gets Its Due," Associated Press, February 10, 2009, www.blackameri caweb.com/?q=articles/news/moving_america_news/6676/1.
9. *Browder v. Gayle*, 142 F. Supp. 707 (1956).

10. Bill Brubaker, "Civil Rights Leader Convicted of Incest," *Washington Post*, April 11, 2008, www.washingtonpost.com/wp-dyn/content/article/2008/04/10/AR2008041002222.html.

11. Eldridge Cleaver, *Soul on Ice* (Delta Books, 1999).

12. Pearl Cleage, *Mad at Miles: A Black Woman's Guide to Truth* (Cleage Group, 1990), 27–28.

13. You can find discussions on this theory in various online forums, including at DVDtalk.com/forum and at www.boxingforum.com/boxing-forum-general-discussion/4460-did-mike-tyson-actually-rape-desiree-washington-who-ya-voting.html.

14. From an email to the author, received February 5, 2009.

15. "Teen Gets Five Years in Group Sex Assault on Girl, 11," Associated Press, July 2, 2008, www.msnbc.msn.com/id/25500810.

16. Johnnetta Betsch Cole and Beverly Guy-Sheftall, *Gender Talk: The Struggle for Women's Equality in African American Communities* (One World/Ballantine, 2003), 147.

17. Linda A. Foley and Nicole Varelas, "Blacks' and Whites' Perceptions of Interracial and Intraracial Rape," *Journal of Social Psychology* 38 (June 1998), 392–400, accessed at www.highbeam.com/doc/1G1-20615256.html.

18. Kennedy, *Interracial Intimacies*, 181.

19. Dorian Block, "20 Years Later, Tawana Brawley Has Turned Back on Past," New York *Daily News*, November 18, 2007, www.nydailynews.com/news/2007/11/18/2007-11-18_20_years_later_tawana_brawley_has_turned.html?page=0.

20. Aaron Beard, "Disbarred Duke Prosecutor Future Dim," *Washington Post*, June 18, 2007, www.washingtonpost.com/wp-dyn/content/article/2007/06/17/AR2007061700687.html.

21. Kennedy, *Interracial Intimacies*, 45–48.

22. Ibid., 76.

23. Aaron Gullickson, "Black-White Interracial Marriage Trends 1850–2000," *Journal of Family History* 31, no. 3 (2006), 1–24, http://paa2006.princeton.edu/download.aspx?submissionId=60719.

24. Kennedy, *Interracial Intimacies*, 72, citing other sources.

25. Allison Davis, Burleigh B. Gardner, and Mary R. Gardner, *Deep South: A Social Anthropological Study of Caste and Class* (University of Chicago Press, 1941), 33–34.

26. Kennedy, *Interracial Intimacies*, 207.
27. Tunde Obadina, "Slave Trade: A Root of Contemporary African Crisis," *African Economic Analysis* (2000), www.afbis.com/analysis/slave.htm.
28. Lisa Vazquez, "Our Mess and His Majesty," www.blackwomenblow thetrumpet.blogspot.com, July 7, 2009.
29. Nathaniel Branden, *The Six Pillars of Self-Esteem* (Bantam, 1994), 120.
30. Vazquez, "Our Mess and His Majesty."

Notion 2: I'm Looking for My Good Black Man

1. Krissah Williams, "Singled Out: In Seeking a Mate, Men and Women Find Delicate Imbalance," *Washington Post*, October 8, 2006.
2. Theodore McClendon, *How to Find a Good Black Man* (McClendon Report, 2003).
3. "Where Have All the Good Black Men Gone?" *Tyra Show*, Warner Bros., May 23, 2008, http://tyrashow.warnerbros.com/2008/05/where_have_all_the_good_black.php.
4. United States Census Bureau, "2008 American Community Survey," http://factfinder.census.gov.
5. "The Power of Higher Education to Close Black/White Income Gap," *Journal of Blacks in Higher Education* 30 (April 2007), 34–36.
6. A study of the ratios of black men to white men serving in Vietnam refutes this theory, but it is still popularly held; see Charles C. Moskos and John Sibley Butler, *All That We Can Be: Black Leadership and Racial Integration the Army Way* (Basic Books, 1997).
7. Racial disparities in sentencing are tracked and examined through the nonprofit group the Sentencing Project; their most recent figures are found at www.thesentencingproject.org.
8. Devah Pager, "The Mark of a Criminal Record," *American Sociological Journal* 67 (2003), 526–46.
9. "African Americans Continue to Make Solid Gains in Bachelor and Master Degree Awards: But Professional and Doctoral Degrees Show Declines," *Journal of Blacks in Higher Education* (2008), www.jbhe.com/features/60_degreeawards.html, retrieved July 14, 2009.
10. Raymond Fishman, Sheena Iyengar, et al., "Racial Preferences in Dating," *Review of Economic Studies* 75 (2008), 117–32.

11. Lisa Vazquez, "The Intersectionality of Strategic Marriage and Power," www.blackwomenblowthetrumpet.blogspot.com, June 1, 2009.

12. "If Only Black Women Made the Double Standards," posted by Cherry_darling, October 26, 2008, 11:53:59 p.m., www.dearblackman.com/discussion_boards/index.php?topic=545.msg5495#msg 5495.

13. "Emmett Till," www.wikipedia.org/wiki/Emmett_Till, retrieved July 10, 2009.

14. Steve Sailer, "Census Shows Interracial Marriage Gender Gaps Remain Large," United Press International, March 14, 2003, www .isteve.com/2003_census_interracial_marriage_gender_gap.htm.

15. Kellina Craig-Henderson, *Black Men in Interracial Relationships* (Transaction Publishers, 2006), 40.

16. Lisa Vazquez, "Who Cares If Brothas Want White Women?" www .blackwomenblowthetrumpet.blogspot.com, July 8, 2008.

17. Carolyn Salazar and Adam Nichols, "Four Marines Face Death Penalty for Murder of Sgt. Jan Pietrzak and Wife," *New York Post*, November 8, 2008, www.nypost.com/seven/11072008/news/regional news/a_few_bad_men_137578.htm.

18. Carolyn Salazar, "A Few 'Bad' Men—Race Eyed in Marine Dual Slay," *New York Post*, November 7, 2008, 12, www.nypost.com/seven/ 11072008/news/regionalnews/a_few_bad_men_137578.htm.

19. Phil Cohen, "But It's Not About Race," November 8, 2008, www .dvrbs.com/world/ButItsNotAboutRace.htm.

20. Discussion post: "Why are white men hesitant to date black women?" www.topix.com/forum/news/sex/T366ANV07J5AQEM 68/p19, retrieved on July 9, 2009.

21. Jewels Logan, "Black Women Fucked Me Up!" July 28, 2008, www .youtube.com/watch?v=mqghhnD4BFk&feature=channel_page.

22. Cleaver, 162.

Notion 3: My Family Would Never Accept Him— and His Would Never Accept Me

1. "After 40 Years, Interracial Marriage Flourishing," Associated Press, April 15, 2007, retrieved from www.msnbc.msn.com/id/18090277, July 14, 2009.
2. Joseph Carroll, "Most Americans Approve of Interracial Marriage," Gallup News Service, August 16, 2007, www.gallup.com/poll/28417/Most-Americans-Approve-Interracial-Marriages.aspx.
3. Fishman, Iyengar, et al., "Racial Preferences in Dating," 119.
4. Rachel Sullivan, "Back by Popular Demand: A Few Notes on Women in Black/White Interracial Relationships," March 13, 2008, www.rachelstavern.com.
5. Rachel Sullivan, "What About the Children? How Biracial Children Affect Family Approval of Interracial Relationships," March 29, 2008, www.rachelstavern.com/uncategorized/what-about-the-children-how-biracial-children-affect-family-approval-of-irs.html.
6. Rachel Sullivan, "Myths About Intraracial Relationships," February 12, 2008, www.rachelstavern.com/race-and-racism/myths-about-intraracial-relationships-pt-1.html.

Notion 4: I Don't Find White Men Attractive

1. Chris Rock, *Kill the Messenger: Chris Rock from New York, London and Johannesburg* (HBO Home Video, 2008).
2. Kevan Wylie and Ian Eardley, "Penis Myths Debunked," *Live Science*, www.livescience.com/health/070601_penis_myths.html.
3. See www.kinseyinstitute.org and www.kinseyinstitute.org/resources/FAQ.html#penis.
4. Kennedy, *Interracial Intimacies*, 190.
5. Ibid.
6. "Lynching Statistics," Tuskegee Institute Historical Archives (1979), as reprinted by the African American Studies Department, University of Buffalo, State University of New York, www.africanamericanstudies.buffalo.edu/ANNOUNCE/vra/lynch/lynchstats.html, retrieved on July 11, 2009.
7. Cole and Guy-Sheftall, *Gender Talk*, 134.

8. "Why Are White Men/Black Women Couples Uncommon?" City-Data, www.city-data.com/forum/relationships/377272-why-white-men-black-women-couples.html, retrieved on July 14, 2009.
9. Cole and Guy-Sheftall, *Gender Talk*, 135–36.
10. Richard Majors and Janet Mancini Billson, *Cool Pose: The Dilemma of Black Manhood in America* (Touchstone Books, 1992), 12.
11. Adrian J. Blow and Kelley Hartnett, "Infidelity in Committed Relationships II," *Journal of Marital and Family Therapy*, April 2005.
12. Audrey Grayson, "Why Nice Guys Finish Last: New Research Points to Biological Reason Why Girls Like Bad Boys," June 19, 2008, http://abcnews.go.com/health/Story?id=5197531&page=1.
13. M. Bahati Kuumba, "Gender Justice," *Progressive Black Masculinities* (Routledge, 2008).

Notion 5: White Men Don't Find Black Women Attractive— Unless They Look Like Beyoncé

1. Fishman, Iyengar, et al., "Racial Preferences in Dating," 119.
2. "Saartjie Baartman," http://en.wikipedia.org/wiki/Saartjie_Baartman, retrieved March 3, 2009.
3. Sal-Anderson, Supposing I Wanted to Date a White Guy . . . ?, 50.
4. Dionne P. Stephens and Layli D. Phillips, "Freaks, Gold Diggers, Divas, and Dykes: The Sociohistorical Development of Adolescent African Americans' Sexual Scripts," 10 *Sexuality & Culture* (Winter 2006), 8.
5. Kathy Russell, Midge Wilson, et al., *The Color Concept* (Anchor Books, 1993).
6. Charles W. Cherry II, "Sean 'Diddy' Combs Beats Down False Internet Rumor That Upscale Brand He Manages Prefers Light-Skinned Women," *Florida Courier*, April 3, 2009.
7. Lisa Vazquez, "Sistas, What Goes Around, Comes Around," June 30, 2009, www.blackwomenblowthetrumpet.blogspot.com.
8. Logan, "Black Women Fucked Me Up!"
9. Eve Sharon Moore, *Black Female Interracial Marriage, Book 1: First and Foremost* (e-book, 2009), www.blackfemaleinterracialmarriage.com.
10. American Obesity Association Fact Sheet, retrieved from http://obesity1.tempdomainname.com/subs/fastfacts/Obesity_Minority_Pop.shtml.

11. Miranda Hitti, "Rich-Poor Gap Narrowing in Obesity," WebMD News Service, May 2, 2005, www.webmd.com/diet/news/20050502/rich-poor-gap-narrowing-in-obesity?pagenumber=1.

12. See Paul Campos, *The Obesity Myth* (Gotham Books, 2004) and National Institutes of Health Weight-Control Information Network statistics, published at http://win.niddk.nih.gov/statistics/index.htm#whydodiffer.

13. Lisa Vazquez, "Black Women's Weighty Issues with Weight," December 20, 2008, www.blackwomenblowthetrumpet.blogspot.com.

14. Moore, *Black Female Interracial Marriage*, 97–98.

15. Deborah R. Greenberg et al., "Racial Differences in Body Type Preferences of Men for Women," *International Journal on Eating Disorders* 19, no. 3 (1998), 275–78.

16. Fary M. Cachelin et al., "Does Ethnicity Influence Body-Size Preference? A Comparison of Body Image and Body Size," *Obesity* 10 (2002), 158–66.

17. Andrea D. Powell and Arnold S. Kahn, "Racial Differences in the Desire to Be Thin," *International Journal of Eating Disorders* 17, no. 2 (1995), 191–95.

18. http://abagond.wordpress.com/2007/11/20/why-i-love-thick-women, retrieved on February 24, 2009.

19. Ibid.

20. bell hooks, *Communion: The Female Search for Love* (William Morrow, 2002), 119–20.

21. Carolyn M. West, "Mammy, Jezebel, Sapphire, and Their Homegirls: Developing an 'Oppositional Gaze' Toward the Images of Black Women," in J. Chrisler, C. Golden, and P. Rozee, eds., *Lectures on the Psychology of Women*, 4th ed. (McGraw Hill, 2008), 286–99.

22. Jane Musoke-Ntyeafas, "Busting the Myth of the Angry Black Woman," *Afro Toronto*, September 15, 2006, retrieved from www.afrotoronto.com/CMS/index.php?option=com_content&task=view&id=203&Itemid=45.

Notion 6: What About the Children?

1. Kennedy, *Interracial Intimacies*, 222–23.

2. Ibid., 223.

3. Kathy Russell et al., *The Color Complex: The Politics of Skin Color among African Americans* (Harcourt, 1992).

4. Kimberly Jade Norwood, "The Virulence of Blackthink™ and How Its Threat of Ostracism Shackles Those Deemed Not Black Enough," *Kentucky Law Journal* 93 (2004–2005), 143.

5. Elliott Lewis, *Fade: My Journeys in Multiracial America* (Carroll and Graf, 2006), 151.

6. Ibid., 5.

7. Randall Kennedy, *Sellout: The Politics of Racial Betrayal* (Pantheon Books, 2008), citing John Blake, 59.

8. Kennedy, "Racial Passing," *Interracial Intimacies*, 223–337.

9. Sullivan, "What About the Children?"

10. Ibid.

11. Ibid.

12. For a recent taste of the discussion surrounding Mr. Woods's ethnicity, see David Swerdlick's "The M Word," first posted on theroot .com, July 30, 2008, www.washingtonpost.com/wp-dyn/content/ discussion/2008/07/28/DI2008072802082.html.

13. Maria P. P. Root, *Love's Revolution: Interracial Marriage* (Temple University Press, 2001) and *The Multiracial Experience: Racial Borders as the New Frontier* (Sage Publications, 1996).

14. U.S. Census Bureau, "Questions and Answers for Census 2000 Data on Race," March 14, 2000, retrieved at www.census.gov/Press-Release/www/2001/raceqandas.html.

15. Tracey Laszloffy and Kerry Ann Rocquemore, *Raising Biracial Children* (AltaMira Press, 2005), 2.

16. Ibid., 5–9.

17. James H. Jacobs, "Identity Development in Biracial Children," *Racially Mixed People in America* (Sage Publications, 1992).

18. Lewis, *Fade*, 40–41.

19. Laura McFarland, "Color and Kids: Heritage Part of Family Lives," *Rocky Mount Telegram* (NC), February 13, 2009, www.projectrace .com/inthenews/archive/inthenews-021509.php.

Notion 7: He Must Have Money:
Black Women as Gold Diggers

1. Stephens and Phillips, "Freaks, Gold Diggers, Divas, and Dykes," 18.
2. "Educational Attainment—People 25 Years Old and Over, by Total Money Earnings in 2005, Work Experience in 2005, Age, Race, Hispanic Origin, and Sex," United States Census Reports, March 2006, http://pubdb3.census.gov/macro/032006/perinc/new03_005.htmv.
3. George A. Yancy and Richard Lewis, *Interracial Families: Current Concepts and Controversies* (Taylor and Francis, 2008), 67–68.
4. Moore, *Black Women*, 33.
5. Interview with Steve Harvey, retrieved on March 15, 2009, from http://hellobeautiful.blackplanet.com/your-man/steve-harvey-talks-about-his-book-part-1.
6. Steve Harvey, *Act Like a Lady, Think Like a Man* (Amistad, 2009), 82–83.
7. Kurt Davis, "The Economics of Love," *Virginia Law Weekly*, February 13, 2008, retrieved from www.lawweekly.org/?module=display story&story_id=1943&edition_id=82&format=html.

Notion 8: You're a Sellout:
Perception of Black Women Who Date White Men

1. Norwood, "The Virulence of Blackthink™," 189.
2. Kennedy, *Sellout*, 4.
3. Norwood, "The Virulence of Blackthink™," 148.
4. Kennedy, *Sellout*, 3.
5. Collins, *Black Feminist Thought*, 163.
6. John McWhorter, "Blackness: A Quick and Dirty Primer," www.the root.com, February 13, 2008, www.theroot.com/views/blackness-quick-and-dirty-primer.
7. John McWhorter, "Blackness Primer Revisited," February 28, 2008, www.theroot.com/views/blackness-primer-revisited.
8. Norwood, "The Virulence of Blackthink™," 161–62.
9. http://en.wikipedia.org/wiki/Black_people, retrieved on September 24, 2009.

10. Elwood Watson, "Defining a Person's Blackness," *Diverse: Issues in Higher Education*, February 12, 2009, www.diverseeducation.word press.com/2009/02.

11. Norwood, "The Virulence of Blackthink™," 175–76.

12. "Parameters of Blackness," February 14, 2008, http://commu nitycheckup.com/2008/02/14/parameters-of-blackness/retrieved February 21, 2009.

13. Lisa Vazquez, "Multiculturalism and the Dangers of White Privilege Idolatry," April 3, 2009, www.blackwomenblowthetrumpet .blogspot.com.

Notion 9: We'd Be Too Different

1. Moore, *Black Female Interracial Marriage*, 27.

Notion 10: It's the Same Story Around the World

1. Peter Carlson, "American Aphrodite," *Washington Post*, August 15, 2004, www.washingtonpost.com/wp-dyn/articles/A3846-2004Aug15 .html, retrieved July 13, 2009.

BIBLIOGRAPHY

Angelou, Maya. *Still I Rise*. New York: Random House, 1978.

Blow, Adrian J., and Kelley Hartnett. "Infidelity in Committed Relationships II." *Journal of Marital and Family Therapy*. April 2005.

Branden, Nathaniel. *The Six Pillars of Self-Esteem*. New York: Bantam, 1994.

Campos, Paul. *The Obesity Myth*. New York: Gotham Books, 2004.

Cleage, Pearl. *Mad at Miles: A Black Woman's Guide to Truth*. Southfield, MI: Cleage Group, 1990.

Cleaver, Eldridge. *Soul on Ice*. New York: Dell, 1968.

Cole, Johnnetta Betsch, and Beverly Guy-Sheftall. *Gender Talk: The Struggle for Women's Equality in African American Communities*. New York: Ballantine Books, 2003.

Collins, Patricia Hill. *Black Feminist Thought*. New York: Routledge Classics, 2009.

Craig-Henderson, Kellina. *Black Men in Interracial Relationships*. Edison, NJ: Transaction Publishers, 2006.

Davis, Allison, Burleigh B. Gardner, and Mary R. Gardner. *Deep South: A Social Anthropological Study of Caste and Class*. University of Chicago Press, 1941.

Fishman, Raymond, Sheena Iyengar, et al. "Racial Preferences in Dating." *Review of Economic Studies* 75 (2008), 117–32.

Foley, Linda A., and Nicole Varelas. "Blacks' and Whites' Perceptions of Interracial and Intraracial Rape." *Journal of Social Psychology* (June 1998), vol. 138(3), pp. 392–400.

Greenberg, Deborah R., et al. "Racial Differences in Body Type Preferences of Men for Women." *International Journal on Eating Disorders* 19, no. 3 (1998), 275–78.

Gullickson, Aaron. "Black-White Interracial Marriage Trends 1850–2000." *Journal of Family History* 31, no. 3 (2006), 1–24.

Harvey, Steve. *Act Like a Lady, Think Like a Man*. New York: Amistad, 2009.

hooks, bell. *Rock My Soul: Black Women and Self-Esteem*. New York: Atria, 2002.

———. *Communion: The Female Search for Love*. New York: Harper Paperbacks, 2002.

Jacobs, James H. "Identity Development in Biracial Children." *Racially Mixed People in America*. Thousand Oaks, CA: Sage Publications, 1992.

Kennedy, Randall. *Interracial Intimacies: Sex, Marriage, Identity, and Adoption*. New York: Vintage Books, 2007.

———. *Sellout: The Politics of Racial Betrayal*. New York: Pantheon Books, 2008.

Kuumba, M. Bahati. "Gender Justice." *Progressive Black Masculinities*. New York: Routledge, 2006.

Laszloffy, Tracey, and Kerry Ann Rocquemore. *Raising Biracial Children.* Lanham, MD: AltaMira Press, 2005.

Lewis, Elliott. *Fade: My Journeys in Multiracial America.* New York: Carroll and Graf, 2006.

Majors, Richard, and Janet Mancini Billson. *Cool Pose: The Dilemmas of Black Manhood in America.* New York: Touchstone Books, 1992.

McClendon, Theodore. *How to Find a Good Black Man.* Gary, IN: McClendon Report, June 2003.

McGuire, Danielle L., "It Was Like All of Us Had Been Raped: Sexual Violence, Community Mobilization, and the African American Freedom Struggle." In Pippa Holloway, ed. *Other Souths.* Athens, GA: University of Georgia Press, 2006.

Moore, Eva Sharon ("Evia"). *Black Women: First and Foremost.* e-book, 2009.

Moskos, Charles C., and John Sibley Butler. *All That We Can Be: Black Leadership and Racial Integration the Army Way.* New York: Basic Books, 1995.

Norwood, Kimberly Jade. "The Virulence of Blackthink™ and How Its Threat of Ostracism Shackles Those Deemed Not Black Enough." *Kentucky Law Journal* 93 (2004–2005), 143.

Powell, Andrea D., and Arnold S. Kahn. "Racial Differences in the Desire to Be Thin." *International Journal of Eating Disorders* 17, no. 2 (1995), 191–95.

Russell, Kathy, Midge Wilson, et al. *The Color Concept.* New York: Anchor Books, 1993.

Sal-Anderson, Halima. *Supposing I Wanted to Date a White Guy . . . ?* e-book, 2008.

Speller, Daamon. *A Box of White Chocolate.* Deer Park, NY: Kensington/ Urban Books, 2008.

Stephens, Dionne, and Layli Phillips. "Freaks, Gold Diggers, Divas, and Dykes: The Sociohistorical Development of Adolescent African Americans' Sexual Scripts." 10 *Sexuality & Culture* (Winter 2002), 6.

West, Carolyn M. "Mammy, Jezebel, Sapphire, and Their Homegirls: Developing an 'Oppositional Gaze' Toward the Images of Black Women." In J. Chrisler, C. Golden, and P. Rozee, eds. *Lectures on the Psychology of Women*. 4th ed. New York: McGraw-Hill, 2008, 286–99.

Yancy, George A., and Richard Lewis. *Interracial Families: Current Concepts and Controversies*. New York: Taylor and Francis, 2008.

ACKNOWLEDGMENTS

Have you ever felt like everything you had ever done, experienced, felt, and believed came together? If you have, then you understand how I felt about writing this book. It was an "Aha Moment" as Oprah says. It was the convergence of so many experiences and thoughts that I can only feel it was something God specifically planned for me. And because of that, so many of the people and resources that I needed came to me almost effortlessly.

The first of those resources is my agent, Audra Barrett. When I called her and told her I wanted to stop writing fiction and do this book, I worried that she might not be interested. But her immediate response was "Are you kidding? Let's go!" She has been an invaluable source of ideas, intelligence, and support. I never thought of myself as the "temperamental artist " sort, but Audra's willingness to listen to the frustrations surrounding the completion of this work makes me wonder if the term applies!

Much thanks also go out to Karen Hunter and her team at Simon and Schuster/Pocket Books. Karen herself is a "ball of fire"—a deeply passionate, hardworking sista who knows where the buttons are in the black community. I am thrilled to be working with her. Brigitte Smith, Jean

Anne Rose, and Kerrie Loyd have worked tremendously hard to "get this book out there"—and I am deeply grateful to them.

This book could not have been written without the dozens of couples and experts who agreed to share their knowledge and experiences with me. In particular, Drs. Rachel Sullivan and Kellina Craig Henderson became my "go-to" women for discussing black women in interracial relationships. Law professor Kimberly Jade Norwood's essay on "blackthink" changed my way of thinking, as did Lisa Vazquez's blog blackwomenblowthetrumpet.blogspot.com and Evia Moore's blackfemaleinterracialmarriage.com. Fleace' Weaver's blackgirltravel.com is a stroke of genius—and I know she will do well. Moore, Angela Shaw, Halima Sal Anderson, Nikki Doughty, Wendy Coakley-Thompson, and Mona Washington were sources of insightful commentary. Each of these women was an immense help to me. Thank you all!

I appreciate the generosity of time and spirit of the women and men who talked with me about their feelings about interracial relationships. All of them were wonderfully, brutally, and totally honest. It's hard to say "I don't like it and here's why" in a culture that often seems to prefer lies in the name of political correctness. I appreciate these men and women for telling it like they see it *now*—and being willing to see it differently in the future.

Many thanks go to the sistas and their husbands who are in interracial relationships for sharing their stories with me. They revealed themselves to be quietly courageous in their own ways, since each had faced some difficulty or hardship over her choice of partner. Their optimism, their commitment to their families, and their willingness to take on some of the knottiest of racial misunderstandings in their own homes remain an inspiration to me.

Paula Langguth Ryan, Michelle Chin, Rachel Schwartz-Hartje, the Goddard School of Gaithersburg, the Montgomery County Public Library system—thank you! And, of course, thanks go out to the Folan and Langhorne families for their ongoing love and support.

Last, but certainly not least, some special thanks go to my husband—the white boy I brought home. Couldn't have written this one without you, babe.